Sixth Edition

LOCATING AND CORRECTING READING DIFFICULTIES

Eldon E. Ekwall
late of University of Texas at El Paso

James L. Shanker
California State University, Hayward

Merrill, an imprint of
Macmillan Publishing Company
New York

Maxwell Macmillan Canada
Toronto

Maxwell Macmillan International
New York   Oxford   Singapore   Sydney

Cover art: © 1992 Clare Wood
Editor: Linda James Scharp
Production Editor: Julie Anderson Tober
Art Coordinator: Lorraine Woost
Text Designer: Susan E. Frankenberry
Cover Designer: Cathleen Norz
Production Buyer: Patricia A. Tonneman
Illustrations: Steve Botts

This book was set in Century Schoolbook by Carlisle Communications, Ltd. and was printed and bound by Book Press, Inc., a Quebecor America Book Group Company.

Macmillan Publishing Company
866 Third Avenue
New York, NY 10022

Macmillan Publishing Company is part of the
Maxwell Communication Group of Companies.

Maxwell Macmillan Canada, Inc.
1200 Eglinton Avenue East, Suite 200
Don Mills, Ontario M3C 3N1

Library of Congress Cataloging-in-Publication Data

Ekwall, Eldon E.
     Locating and correcting reading difficulties / Eldon E. Edwall,
James L. Shanker. — 6th ed.
       p. cm.
     Includes bibliographical references and index.
     ISBN 0-02-332181-4
     1. Reading—Remedial teaching. I. Shanker, James L. II. Title.
LB1050.5.E38 1993
372.4'3 —dc20
                                                                    92-23298
                                                                    CIP

Printing: 1 2 3 4 5 6 7 8 9   Year: 3 4 5 6 7

To Susan

Preface

The sixth edition of this book, like the previous editions, is designed to give busy teachers and students in reading education concrete methods of locating and correcting reading difficulties. It can be used in developmental, corrective, and remedial situations. The major features of previous editions have been retained, with new, up-to-date information added to nearly every chapter. The importance of direct instruction, motivational learning activities, and abundant practice in the act of reading is stressed. Although individual reading skills are still identified, greater emphasis is placed on the use of strategic approaches to the teaching of reading.

This new edition contains additional concrete methods for teaching reading comprehension, including the use of semantic mapping, K-W-L, and other strategies. New material is also included on echo reading, precision reading, and other oral reading strategies, plus activities designed for independent student use with the audio tape recorder. These oral reading approaches have been shown to be unusally effective in developing students' reading efficiency or fluency. This edition includes new material on the direct instruction of basic sight words, specific strategies for teaching structural analysis, new techniques for teaching vocabulary, and activities to assist students to develop the skills of skimming and scanning. Also included in this edition are a description and chart for implementing the *word-attack strategy,* a step-by-step process students can use to attack unknown words on their own.

Although the basic format of each chapter remains the same, the Reading Diagnosis Chart and chapter sequence have been modified slightly in response to suggestions by reviewers. The new sequence more closely matches the logical development of these abilities in readers and corresponds to the order of the chapters.

The sixth edition has been designed so that teachers and students in reading education courses can use the materials in Appendices A through I to construct their own diagnostic kits. These appendices include materials for assessing students' knowledge of the alphabet, basic sight words and phrases, phonics, structural analysis, and the use of context clues. Each of these appendices includes information on how to prepare the materials for classroom use. Specific directions and important points to remember are also included for administering each test or survey instrument. Other materials included in the appendices are a code for marking in oral diagnosis; a quick check to determine if students should be given an entire basic sight word test; the *Quick Survey Word List,* which quickly assesses a student's ability to use phonics and syllabication skills to decode multisyllable words; information on the use of the cloze procedure; comprehensive charts listing the scope and sequence of reading skills as presented in typical basal readers; a phonics primer; an extensive list of phonograms and words for use in teaching phonics; lists of prepositional phrases; lists of the meaning, examples, and uses of prefixes and suffixes; samples of author, title, and subject cards; charts for graphing students' progress in using the technique of repeated readings; and charts for graphing words per minute and comprehension. New to this edition are Appendix D, a new test of basic sight words and phrases that uses the Dolch list rearranged according to the frequency of occurrence of basic sight vocabulary in children's trade books; Appendix N, a list of 110 basic sight word sentences; Appendix R, charts for graphing students' progress in using the precision reading technique; and Appendix T, suggestions for interviewing parents of disabled readers.

You should first turn to the section entitled "How to Use This Book" where you will find an explanation of the format used. In each chapter there is a short section on how to recognize problems with reading skills, a brief discussion of pertinent information on problems, and specific recommendations on how to correct these difficulties. In some areas, you will also find games and activities to help strengthen or reinforce reading abilities. The text alternates use of masculine and feminine pronouns by chapter.

All of the ideas in this text have been tried and proven successful. You should remember, however, that what works well with one student may not be appropriate with another. Furthermore, ideas that are suitable for one grade level may not be suitable for another.

As with the first five editions, this text is not designed to present the theory and philosophy of reading. It is also not a substitute for a good reading methods course. It will, however, provide teachers and students in reading education with concrete procedures that can be successfully implemented in the classroom.

ACKNOWLEDGMENTS

A number of excellent teachers, and other personnel concerned with the teaching of reading, have contributed numerous ideas and suggestions that appear in this book. Although it is not possible to thank each of them individually, their contributions are sincerely appreciated. Special thanks goes to Ethel Murphy for her many contributions to this edition. She possesses a thorough knowledge of the field of reading, an understanding of the learning process, and an ability to help teachers teach children to read.

In addition, I would like to express my appreciation to Linda Sharp, Julie Tober, and Jeff Johnston of the Macmillan staff. Linda skillfully managed this project from beginning to end and contributed not only her exceptional editorial skills but also her unusual knowledge of the fields of reading and education. Julie capably supervised the production of this book, juggling many tasks and demonstrating considerable patience. Jeff Johnston worked closely on previous editions of this book and oversaw the development of this edition from his position as Editor-in-Chief, Education, College Division. Jeff Putnam served as copyeditor on both the fifth and sixth editions of this book. His editing skills and attention to detail have made this a more readable text.

I appreciate the conscientious work of the following individuals who kindly reviewed this edition of the text: W. Gale Breedlove, University of South Carolina; Ralph L. Brown, Midwestern State University; Edward W. Holmes, Towson State University, Kay G. Rayborn, Stephen F. Austin State University; Richard H. Sherman, Calumet College of St. Joseph. They, and reviewers of previous editions, have offered their insights, thoughtful comments, and constructive suggestions to make this a more useful text.

I wish to thank Susan, Michael, and Kenny Shanker for their support and their understanding on those nights when I was late for, or failed to appear at, dinner.

Eldon E. Ekwall passed away in November, 1989. He will be missed by many. Ed Ekwall was a dedicated teacher, scholar, and prolific writer who made enormous contributions to the field of reading. Of the many articles and books that he wrote or contributed to, this "little red book" was his favorite. His influence on the lives of the students he taught and the youngsters he assisted directly and indirectly through his teaching and his writing stand as testimony to the many accomplishments of this remarkable man.

—J.L.S.

Contents

How to Use This Book

Begin by reading the Definition of Terms in the next section to be sure you are familiar with all of them before you read the text. Then read the Reading Diagnosis Chart, (p. xxii), which lists 28 reading or reading-related abilities. After looking over the Reading Diagnosis Chart, skim the entire book from beginning to end to ensure familiarity with the contents. Each of the first 28 chapters has a similar organization. First, an explanation is given on how to recognize the difficulty with the specific ability. Then a discussion explains any pertinent problem. Specific recommendations for correcting any weaknesses in each of the abilities follow the discussion. Finally, in some chapters, a list of games and exercises is presented to help correct these reading difficulties. In most cases you could not, or would not, be able to attempt everything listed as a recommendation; however, you can choose the techniques that seem most appropriate for your situation.

The Reading Diagnosis Chart is constructed to give you an opportunity to check each of the 28 abilities three times during the year. The time period between checks will depend on the intensity of the help or the normal teaching program. It could be as often as once a month or once during each semester of the school year. You should attempt to locate student difficulties as early in the year as possible. The "Recognized By" section in each chapter will be helpful in determining whether certain skills are deficient. After determining which abilities are weak, tally the total number of students who are weak in each area. If possible, group the students who need reading instruction in similar areas. In some cases, you may base your instruction on those areas in which the class as a whole is weakest. Then turn to the "Recommendations" and the "Games and Exercises" sections to use the suggestions given there.

Before initiating actual instruction, read the section entitled "Principles of Effective Instruction" at the beginning of Chapter 29. The suggestions in this section will guide you in selecting the most appropriate recommendations in each chapter for your student or students.

The checklist does not categorize reading difficulties by the severity of the problem. Be aware, however, that some of the items listed are more serious than others. Each discussion section explains how to determine whether the difficulty needs treatment or is only a symptom of a more serious problem. For example, word-by-word reading, improper phrasing, and repetitions usually are symptoms of more serious problems, such as difficulty in one or more of the following areas: decoding, efficiency skills, or comprehension. In this situation, treatment for these larger problems probably would cause the symptoms of word-by-word reading, improper phrasing, and repetitions to disappear automatically. Read each discussion section carefully to ensure adequate diagnosis and to determine the proper improvement procedure.

After noting on the Reading Diagnosis Chart the skills in which your students are weak, turn to the Table of Contents. This will help you to quickly locate corrective procedures for each of the problems listed. The numbers on the Reading Diagnosis Chart correspond to the chapter numbers for each difficulty noted. For example, students who have difficulty with basic sight words can be helped by using the corrective procedures in Chapter 12, those who are unable to skim or scan can be helped by using the procedures in Chapter 25, and so on.

Following the Reading Diagnosis Chart is a section entitled "Making Your Own Diagnostic Kit from the Appendices." Become familiar with this section, so you can make your own diagnostic kit as you read the various sections for which testing or assessment materials are included in the appendices. After becoming familiar with the text, you may wish to reproduce copies of the Reading Diagnosis Chart so you will have a record for each member of the class, or for each student with whom you are working.

It will be easier to locate certain difficulties if you use the code for marking in oral diagnosis, which is described in Appendix A. This code will enable you to find exactly what type of mistakes students make in their reading. With a little practice, you will become adept at transcribing the student's oral reading. You will, of course, need a copy of what the student is reading (preferably double-spaced) to mark as the student reads. You will also find this marked or coded copy useful in rechecking a student's reading to record progress in overcoming earlier difficulties. In selecting material for the student to read, try to find material that will cause the students to make 5 to 10 errors per page. If the material is too easy and the students are able to read it without error, you obviously will be unable to determine the nature of the reading difficulties. On the other hand, if students make more than about 10 errors per page, the material may be so difficult and frustrating that they will guess wildly and lose their ability to apply the reading skills they do possess. This instruction applies to the selection of reading material for *testing* purposes only. The difficulty of the reading material will vary according to the purpose for which it is used. The student should be able to decode at least 95% of the words in material you use for *instructing* the student and at least 98% of the words in material that the student reads *independently*.

   Sometimes a particular suggestion will be appropriate with a younger child but inappropriate for an older student. We have not listed the various suggestions as appropriate for certain grades or age levels. Exercise your own judgment based on the severity of the problem and the age and attitude of the child. We have, however, noted that some problems are beyond the beginning-reading stage.

Definition of Terms

Affix A term meaning to fasten, usually applied to suffixes and prefixes collectively.

Basal Reader A reading textbook designed for a specific grade level. These usually contain material designed to enhance specific skills, such as word-attack, vocabulary, and comprehension skills.

Basic Sight Words or **Basic Sight Vocabulary** These are words that appear most often in the reading material written for children and adults. For a student to master a basic sight word, he must recognize and pronounce the word instantly (one second or less) every time he sees it. One of the most common basic sight word lists is the Dolch Basic Sight Vocabulary,* which contains no nouns but is a 220-word list of "service words." In Appendix D you will find a modified version of this list, along with instructions for assessing students' knowledge of these words.

Basic Sight Word Phrases These are basic sight words that are grouped together in phrase units. When students learn to read these phrases quickly and smoothly, they usually transfer their ability to recognize basic sight words in isolation to reading them in context.

Choral Reading Reading done orally by two or more students from the same passage at the same time.

Cloze Passage A reading passage of approximately 250 words in which, beginning after the 25th word, every 5th word is omitted. Students read the original passage, then fill in the exact word, if possible. Independent, instructional, and frustration levels may be calculated based on the percentage of correct words filled in.

---

*Dolch, E.W. (1955). *Methods in reading* (pp. 373–374). Champaign, IL: Garrard Publishing.

Cloze Procedure   A process of matching students to materials at their appropriate grade level. Cloze passages may be used to test the students' comprehension of selected passages to determine placement, to teach context clues, or to teach students to better comprehend what they read.

Comprehension   Meaning gained from what is written on a page (when read) or heard (when spoken).

Consonant Blend   Combinations of two or three consonants blended together into sounds while retaining the sounds of the individual letters, e.g., *cr* in *crayon* and *pl* in *plate*.

Consonant Cluster   A term meaning both consonant **digraphs** and **consonant blends.**

Context Clues   Clues to the meaning and/or pronunciation of an unknown word derived from the words preceding or following that word. For example, one can use context clues to determine that the missing word in the following sentence is *dog:* The _____ was barking all night and kept me awake.

Critical Reading   Evaluating on the basis of the reader's experience the meaning and implications of what is read.

Decoding   The process of taking words in print and changing them to spoken words. This is accomplished when the reader applies one or more of the following: sight word recognition, phonics, structural analysis, and context clues.

Diagnosis   A careful investigation of a problem carried out to determine the amount and sequence of remediation needed by a student with reading difficulties.

Digraph   A combination of two letters recording (representing) a single sound. There are *consonant digraphs* and *vowel digraphs*. An example of a consonant digraph is *ph* in the word *digraph*. In this case, the *ph* stands for the /f/ sound. (When a letter is found between two slash marks, as the *f* above, it means the sound for which the letter stands.) An example of a vowel digraph is the *ea* in the word *each*. In saying the sound (phoneme) represented by the letters of a digraph, one does not change the position of the mouth from the beginning to the end of the sound.

Diphthong   A combination of two vowel letters that are both heard in making a compound sound, e.g., *oa* in *boat* and *oy* in *boy*. In pronouncing a diphthong sound, the position of the mouth is moved from the beginning to the end of the diphthong.

Direct Instruction   A teaching approach that is academically focused, sequential, and structured. The teacher presents information to the students and monitors the pacing and learning of the material.

Echo Reading   A recommended technique for improving efficiency skills in reading. This technique can work on a one-to-one basis or with a tape recorder. Students may also use this technique when reading in pairs. The teacher reads a passage aloud, then the student attempts to duplicate the passage using the same phrasing and intonation.

Efficiency Skills Beyond the ability to merely decode words, the ability to use punctuation and other cues to read smoothly and easily, with proper speed, accuracy, and phrasing. This term is often used synonymously with **fluency.**

El Paso Phonics Survey An informal instrument used to determine whether students know sound-symbol, or phoneme-grapheme, correspondence for the most phonetically regular **phonic elements.**

Engaged Time or **On-task Time** The amount of time a student is involved or engaged in the learning task.

Flexible Reading Adjusting reading speed to fit the requirement of understanding the text. The purpose for reading and the type of material to be read dictate appropriate speed.

Fluency See **efficiency skills.**

General Sight Words or **General Sight Vocabulary** *Any* word that a reader has seen many times in the past and is able to recognize instantly without using word-attack skills. This term should not be confused with **basic sight words,** which refers only to words that appear on a list of the most frequently occurring words.

Grapheme A grapheme is the written representation of a phoneme, e.g., the word *dog* has three distinct sounds that are represented by the graphemes *d, o,* and *g.* The word *straight* has five phonemes that are represented by the graphemes *s, t, r, aigh,* and *t* (See **phoneme**).

Holistic Approach A teaching-learning approach that emphasizes wholes of subject matter. A completely holistic approach to teaching reading would include few or no subskills of reading. Also called *whole language approach.*

Interactive Model of Reading A model of reading that describes it as being both concept- and text-driven, in which the reader and the text work together to elicit meaning. The reader comprehends through the use of both decoding skills and prior knowledge.

Kinesthetic Method The use of touch, hearing, sight, and muscle movement to teach letters or words. The approach usually involves tracing over words with the index and middle fingers while sounding the part being traced.

K-W-L Strategy For reading in the content areas, finding out what the students *know* about the subject to be read (K), assessing what they *want* to learn (W), and finally what they *learned* from reading the passage (L).

Language Experience Approach (LEA) The student's or group's own words are written down and used as material for instruction in reading, writing, spelling, listening, and speaking. The approach relies on children's oral language background to develop their reading skills and is considered more personalized and motivating, though less systematic or sequential, than other approaches.

Letter Knowledge The ability to discriminate, recognize, and name the letters of the alphabet.

Letter-sound Correspondence The relationship between a letter and the sound it stands for.

Levels of Reading

Independent or **free reading level** The student can function adequately without the teacher's help at this level. Comprehension should average 90% or better, and word recognition should average 99% or better.

Instructional reading level The student can function adequately with teacher guidance and yet be challenged to stimulate his reading growth. Comprehension should average 75% or better, and word recognition should average 90% or better.

Frustration reading level The student cannot function adequately. In reading at this level, the student often shows signs of tension and discomfort. Vocalization is often present. Comprehension averages 50% or less, and word recognition averages 90% or less.

Literature-based Reading Program Teaching reading using children's stories, nonfiction pieces, and poetry. This may range from an in-depth study of core literary works to extension of core work together with recreational and motivational reading that is based on the student's natural curiosity.

Meaning Vocabulary Sometimes called simply **vocabulary**, it refers to the student's knowledge of the *meanings* of words in her listening, speaking, and reading vocabularies.

Metacognition Knowledge of one's own thought processes while reading. This implies that the student can select reading strategies that will help her to comprehend the material.

Neurological Impress Method The teacher sits beside the student and points to each word, reading it aloud. The student follows along with his eyes and reads aloud with the teacher.

Phoneme The smallest unit of speech sound in a language, e.g., in the word *dog* there are three phonemes: /d/, /o/, and /g/.

Phonic Elements Phonic elements are initial consonants, consonant digraphs, consonant blends, vowels, vowel combinations, or special letter combinations to be learned in the study of **phonics**.

Phonics The study of sound-symbol (phoneme-grapheme) relationships as they apply to the teaching of reading; usually used in beginning reading.

Phonogram A series of letters that begin with a vowel and are often found together, e.g., *all, ell, old, ime,* etc. A phonogram is sometimes referred to as a *graphemic base, word element, word family, vowel family,* or *graphoneme.*

Precision Reading A method used to help students overcome difficulties with reading efficiency. A segment of a book is selected and the student is told to practice reading these sentences as accurately as possible. Later, the oral reading of the sentences is scored and the results are graphed.

Reading Programs

Developmental The normal classroom instructional program followed by the teacher to meet the needs of students who are progressing at a normal rate in terms of their capacity.

Corrective A program of instruction, usually conducted by a classroom teacher within the class setting, to correct mild reading difficulties.

Remedial A program of instruction, usually carried on outside the regular classroom, to teach specific developmental reading skills to students with severe reading difficulties.

Semantic Mapping Organizing concepts into a cognitive structure or hierarchy for better comprehension.

Story Frame A device used to build comprehension. It provides structure to a variety of content material. In a story frame, the teacher begins a sentence about the story's content and the student must complete the sentence. Story frames may become more elaborate and deal with character, plot, and setting as students become more skilled in completing them.

Structural Analysis Now often referred to as *morphology,* which is concerned with the study of meaning-bearing units such as root words, prefixes, suffixes, possessives, plurals, accent rules, and syllables.

Vocabulary Most often this term is synonymous with **meaning vocabulary**; sometimes it is used to refer to the number of words a reader recognizes, or a reader's *sight vocabulary.*

Whole Language Approach Reading and writing instruction that uses complete texts in communicative situations, as contrasted with focused skills practice or the use of phonics or isolated drilling of language. This approach may also incorporate speaking, listening, and spelling, and use materials such as newspapers, children's books, notes, and memos.

Word-analysis Skills Sometimes called *word-attack skills,* these are the skills a reader must use to determine how to pronounce a word when it is not recognized instantly. (The three important word-analysis skills are phonics, structural analysis, and context clues.)

Word-recognition Skills The ability of a reader to recognize words, usually referring only to recognition by sight or recognition without the aid of word analysis.

Reading Diagnosis Chart

NAME ——————
GRADE ——————
TEACHER ——————
SCHOOL ——————

#	1st Check	2nd Check	3rd Check	Description	Category
1				Lacks Knowledge of the Alphabet	Pre-Reading
2				Word-by-Word Reading	Oral Reading
3				Incorrect Phrasing	
4				Poor Pronunciation	
5				Omissions	
6				Repetitions	
7				Inversions or Reversals	
8				Insertions	
9				Substitutions	
10				Guesses at Words	
11				Voicing-Lip Movements, Finger-Pointing, and Head Movements	
12				Basic Sight Words Not Known	Decoding
13				General Sight Vocabulary Not up to Grade Level	
14				Phonics Difficulties: Consonants	
15				Phonics Difficulties: Vowels	
16				Phonics Difficulties: Blends, Digraphs, or Diphthongs	
17				Structural Analysis Difficulties	
18				Contractions Not Known	
19				Inadequate Ability to Use Context Clues	
20				Vocabulary Inadequate	Comprehension
21				Comprehension Inadequate	
22				Low Rate of Speed	Study Skills
23				Inability to Adjust Reading Rate	
24				High Rate of Reading at the Expense of Accuracy	
25				Inability to Skim or Scan	
26				Unable to Locate Information	
27				Undeveloped Dictionary Skills	Other
28				Written Recall Limited by Spelling Ability	

D—Difficulty recognized
P—Pupil progressing
N—No longer has difficulty

The items listed above represent the most common difficulties encountered by pupils in the reading program. Following each numbered item are spaces for notation of that specific difficulty. This may be done at intervals of several months. One might use a check to indicate difficulty recognized or the following letters to represent an even more accurate appraisal:

Making Your Own Diagnostic Kit From the Appendices

Materials are included in Appendices B through I for developing your own diagnostic kit for use in locating students who have difficulties in reading. Each appendix is arranged as follows:

Preparing for the Test.　In this section you will find instructions for preparing the material in this book for use in testing. In most cases, the directions include removing an answer sheet, which is to be duplicated. Directions are also included for removing and laminating a stimulus sheet. It is suggested that you file material in each of these appendices so that you may easily retrieve them. You may wish to file each test or assessment device in a large manila envelope and then label each envelope like a file folder. These may then be kept in a portable file box, and easily transported from place to place as needed in various testing situations.

Specific Directions for Giving Each Test or Assessment Device.　In this section, you will find specific directions to use in administering each test or assessment device.

Important Points to Remember.　In administering any test or assessment device, there are certain techniques that you will find helpful and others that should be avoided. This section, found in each appendix, includes this information.

Following is a list of appendices and testing or assessment devices that you should have in your kit when it is completed.

Appendix B　A test of letter knowledge.

Appendix C　The *Quick Check for Basic Sight Words.*

Appendix D　The Basic Sight Word Test and Basic Sight Word Phrases Test.

Appendix E   *Quick Survey Word List* and the *El Paso Phonics Survey.* The *Quick Survey Word List* is used to determine whether students who are expected to read at approximately the fourth-grade level or above would need to be given a phonics test and other corresponding tests such as the one in Appendix F. Students who do well on the *Quick Survey Word List* would not need further phonics testing. Therefore, the use of this survey can sometimes save considerable time in the diagnostic process.

Appendix F   Materials for testing students' knowledge of vowel rules and syllable principles.

Appendix G   A test for students' knowledge of contractions.

Appendix H   A test for students' ability to use context clues.

Appendix I   Passages for using the cloze procedure (optional).

I

PRE-READING ABILITY

1

Lacks Knowledge of the Alphabet

RECOGNIZED BY

The student is unable to recognize the letters of the alphabet when shown the letters, is unable to point to the letters of the alphabet, is unable to match uppercase and lowercase letters, or is unable to match one uppercase or lowercase letter with another letter that looks exactly the same.

DISCUSSION

Research has consistently shown that a child's ability to recognize and name the letters of the alphabet is highly correlated with, and usually predictive of, later reading success. Students who, when given an informal reading inventory, know very few words, or students who appear to be severely disabled in reading, should be given a test for letter knowledge. Keep in mind that there are various levels of difficulty in testing for letter knowledge. The materials listed in Appendix B will enable you to determine whether the student has difficulty with the alphabet and, if so, the level of difficulty at which the student is weak. For example, it is more difficult for a student to name letters in random order than it is to point to the letters named by the teacher.

RECOMMENDATIONS

A. Teach the student the alphabet song. Then, present a copy of the alphabet (in alphabetical order) and as the student sings the song, ask the student to point to each letter.
B. Present a letter and discuss its characteristic shape, e.g., that it has an ascender, such as the letter *h,* or a descender, such as the letter *p.* The speed at which students can learn the letters is highly variable. Some students can learn several letters at a time, while some beginning readers can learn only one letter per week.
C. Make a tape recording of the letters of the alphabet to accompany an alphabet book such as *Animalia* by Graeme Base. Students will find this entertaining, and it provides a way for the student to learn the letters in context.

D. Make a list of the first third of the alphabet:

1. A	5. E
2. B	6. F
3. C	7. G
4. D	8. H

Then make a recording for the student to take home or work with in the classroom. The tape-recorded script can be as follows: "Look at the letter by number one. This letter is A. Point to it and say 'A.' Look at it very carefully and say 'A' again. The next letter by number two is B. Point to it and say 'B.' Look at it very carefully and say it again," and continue through the list. You may wish to modify this script to have the student also write the letter. In this case the script would be as follows: "Look at the letter by number one. This letter is A. Point to it and say 'A.' Look at it very carefully and say it again. Now write the letter and say 'A' as you write it," and so on. This presentation will be successful only with students who are able to learn the letters easily and rapidly. For other students the presentation can be simplified by presenting only one or two letters at a time.

E. If some letters are reversed, or if the student seems to have a difficult time learning them, prepare letters cut from fine sandpaper and have the student feel the letters as he pronounces them. This can also be done with three-dimensional letters made of felt or similar material.

F. Place a thin layer of salt or fine sand in the bottom of a shoebox lid and ask the student to trace letters with his finger in the sand or salt.

G. When teaching the alphabet, be sure that it appears on a chart where children can constantly see it. Using just a few letters at a time, work with students until they can instantly tell you which letter comes before or after any other letter. For example, if you say, "Which letter comes before *g?*" and point to a child, he should instantly say '*f.*' Most adults can instantly give the letter that immediately *follows* another; however, they usually pause a few seconds before they tell which letter *precedes* another. Knowing the order of the letters will save time later when students are using the dictionary.

GAMES AND EXERCISES

Alphabet Race

Purpose: To teach knowledge of the alphabet

Materials: A race track gameboard
Flash cards containing each letter of the alphabet (or each letter to be learned)
A marker and a die

Procedure:

A student throws the die and can then move that many spaces if he can identify the letter on the flashcard. To provide more practice, modify the rules so that the student must identify one flashcard for each space he moves.

Newspaper Search

Purpose: To teach knowledge of the alphabet

Materials: A newspaper page and a crayon for each student

Procedure:

The teacher or a student names a letter and the remaining students search their newspaper pages to find the letter and circle it with the crayon. Then have them hunt for another letter and continue in the same manner. Additional practice may be provided by having the students search for both uppercase and lowercase examples of the letter named.

Letter Bingo

Purpose: To teach knowledge of the alphabet

Materials: A bingo card filled with alphabet letters
Markers for each child

Procedure:

The caller names a letter and holds up the matching card while the students search for and cover the named letter on their cards. The first player to cover a row calls "bingo."

II

ORAL READING

2

Word-by-Word Reading

RECOGNIZED BY

The student pauses after each word and does not allow the words to flow as they would in a conversation.

DISCUSSION

Word-by-word reading may be caused by one or more of the following: (1) failure to apply decoding skills effectively (these include basic sight vocabulary, phonics, structural analysis, and context clues); (2) failure to comprehend adequately; or (3) poor reading-efficiency skills (lack of fluency). Young students who are beginning to read are often word-by-word readers. However, as their sight vocabulary continues to grow and their word-analysis skills are refined, they should lose this habit.

You should determine which of the previously listed factors is causing the word-by-word reading. Make this determination as follows: Give the student something to read at a lower reading level than she is capable of. If she continues to read poorly, the problem may then be assumed to be poor efficiency skills. If she immediately improves, the problem can generally be considered one of either decoding or comprehension. You must then decide between these two difficulties. Ask the student questions about the more difficult material she was reading word-by-word. If the student can answer approximately 75% or more of the questions correctly, then her problem probably lies in the area of decoding. If she cannot answer approximately 75% of the questions correctly, she may be having trouble with comprehension. You may also take a few of the more difficult words from the reading passage and put them on flash cards to see if the student can recognize these words in isolation.

If the student is unable to decode the words, the recommendations listed in items A through G will be helpful. If the difficulty results from poor efficiency skills, the recommendations under items H through S will be more helpful. However, if the student is having difficulty with comprehension, you should follow the suggestions listed under "Comprehension Inadequate," Chapter 21.

Remember that students can only read efficiently (fluently) when they are thoroughly familiar with the vocabulary in the material that they are required to read. Therefore, if a student is having difficulty with the vocabulary in the material, you should not try the types of suggestions listed in items F through Q. You would be treating the symptoms rather than the actual cause of the difficulty.

RECOMMENDATIONS

For students whose word-by-word reading is caused by inadequate decoding ability:

A. Use reading material on a lower level of difficulty.

B. Do not expect students to read material above their meaning-vocabulary level. Generally use *easy* materials and encourage students to read in great quantity.

C. Have the students dictate or write their own stories and read them aloud. Tape-record their readings of these stories and contrast the recordings with their readings of less familiar stories. Discuss the differences and their need for smooth fluent reading. (This is an adaptation of the language-experience approach.)

D. Use other aspects of the language-experience approach as described in Chapter 29.

E. If word-by-word reading is caused by an insufficient sight vocabulary, you should follow the suggestions listed under "Incorrect Phrasing," Chapter 3, item A, and those listed in Chapters 12 and 13.

F. If the student is unable to use phonics or structural analysis sufficiently for decoding, then the recommendations in Chapters 14 through 18 will prove helpful.

G. To help students use their existing decoding skills effectively, teach the following *word-attack strategy:*

WHEN YOU COME TO A WORD YOU DON'T KNOW:

1. Say the beginning sound.
2. Read the rest of the sentence. THINK.
3. Say the parts that you know. GUESS.
4. Ask someone or skip it and go on.

This strategy and effective ways to teach it are described in Chapter 19, which also presents a number of other recommendations for teaching students to use context clues.

For students whose incorrect phrasing is caused by other poor efficiency skills:

H. If the student seems unaware of her word-by-word reading, it is often helpful to tape-record the student while she is reading orally. Then play back the recording so she can become aware of the specific problem. If necessary, take time to demonstrate both the inappropriate (word-by-word) and fluent reading.

I. In recommendation B, we suggested that you urge students to read in great quantity. This suggestion was aimed at readers whose word-by-word reading results from poor decoding skills. This recommendation is equally valuable for students whose word-by-word reading results from poor efficiency skills. The recommendation bears repeating: Provide abundant opportunities for students to receive practice in the act of reading, both orally and silently.

J. Use one or more of the following oral reading techniques: neurological impress method (NIM), echo reading, repeated readings, and precision reading. These procedures, which are highly effective with a variety of oral reading difficulties, are described in detail in Chapter 29. A number of other oral reading activities are also described briefly in Chapter 29.

K. Allow students to preread material silently before asking them to read it orally. You might allow students to ask you for assistance with difficult words during the silent reading phase. If they ask for help on more than 10% of the words, then the material is too difficult and should be replaced with easier material.

L. Using an audio tape recorder may also serve as an excellent way for students to practice oral reading. The teacher might set up a "recording studio," providing a tape recorder, microphone, and cassette tapes for the students. The following activities are effective:

1. The student reads orally into the tape recorder, plays back the tape, and
   a. listens to the recording noting errors
   b. reads along silently, or
   c. reads along orally
2. The teacher or another person reads a selection into the tape recorder and the student plays it back as in item 1. The teacher may make purposeful errors or exhibit poor efficiency skills, such as word-by-word reading. The student evaluates the teacher's performance and tries to apply this to her own reading.
3. Two or more students read into a tape recorder together, using some of the above techniques.

M. Provide experience in choral reading. This activity may be done with as few as two students or with the entire class.

N. Give a series of timed silent-reading exercises. The addition of the time factor will often make the student aware of the word-by-word reading.

O. Allow students to choose stories that they feel are exciting and then let them read their selections aloud.

P. Have the children read and dramatize conversations.

Q. Have the children read poetry. They should read it over until it becomes easy for them.

R. Use commercial materials, such as *Plays for Echo Reading* published by Harcourt Brace Jovanovich, that are designed to develop expressive, fluent oral reading.

3

Incorrect Phrasing

RECOGNIZED BY

The student fails to read in natural phrasing or linguistic units. He may fail to take a breath at the proper place and will often ignore punctuation, especially commas.

DISCUSSION

The causes of incorrect phrasing may be inadequate decoding ability, insufficient comprehension, or poor efficiency skills. You should first determine the cause. Give the student a disorganized list of all the words from a passage that he will read later. The passage should be at a reading level at which the student is experiencing difficulty. If he does not recognize approximately 95% of the words on the list, you can assume that inadequate decoding ability is contributing to the problem of incorrect phrasing. If the student does recognize at least 95% of the words on the list, then have him read the story from which the words came and answer at least six questions about that story. If the student phrases incorrectly and fails to answer at least 75% of the questions (but knows 95% or more of the words), comprehension difficulties are probably a major contributor to the problem.

Reading material is probably not too difficult for a student if he has instant recognition of 95% or more of the words and can answer at least 75% of questions about the passage. If the material is *not* too difficult in terms of vocabulary and comprehension, and a student continues to phrase incorrectly, you may assume that either he does not understand the meaning of various punctuation marks or he has other poor efficiency skills.

If insufficient decoding skills are a contributing factor in incorrect phrasing, then the suggestions in items A through G should be beneficial. If the cause of incorrect phrasing is a lack of comprehension, consult item H in the recommendations and refer to the appropriate chapter. If incorrect phrasing is caused by a failure to understand the meaning of certain punctuation marks, the suggestions listed under items I through O are appropriate. If incorrect phrasing is caused by other poor efficiency skills, then consult items P through X.

If the incorrect phrasing is caused by either a lack of decoding ability or a lack of comprehension, you would be treating only the symptom and not the cause by using the recommendations listed in items I through X.

RECOMMENDATIONS

For students whose incorrect phrasing is caused by inadequate decoding ability:

A. If the cause of incorrect phrasing is a lack of knowledge of basic sight vocabulary or a limited number of other words in the student's sight vocabulary, then the suggestions recommended in Chapters 12 and 13 will be helpful. A word becomes a sight word after it has been read many times. Some writers and researchers have estimated that it takes from 20 to 70 exposures to a word before it actually becomes a sight word. A student who has not built up a sight vocabulary equivalent to his grade level must read and read and read to expose himself to as many new words as many times as possible.

B. Have the student practice reading sight phrase cards such as those described for testing basic sight-word phrases in Appendix C.

C. Compile lists of common prepositional phrases and have the students practice reading these phrases. (See Appendix M.) Follow this practice, and that described in item B, with timed tests of the students' ability to read the phrases off flash cards. Such tests can be administered by the teacher, another adult, or other students. Be sure to mix up the phrases before flashing them. Provide a penalty for missed phrases. After the test, graph and display the students' performance, so that they can see their improvement. It is important to emphasize to the students that they are competing only against themselves, not against one another.

D. Have the student read the Basic Sight Word Sentences, presented in Appendix N, with appropriate phrasing.

E. Use one or more of the tape-recorder activities described in Chapter 2, item J.

F. If the cause of incorrect phrasing is weakness in other decoding skills (phonics, structural analysis, or context clues), then the suggestions recommended in Chapters 14 through 19 will be helpful.

G. Use material that presents no vocabulary problem, allowing the student to concentrate on phrasing without experiencing difficulty in word attack.

For students whose incorrect phrasing is caused by insufficient comprehension:

H. The recommendations in Chapter 20, "Vocabulary Inadequate," or Chapter 21, "Comprehension Inadequate," will be helpful if incorrect phrasing is caused by a lack of comprehension.

For students whose incorrect phrasing is caused by a failure to understand the meaning of certain punctuation marks:

I. Review the meanings of various punctuation marks and discuss how these help the students to phrase properly. It often helps to draw an analogy between traffic signs and punctuation marks; i.e., commas are likened to yield the right-of-way signs and periods are likened to stop signs. Another option is to use guides: three counts for periods, two for commas.

J. Prepare a paragraph with no punctuation marks. Have the student try to read it. Then you and the student together punctuate and read the selection.

K. Use short written paragraphs to demonstrate how punctuation affects the pitch and stress of your voice. Have the student repeat and then reread the paragraphs.

L. Use an overhead projector with paragraphs without punctuation. Together with the student, fill in appropriate marks and read.

M. Dictate simple paragraphs. The student provides the punctuation, in part by listening to the inflections of your voice.

N. Use the language-experience approach (see Chapter 29) and leave out all punctuation marks from the student's dictated story. Then have the student fill them in.

O. Provide cards with words or phrases and cards with punctuation marks. Have the student arrange them properly.

For students whose incorrect phrasing is caused by other poor efficiency skills:

P. Demonstrate proper phrasing by reading to the class.

Q. Reproduce certain reading passages divided into phrases as in the following sentence:

> *Fred and Mary   were on their way   to the movies.*

In doing this, you may find that there is more carryover if a space is left between the phrases rather than using a dash(—) or a slash(/) to separate the phrases.

R. An alternative to the previous suggestion is to write the sentences using crayons or markers. Make each phrase a different color. After they read sentences in color, have the students read them in black and white print. In the following example the different styles of type represent different colors.

> **Fred and Mary**   *were on their way*   to the movies.

S. Have the children read and dramatize conversation.

T. Provide choral-reading with several readers who phrase properly.

U. Photocopy songs. Have the students read these without the music.

V. Have students read orally phrases that extend only to the end of the line. After practicing with these phrases, have students read phrases that carry over onto the next line (however, leave more than the normal amount of space between each phrase). Gradually go from this style to normal writing.

W. Use commercial materials, such as *Plays for Echo Reading* published by Harcourt Brace Jovanovich, that are designed to promote fluent oral reading.

X. Use one or more of the following oral reading techniques: neurological impress method (NIM), echo reading, repeated readings, and precision reading. These procedures, which are highly effective with a variety of oral reading difficulties, are described in detail in Chapter 29. A number of other oral reading activities are also described briefly in Chapter 29.

GAMES AND EXERCISES

Bouncing for Words

Purpose: To provide practice on basic sight words, other sight words, or sight phrases

Materials: Group-size (6″ × 3″) cards for the basic sight words, sight words in general, or sight phrases to be learned
A chair for each child
A basketball or volleyball

Procedure:

Each child is given one phrase card. He stands behind a chair and places his card face up on the seat of the chair. The leader, one of the children in the group, bounces the ball to the first child. As the child catches the ball, he says the phrase. If the student says it correctly, he then picks up the card. If the student misses the phrase, the card remains on the chair. Play continues until all the children have a turn at their phrases. At the end of the game, the children exchange cards and play continues. Any child who could not say the phrase when he caught the ball is told the phrase and keeps the phrase card until all the cards are exchanged at the end of the next game.

   As variations, use sight word cards instead of phrase cards, or use two teams. Instead of beginning with the children in a circle, have opposite teams face each other with 8 or 10 feet between each team. The leader then rotates the bounces between teams. The team with the least number of cards on its chairs after a certain number of sets or games is the winner.

Search

Purpose: To provide practice on the basic sight words or on phrasing

Materials: Three or more identical packs of word cards or three or more identical packs of sight phrase cards

Procedure:

Three or more children sit around a table, each with a pack of phrase or word cards that are identical to those of the rest of the players. One child looks at his pack and calls a phrase. The remaining players then see who can find the same phrase. The child who finds the phrase first places the card face up in the middle of the table and scores a point for himself. Play continues until a certain number of points are scored by an individual.

Pony Express

Purpose: To provide practice on phrasing

Materials: Pocket chart
              Sight phrase cards

Procedure:

Fill a pocket chart with sight cards. Each word may represent a letter in the pony express saddlebag. The children come one at a time to claim their letters and read them to the rest of the class. After all cards have been removed from the chart, the children exchange cards (letters) and begin again by mailing their letters (placing them back in the pocket chart).

A Phrasing Scope

Purpose: To provide practice in proper phrasing

Materials: Pieces of paper about 5" wide
              A piece of cardboard a little larger than the strips of paper
              Two dowel pins about 1/2" in diameter and 7" long

Procedure:

Paste the pieces of paper into a long strip. Type a story, either original or from a book, on the strip. Type only one phrase on a line and double-space the lines. Next, fold the piece of cardboard and seal the sides, leaving the top and bottom open. Cut a window near the top of the cardboard. Slide the strip of paper through the cardboard and attach a round stick (1/2" dowel) at each end of the strip of paper. The pupil rolls the paper from the bottom to the top and reads the story as each phrase passes through the window's opening. See example on next page.

Sets

Purpose: To learn new phrases and to provide practice on reading those already known

Materials: Two decks of identical phrase cards; number of cards used depends on the number of players, use four phrase cards for each player

Procedure:

Deal one deck of phrase cards, so each player has four different phrases. Place all duplicate phrases from the second deck faceup in several rows on the table.

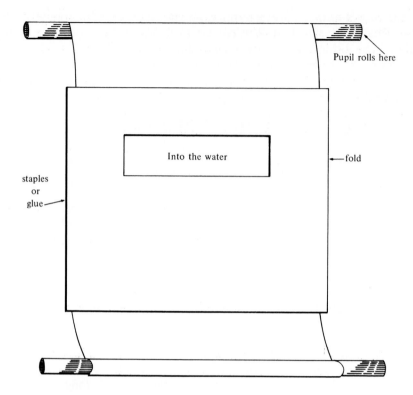

Begin by pointing to a phrase and saying it. The student who has the matching phrase picks it up and says it as he places it in his hand to make a matching "set." Play continues until one player has a complete set of four matches. The student must then read all of the phrases in his hand as they are placed on the desk or table. If the student cannot read them, play continues until another student has a complete matching set and *can* read them without help. The winner is the first student who obtains a complete matching set and is able to read all phrases from the set in his hand.

Drawing for Phrases

Purpose: To provide practice in reading basic sight words and phrases

Materials: Three small boxes
             1″ squares of tagboard

Procedure:

In this game it is beneficial to have a disabled reader work with a good reader. Write a number of different prepositions on 1″ squares of tagboard and place them in box one. Use words such as *with, in, under,* and *over* that would fit with almost any noun. In box two place 1″ tagboard squares with the words *the* and *a.* In box three place a few 1″ tagboard squares with nouns on them such as *house* and *chair.* Ask students to draw one square from each box to form a phrase. After all squares have been drawn and the phrases read, the squares may then be rearranged to form more phrases. You may wish to have the students write down the phrases to see who can create the most phrases. The written list is also useful for reviewing the phrases at a later date.

4

Poor Pronunciation

RECOGNIZED BY

The student fails to pronounce a word correctly.

DISCUSSION

Mispronunciation of words is one of the most serious reading problems of disabled readers. The problem may be caused by one or a combination of the following factors: (1) the student is weak in knowledge of phonics or structural analysis;[*] (2) the student possesses, but does not use, knowledge of phonics or structural analysis; (3) the student has poor efficiency skills; or (4) the student has a hearing, speech, or language difficulty. In any case, a careful diagnosis is called for before a program of correction is started. The following paragraphs suggest ways to diagnose the various reasons for poor pronunciation.

The student lacks knowledge of phonics or structural analysis. The El Paso Phonics Survey found in Appendix E can be used to quickly spot those areas of weakness in the student's knowledge of phonics. Teachers should be especially careful in selecting a phonics test to use. Extensive research at the Reading Center at the University of Texas at El Paso has shown that group phonics tests simply do not measure what a student actually does in applying phonic word-attack skills in the act of reading. Therefore, such tests do not aid diagnostic teaching. This inadequacy is also true of some individual phonics tests. However, the El Paso Phonics Survey does require the student to respond in a situation similar to the actual application of skills. The tests found in Appendices F and G will enable you to determine if the student is having difficulty with structural-analysis skills.

The student has phonics or structural-analysis knowledge but does not use it

---

*If the student has difficulty pronouncing *one-syllable* words, then she is likely to have a problem with phonics. If the student has difficulty pronouncing words of *two or more syllables,* then she is likely to have a problem with structural analysis. These are analogous decoding skills. When using phonics, the student visually divides a one-syllable word into individual sounds *(phonemes),* pronounces each sound, and blends the sounds together. When using structural analysis, the student visually divides a word of two or more syllables into pronounceable parts *(morphemes),* pronounces each part, and blends the parts together. In using both skills, the student must perform the three acts quickly. A third decoding skill, using context clues, enables the student to use the meaning of other words in a sentence to help in figuring out the unknown word. Skilled readers use all of these skills together, along with sight word recognition, to decode effectively.

properly. The El Paso Phonics Survey actually tests the student's ability to use phonics as well as phonics knowledge itself. The teacher may want to supplement test results by observing the ways in which the student attacks or fails to attack one-syllable words. To determine whether the student applies structural-analysis skills, the teacher should observe the student when she reads material containing words of two or more syllables.

Poor efficiency skills. You should stop the reader at a mispronounced word and ask for the correct pronunciation. If the student usually says it correctly, she may lack reading fluency (poor efficiency skills). This would still not exclude the possibility that training in various forms of word analysis might be beneficial.

Hearing, speech, or language differences. An auditory-discrimination test is easy to administer and will determine if a student has difficulty discriminating between somewhat similar sounds. The inability to discriminate between certain sounds can lead to the mispronunciation of words. This knowledge, supplemented with informal hearing tests, such as determining if the student hears a normal voice at the distance most students hear it, will help you decide if a hearing defect is contributing to the reading difficulty. Students indicating difficulty in any of these areas should be examined further by a specialist. To determine if the student has a speech difficulty, ask the student to repeat sentences that are given orally. Use words that were mispronounced in previous reading. Words read incorrectly, but spoken correctly, are not speech problems. Some students may mispronounce words because their first language is not English. This may also occur if the student speaks a nonstandard dialect of English. This need not be cause for concern. If the mispronunciation does not cause loss of meaning (comprehension), then it is not necessary to remediate this difficulty. You can determine whether meaning is affected by using the procedure described in the previous chapter to check comprehension. Teachers of students who are limited-English speakers or speakers of nonstandard dialects should become familiar with the differences in pronunciations that will occur in the language or dialect spoken. With this knowledge and some experience, you will have little difficulty in determining whether problems in mispronunciation of words affect reading comprehension.

If the student lacks knowledge of phonics or structural analysis, then the suggestions in items A through E in the recommendations section should be beneficial. If the student has knowledge of phonics or structural analysis but does not use these skills properly when reading, consult items F and G. If the pronunciation difficulties are caused by poor efficiency skills, the suggestions listed under items H through J are appropriate. Finally, if poor pronunciation is caused by hearing, speech, or language differences, then consult items K through N.

RECOMMENDATIONS

For students who need help in phonics or structural-analysis knowledge:

A. Teach the phonics or structural-analysis skills in which a weakness is indicated by the El Paso Phonics Survey (see Appendix E) or the structural analysis tests (Appendices F and G). Then refer to the appropriate chapters (14 through 18) for corrective procedures.

B. Use the phonogram list in Appendix L as suggested under "Using the Phonogram List to Teach Phonics."

C. Have students make their own lists of common letter combinations that are generally phonetically regular such as *-tion, -ance,* and *-edge* as they are encountered and learned.

D. Make lists of prefixes and suffixes; however, do not expect the students to learn the meaning of many of these. Focus only on the students' correct pronunciation of these affixes. (See list of prefixes and suffixes in Appendix O.)

E. Have the students make word cards or lists and build their own file of words that they habitually mispronounce. Allow for periodic, independent study of these words. An old shoe box makes an excellent file box for indexing word cards.

For students who possess knowledge of phonics or structural analysis but do not use this knowledge properly:

F. Use the phonogram list in Appendix L as follows:

1. Have the student first pronounce *sent*; then give her a number of other words and nonsense words to pronounce that end in *-ent,* such as *dent, pent,* and *bent.* This exercise will give the student practice in using various consonant sounds in conjunction with various word endings.

2. Do the same as in 1, using consonant blends with various combinations; for example, pronounce *slash,* then give a number of other words and nonsense words ending in *-ash,* such as *crash, flash,* and *scash.* As the student reads, ask her to try to pronounce difficult words aloud. You should determine which sounds she knows but is not using. Use these sounds to construct exercises similar to the two shown previously or others appropriate for improving the particular phonic elements not being used correctly.

G. To help students use their existing decoding skills effectively, teach them to use the *word-attack strategy.* This strategy and effective ways to teach it are described in Chapter 19, which also presents a number of other recommendations for teaching students to use context clues.

H. For longer, more difficult words, first teach the student to use *structural analysis,* then teach the student the *word-attack strategy* that will enable her to use the various word-attack skills together when she meets unfamiliar words in the act of reading. For structural analysis, the student must learn to identify word parts, visually separate word parts, pronounce word parts, and blend the parts together to form the whole word. Procedures for doing this are presented in Chapter 17.

For students who have poor efficiency skills:

I. When the student mispronounces a word in oral reading, call attention to the correct pronunciation with as little fuss as possible. Ignoring the mistake tends to reinforce the wrong pronunciation with the student as well as with any other members of the class who are listening. If the student misses the same word more than once, reinforce the student's pronunciation as follows:

1. After you pronounce the word for the student for the second time, ask her to focus her eyes on the word and repeat it five times, then say it loudly.
2. A few minutes later, come back to the word, point to it, and have the student pronounce it. If she says it correctly, lavish the student with praise. If she has again forgotten the word, have her write it carefully on two flash cards or slips of paper. Have her keep one of the cards or slips of paper to use for practice while you keep the other. Later that day or the next, show her your copy of the flash card or slip of paper. If she says it correctly this time, praise the student emphatically. (This procedure will work with only a few words at a time. If the student is missing more than a few words of the material being read, then the material is probably too difficult and should be replaced by easier reading material.)

J. Use commercial materials designed to promote fluent oral reading, such as *Plays for Echo Reading* published by Harcourt Brace Jovanovich.
K. Use one or more of the following oral reading techniques: neurological impress method (NIM), echo reading, repeated readings, and precision reading. These procedures, which are highly effective with a variety of oral reading difficulties, are described in detail in Chapter 29. A number of other oral reading activities are also described briefly in Chapter 29.

For students whose pronunciation difficulties are caused by hearing, speech, or language differences:

L. To teach certain sounds with which students are having difficulty:

1. Set up pairs with only one different sound, e.g., hit—heat.
2. Make sure the students can hear the sound differences.
3. Make sure the students can say the words.
4. Use each word in a sentence and then have the students say the single sound following that sentence.

M. Have students hold their throats with their hands to feel the difference in vibration from one word to another or from one letter to another.
N. Play games that deal with sounds. For example, the first student says, "I am a *ch*." The rest of the students then guess whether she is a chicken, chipmunk, etc. This gives all students many exposures to word beginnings.
O. Refer to a speech, hearing, or language specialist, if available, for suggestions or direct services to the student.

5

Omissions

RECOGNIZED BY

The student omits words, phrases, or both.

DISCUSSION

Omissions in reading are usually caused by inadequate decoding skills. The student encounters a word or phrase he cannot pronounce and skips over it. The student may or may not pause before omitting the word or phrase. Often such a student is fearful of mispronouncing a word when reading orally. In some cases, omissions result from poor efficiency skills. The student may read too rapidly or carelessly. In either case, the omissions are likely to lead to reduced comprehension, which is a serious problem. Occasionally, omissions result when students purposely skip over unknown words because they have been taught to do so. (This is an appropriate decoding strategy in some circumstances. See the section in Chapter 29 that describes the word-attack strategy.) Omissions are the second most common type of miscue.

Before beginning a program of help, you should determine the cause. To determine if the omission of words is caused by decoding difficulties or poor efficiency skills, ask the student to pronounce any words omitted after he has read a passage. If the student still does not know the word or words, then the problem is likely to be lack of decoding skills. If the student now knows the word or words, assume that the problem is one of poor efficiency skills. You might also have the student read the material at the level in which he is making omissions and note the percentage of words omitted. Then have the student read an easier passage, and note whether omissions still occur. If the percentage of omissions decreases markedly, assume that the student has insufficient decoding skills. If, however, the omissions continue with approximately the same percentage of occurrence, assume that they are a result of poor efficiency skills.

The student may lack word-analysis skills in the areas of phonics, structural analysis, or context clues, or he may to some extent lack comprehension. If the problem stems from one of these difficulties, the suggestions in items A through I will probably be of little or no value, since the omissions are actually only symptoms of a larger problem with word analysis or comprehension. It is then necessary to determine in which of these areas the student is deficient. The procedures and suggestions recommended for each area are given in the following chapters:

> Phonics—Chapters 14, 15, and 16
> Structural Analysis—Chapters 17 and 18
> Context Clues—Chapter 19
> Comprehension—Chapter 21

The word-attack strategy presented in Chapter 19 will prove especially useful to students whose omissions result from inadequate word-analysis skills.

If the student is able to analyze new words but does not have instant recognition of words that, for his grade level, should have become sight words, he probably lacks word-recognition skills. It would then be necessary to help the student build a sight vocabulary. To improve this area, see Chapter 13.

If the student's problem is determined to be one of poor efficiency skills, the suggestions listed under items A through I should be helpful. Also keep in mind that unless the student's errors are rather frequent and affect comprehension to some extent, they may not be worth worrying about.

Some of the recommendations that follow may encourage the student to substitute temporarily one symptom for another. For example, in item D below, the student is encouraged to use finger-pointing to eliminate omissions. The use of such crutches should not be a problem. As the student's reading ability improves, the new behavior (in this case, finger-pointing) will no longer be necessary.

RECOMMENDATIONS

A. Call the reader's attention to omissions when they occur. Making an immediate correction is the first step toward breaking the habit.

B. Allow students to preread material silently before asking them to read it orally. You might allow students to ask you for assistance with difficult words during the silent reading phase. If they ask for help on more than 10% of the words, then the material is too difficult and should be replaced with easier material.

C. Use one or more of the following oral reading techniques: neurological impress method (NIM), echo reading, repeated readings, and precision reading. These procedures, which are highly effective with a variety of oral reading difficulties, are described in detail in Chapter 29. A number of other oral reading activities are also described briefly in Chapter 29. After calling the student's attention to the problem as mentioned in A, you may find that these methods are extremely effective.

D. If whole words or phrases are consistently skipped, you might require the student to point to each word as he reads it. It is helpful to ask the student to pick up his finger and then bring it down on each word as it is read. This keeps the student from pointing to words that are ahead of the actual word being read. This technique also should be stopped as soon as possible.

E. Have several children choral-read or let one child read with a tape recording of a reading passage.

F. Use commercial materials, such as *Plays for Echo Reading* published by Harcourt Brace Jovanovich, that are designed to promote fluent oral reading. Participation in the reading of a play or a readers' theater activity will strongly encourage students to read each word that is written.

G. Ask detailed questions that require thorough reading. Ask about only a sentence or paragraph at a time. Students often will omit adjectives. In this case, it is often helpful to give the student a list of questions such as, "Was the bear big or little?" and "What color were the flowers?" The student will be forced to focus on adjectives that could otherwise easily be omitted.

H. To focus attention on words omitted by the reader, tape-record a passage and then give the student a copy of the material as it is played back to him. Have the student follow along and point to each word as it is read. Have him circle all words omitted. After the reading, discuss possible reasons for his omitting the words and the importance of not doing so. Suggestions for additional tape-recorder activities appear in Chapter 2, item L.

I. As the student reads, ask him to outline the first letter of each word read as follows:

$$\mathcal{S}\text{am } \mathcal{P}\text{lays } \mathbf{b}\text{aseball } \textit{in} \mathsf{t}\text{he } \mathcal{P}\text{ark.}$$

This will be helpful for students who make many omissions. You will, of course, want to discontinue this as soon as the student stops making omissions. Another variation of the previous procedure is to have the student underline the first letters of words as follows:

<u>M</u>ary <u>w</u>ent <u>w</u>ith <u>h</u>er <u>m</u>other <u>t</u>o the <u>s</u>tore.

Following this you may wish to have the student draw lines over or below words in phrases or natural linguistic units as he reads:

<u>Fred has</u> a <u>large brown cat.</u>

6

Repetitions

RECOGNIZED BY

The student rereads words or phrases.

DISCUSSION

The most common causes of repetitions in a student's reading are similar to the causes of omissions in reading, that is, poor word-recognition skills, poor word-analysis skills, or poor efficiency skills. Of these, a problem with word-recognition skills (sight vocabulary) occurs most often. It should be pointed out, however, that sometimes a student repeats certain words in order to correct a reading error or to gain time so as to avoid making an error. This may be a stalling tactic the student uses while she mentally works on the upcoming word. If this happens only on certain words that you know are new or difficult for the student, you should, in most cases, ignore it. If the words the student does not recognize are ones that normally should be sight words for that student, you can assume that she is deficient in word-recognition skills. In this case, the recommendations in Chapter 13 should be beneficial.

The problem of word-analysis difficulties may be in any of the following areas: (1) phonics; (2) structural analysis; (3) or use of context clues. Occasionally the student will need assistance with dictionary skills. If the problem is in one of these areas, some of the recommendations that follow will probably be of little or no value since the repetitions are only a symptom of the larger problems of word-recognition or word-analysis difficulties. You would need to determine in which area of word analysis the student was deficient. These procedures and the suggestions recommended in each case are given in the following chapters:

> Phonics—Chapters 14, 15, and 16
> Structural Analysis—Chapters 17 and 18
> Context Clues—Chapter 19
> Dictionary Skills—Chapter 27

The word-attack strategy presented in Chapter 19 will also prove useful to students whose repetitions result from inadequate word-analysis skills.

You can determine, to some extent, whether poor word-recognition or word-analysis skills is the cause of repetitions by having the student read material at the level in which she is making repetitions. Note the percentage of words or phrases repeated. Then give the student a much easier passage and note whether there is a definite decrease in the percentage of repetitions. If there is, the problem is probably insufficient word-recognition or word-analysis skills. If, on the other hand, a student continues to make as many repetitions as she did on the more difficult passage, then the problem is probably poor efficiency skills.

If you determine that the problem results from poor efficiency skills, then the recommendations listed under items A through G should prove beneficial. Also, the suggestions listed under items H and I may give the student the confidence she needs to begin reading fluently.

RECOMMENDATIONS

A. Call the repetitions to the student's attention. This is the initial step in breaking the bad habit.

B. Use one or more of the following oral reading techniques: neurological impress method (NIM), echo reading, repeated readings, and precision reading. These procedures, which are highly effective with a variety of oral reading difficulties, are described in detail in Chapter 29. A number of other oral reading activities are also described briefly in Chapter 29.

C. Have the students choral-read.

D. Use mechanical devices that are designed to project a certain number of words per minute and that prevent the reader from regressing. When working with children in the primary grades, you should not worry about speed itself. You must make sure the instrument does not move at a rate faster than the normal reading rate of the reader. It is almost always better for the student to first read accurately, then read faster.

E. Have the student set a certain pace with her hand and keep up with this pace as she reads. Do not let the eyes pace the hand.

F. To focus attention on words repeated by the reader, tape-record a passage that she reads and then give the student a copy of the written material as it is played back to her. Have the student follow along pointing to each word and underlining any words as they are repeated. After completing the passage, discuss any reasons that the student believes are causing her to repeat words or phrases.

G. Follow the other suggestions for using the tape recorder, listed in Chapter 2, item J.

H. Provide easier or more familiar material in which the vocabulary presents no problem.

I. Let the students read the material silently before they attempt to read orally.

7

Inversions or Reversals

RECOGNIZED BY

The student reads words from right to left instead of the normal left-to-right sequence, e.g., *was* for *saw*, or *pot* for *top*.

The student reads letters in reverse, e.g., *d* for *b*, or *p* for *g*. The student makes partial reversals in words (the letters within words), e.g., *ant* for *nat*.

The student reverses words within sentences, e.g., the *rat* chased the *cat*," instead of "the *cat* chased the *rat*."

DISCUSSION

Reversals are a normal symptom of poor decoding skills regardless of the age of the reader. An adult who reads at a first-grade level is likely to make the same reversal errors as a 6-year-old reading at a first-grade level, especially when reading words in isolation. As decoding ability improves, reversals almost always disappear.

Reversals or inversions may be caused by a number of factors. The student may have failed to develop a left-to-right eye movement or a left-to-right reading pattern. (This problem, if and when it exists, is difficult to determine.) The student may not have developed a strong enough visual image for the word and may miscall the word because he is not sufficiently focused on the context. The student may suffer from some neurological impairment, or he may fail to realize that the order or position in which letters appear does make a difference. Another possible factor is immaturity. (It is much more common for a student of 5, 6, or even 7 years old to make inversions or reversals than a child who is 8 years old.)

Observation and questioning will, in some cases, help locate the cause of the reversals. However, unless the problem is a difficult one caused by a neurological dysfunction, you need not be concerned with which of the above causes is the major contributor. The recommendations are the same in any case. Many children who make reversals tend to outgrow the problem after a few months of school. However, if the problem persists after several weeks of instruction and the student is making normal progress otherwise (especially if the student is older than 8 years of age), you may wish to refer the student to a psychologist or neurologist. However, be prepared to receive advice that you continue doing the things listed in the following "Recommendations" section.

For many years reading teachers believed that students who made many reversals or inversions tended to have more severe difficulties than students who made other types of errors. More recent research has tended to refute this belief. We now believe that, if checked carefully, you are likely to find that children who make numerous reversals will also make just as high a percentage of other types of errors.

RECOMMENDATIONS

Probably the most important thing you can do to help the student correct the problem is to call his attention to the context in which the word is used. If the student is made aware of the context, then he will have a tendency to correct the problem on his own. To do this, give the student a number of sentences in which the word or words being reversed could only logically be used in one context. It may be helpful to have the student work at the sentence level, rather than at the paragraph or passage level, so he can focus more on the context. The following is an example:

> Fred *was* going with Tom to the movies.
> Lori *saw* a big dog on the way home.

A. Use Big Books for beginning readers to point out left-to right progression (as well as other skills, such as sequencing of words and common sight words). The larger print and the high interest level of most of these books enhance motivation for learning these skills.

B. After discussing the problem with the student, give him sentences in which words that he tends to reverse are covered by a small piece of paper. Allow him to read to the end of the sentence, using the context to determine the word he thinks should be in the sentence. Then allow him to uncover the word and check the accuracy of his use of context.

C. Emphasize left-to-right in all reading activities. The following methods may be helpful:

   1. Cover words or sentences with your hand or a card and read the word or sentence as you uncover it. Then have the student do the same. The student may find it helpful to make a window marker as shown. The child uses it as he would a regular marker but lets the line of print show through the slot.

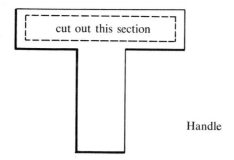

cut out this section

Handle

2. Have the student underline the word or sentence, sounding the word as it is underlined or reading the sentence as it is underlined.
3. Teach the child to pace his reading with his hand, practicing a left-to-right movement.
4. Draw arrows pointing from left to right under troublesome words.

D. Let the child use a typewriter or computer to practice words with which he has difficulty. This will enable him to see the word formed from left to right as he types.
E. Pair the letters that are causing difficulty (such as *p* and *q*). Have the student trace the letters with his index and middle fingers, sounding each letter as it is traced.
F. If whole words are reversed, you can have the student trace the word and then attempt to write it from memory.
G. Use a magnetic board with three-dimensional letters. Have the student manipulate letters to form words commonly reversed.
H. Write in pairs the words sometimes reversed (was/*saw*, net/*ten*, war/*raw*, trap/*part*). Use one word in a sentence and ask students to point to or write the word used.
I. Use a colored letter at the beginning of words commonly confused. Discontinue this practice as soon as the word no longer presents any difficulty for the child.
J. Blindfold the student and form letters or words with which he is having difficulty, using three-dimensional letters. Have the student trace the letter and say it as you trace it on his back, making sure that your finger follows the same part of the letter on the student's back that his does in tracing the three-dimensional letter.
K. To help make the student aware of the importance of sequence of words commonly reversed, place one word commonly reversed over another. Then have the student draw lines from the first letter of the top word to the first letter of the bottom word. Have the student say

each letter as he begins to draw the line from it and each letter as the line reaches it:

L. Write two words commonly reversed side by side. Ask the student to number the letters in the first word by placing a number under each letter. Then ask him to assign the same numbers to the letters in the second word:

```
s a w   w a s       o n   n o
1 2 3   3 2 1       1 2   2 1
```

8

Insertions

RECOGNIZED BY

The student adds words that are not present in the sentences. For example, in the sentence, "The dog chased the little boy," the student may add *big* to make the sentence read, "The *big* dog chased the little boy."

DISCUSSION

Insertions are the third most common type of miscue made by students in oral reading. They are often not as serious as other types of errors. A possible cause of insertions is that the student's oral language development may surpass her reading level or that she may anticipate what is coming next and read that instead of what actually is written. Insertions that make sense within the context of the sentence indicate the student's awareness or comprehension of the material being read. In this case, you may assume the insertions are caused from either poor efficiency skills or oral language development beyond the reading level of the student. When insertions do not make sense within the context of the sentence, you may assume that comprehension problems are involved. The recommendations listed in items A through I are appropriate when the problem is poor efficiency skills or when the oral language development of the student surpasses her reading ability. If students make these types of insertion errors, you should first determine whether they appear often, or are serious enough, to cause concern. If they appear rather seldom, it may be best to ignore them. If the cause of the insertions is a lack of comprehension, then the recommendations in "Comprehension Inadequate," Chapter 21, are recommended.

RECOMMENDATIONS

A. Call the student's attention to the insertion. Sometimes she is not aware of the habit. Allowing the student to continue only provides reinforcement for the mistakes.

B. Encourage the student to read more slowly. Students often believe erroneously that good reading is fast reading. When students try to read more quickly than they are able, insertions may result.

C. Use commercial materials, such as *Plays for Echo Reading* published by Harcourt Brace Jovanovich, that are designed to promote fluent oral reading.

D. Use one or more of the following oral reading techniques: neurological impress method (NIM), echo reading, repeated readings, and precision reading. These procedures, which are highly effective with a variety of oral reading difficulties, are described in detail in Chapter 29. A number of other oral reading activities are also described briefly in Chapter 29.

E. Ask questions that require an exact answer. If the student usually follows a certain pattern in making insertions (such as adding adjectives), you may wish to provide questions for the student to review before reading the story. These questions can focus on the objects in the story described by the adjectives that are often inserted. This will cause the student to read more carefully. Use questions such as: "Does it say how big the frog was?" and "Was it a sunny, warm day, a sunny, cold day, or just a sunny day?"

F. Have students choral-read.

G. Play a tape recording in which the student made insertions. Ask the student to follow the written passage stopping the tape recorder as often as necessary. Have the student write on the written passage the insertions that she made on the oral reading of the material. Use the student-corrected passages as a basis for discussing the problem.

H. Have the student read along with a passage that has been tape-recorded. See Chapter 2, item L, for additional activities using the audio tape recorder.

I. If the student makes many insertions, have her point to each word as it is read. Have the student lift her finger up and bring it down on each word as it is read. Do not allow the student to continue this technique after the habit has disappeared.

9

Substitutions

RECOGNIZED BY

The student substitutes one word for another.

DISCUSSION

Substitutions are the most common type of miscue or oral reading error. The student who substitutes one word for another is either a reader who has not developed adequate decoding skills or one with poor efficiency skills. Some readers make substitutions that are nearly correct within the context of the material being read, e.g., "The man drove the *automobile*" might be read, "The man drove the *car*." If these minor mistakes do not appear too often, it may be best to ignore the problem. If, however, they consistently occur, some steps should be taken. These errors do matter. As students grow older and read increasingly difficult content materials, even contextually appropriate substitutions can result in lowered comprehension.

Substitutions that are not in the proper context of the sentence usually are caused by decoding difficulty. When help is given with decoding skills, the problem of substitutions usually disappears. You should determine whether substitutions are caused by inadequate decoding skills or inefficient reading and plan help accordingly.

The recommendations in items A through H should be helpful for students whose substitutions are caused by decoding difficulties. If, however, the substitutions are caused by poor efficiency skills, then the recommendations under items I through S should be helpful.

RECOMMENDATIONS

For students whose substitutions are caused by inadequate decoding ability:

A. Use reading material on a lower level of difficulty.
B. Do not expect students to read material above their meaning-vocabulary level. Generally, use *easy* materials and encourage students to read in great quantity.

C. If there are many words that are not known, the suggestions listed under Chapters 12 and 13 should be used. When the student's sight vocabulary is brought up to grade level, the problem of making substitutions will probably disappear.

D. If the student is unable to use phonics or structural analysis sufficiently for decoding, the recommendations in Chapters 14 through 18 will prove helpful.

E. To help students use their existing decoding skills effectively, teach the following *word-attack strategy:*

WHEN YOU COME TO A WORD YOU DON'T KNOW:

1. Say the beginning sound.
2. Read the rest of the sentence. THINK.
3. Say the parts that you know. GUESS.
4. Ask someone or skip it and go on.

This strategy and effective ways to teach it are described in Chapter 19, which also presents a number of other recommendations for teaching students to use context clues.

F. Sometimes students feel they must make a continual response while they are reading. When such students do not know a strange word, they are likely to substitute whatever word comes into their minds rather than take the time to use the word-attack strategy. Assure these students that they will be given ample time to attack a word before you or a classmate tell them the word.

G. Use the difficult words in multiple-choice sentences, such as the following examples:

1. John's father gave him a (watch, witch, water) for his birthday.
2. He (though, thought, through) he would be the tallest boy in the class.
3. He asked his father (what, where, when) they would leave.
4. She said, "The books belong to (them, that, this)."

H. Use the words in sentences where the student must complete the word to make the sentence sensible:

1. Can you tell me wh _____ they will be home?
2. Does th _____ book belong to Lori?
3. The stunt driver drove his car thr _____ the wall of fire.
4. Jamie said, "That funny l _____ dog belongs to me."

For students whose substitutions are caused by poor efficiency skills:

I. Call attention to the mistake and correct it when it occurs.

J. In item B above, we recommended that you urge students to read in great quantity. This suggestion was aimed at readers whose substitutions result from poor decoding skills. The suggestion is equally valuable for students whose substitutions result from poor efficiency skills. Thus, the recommendation bears repeating: Provide abundant opportunities for students to receive practice in the act of reading, both orally and silently.

K. Allow students to preread material silently before asking them to read it orally. You might allow students to ask you for assistance with difficult words during the silent reading phase. If they ask for help on more than 10 percent of the words, then the material is too difficult and should be replaced with easier material.

L. Use commercial materials, such as *Plays for Echo Reading* published by Harcourt Brace Jovanovich, that are designed to promote fluent oral reading.

M. Use one or more of the following oral reading techniques: neurological impress method (NIM), echo reading, repeated readings, and precision reading. These procedures, which are highly effective with a variety of oral reading difficulties, are described in detail in Chapter 29. A number of other oral reading activities are also described briefly in Chapter 29.

N. Have the student trace over the first letter or underline the first letter of each word in the sentence as shown:

Debbie went with Tom to the movies.
Debbie went with Tom to the movies.

Do not ask the student to continue this practice for a long period of time. Use it only to break the habit and then stop using it.

O. Have the students choral-read.

P. Have the students follow a printed copy of what they have read as it is played on a tape recorder. As they listen, have them circle words for which substitutions were made. Use this student-corrected material when discussing the problem.

Q. Have the students read along with a passage that has been tape-recorded. Suggestions for additional tape-recorder activities appear in Chapter 2, item L.

R. Ask questions about the subject matter that will reflect the student's mistakes. Have him read to make corrections.

S. Some students, especially when they are under pressure during a test or in a situation somewhat different from their normal environment, will feel pressure to read rather rapidly. If you sense that a student is reading more rapidly than he should or normally does, stop him and explain that it is not necessary to read faster than usual.

10

Guesses at Words

RECOGNIZED BY

The student guesses at new words instead of analyzing the correct pronunciation.

DISCUSSION

Guessing at words is similar to, and often difficult to distinguish from, substitutions (Chapter 9). Accordingly, the suggestions offered in the previous chapter should also be effective for correcting this problem. Guessing at words may be the result of one or several factors. The student may not possess a knowledge of the decoding skills of phonics or structural analysis. She may not know how to systematically analyze a word, or she may not be using context clues. Before attempting to help the student, you should determine which of the factors are responsible for her guessing at words. An effective way of determining why a student guesses at words is to ask her. You should ask whether she knows the sound of the first letter, the blend, the vowel combinations, the first syllable, and so forth. Also, you should check to see whether the student knows how to blend sounds together rapidly. Finally, ask questions to determine whether she is aware of the context in which the word is used. If you are unsure about the student's ability to use phonics, structural analysis, or context clues, follow the suggestions listed under item A. If she has knowledge of phonics and structural analysis, but does not use these skills to decode, the suggestions listed under items B through G will be helpful. Students who do not make use of the context should be given help as recommended in items H through L.

RECOMMENDATIONS

A. If the student guesses at one-syllable words, administer the El Paso Phonics Survey (Appendix E) or a similar test that tests knowledge that approximates what the student would have to do if actually reading in your classroom. Give help where needed according to the results of the test. If the student guesses at words of more than one syllable, you can test for knowledge of syllable principles (Appendix F). Because an inability to use context clues can cause the student to guess at both one-syllable and multisyllable words, testing for the student's ability to use context clues (Appendix H) is also recommended. Recommendations for correcting difficulties in the areas of phonics, structural analysis, and context clues are found in the following chapters:

> Phonics—Chapters 14, 15, and 16
> Structural Analysis—Chapters 17 and 18
> Context Clues—Chapter 19

B. While the student is reading orally, the teacher should call attention to the words at which she guesses. At the same time, help should be given in the systematic analysis of the word. This will assist the reader in developing the habit of analyzing her own difficult words. Help the student to sound the first sound, the second, and on through to the end of the word. Then give help in blending these sounds together. In doing this with older students, you may find it helpful to practice on phonetically regular "nonsense" words. To make phonetically regular nonsense words, use phonetically regular "real" words and replace the consonants, e.g., from the two-syllable word *tulip,* make the nonsense word *lupit.*

C. Teach the *word-attack strategy* presented in the previous chapter and described in more detail in Chapter 19.

D. Do not expect the student to read material above her meaning-vocabulary level. Generally, use *easy* materials and encourage the student to read in great quantity, both orally and silently.

E. Use one or more of the following oral reading techniques: neurological impress method (NIM), echo reading, repeated readings, and precision reading. These procedures, which are highly effective with a variety of oral reading difficulties, are described in detail in Chapter 29. A number of other oral reading activities are also described briefly in Chapter 29.

F. Allow the student to preread material silently before asking her to read it orally. Encourage the student to ask you for assistance with difficult words during the silent reading phase. If the student asks for help on more than 10% of the words, then the material is too difficult and should be replaced with easier material.

G. Have the student trace over or underline the first and last letters and middle vowel or vowels of words at which she pauses:

> It was a very **h**u**mi**d **d**ay.
>
> It was a very hum̲i̲d day.

H. As the student reads, circle or underline the words that she guesses. Replace these words with blank lines and have the student reread the material. Ask her to fill in the correct words from context.

I. Encourage the student to develop the habit of rereading several words preceding the difficult word and sounding out at least the first one or two sounds of the difficult word. Then have the student read several words following the difficult word. This strategy will develop the habit of using context as well as the beginning sounds. The student will learn to sound more of the word than the first syllable as the need arises. For example: "The large black dog was ch _____ on the bone." If the student has read *on the bone* and hears the sound of *ch,* she will in most cases say *chewing.*

J. Give the student sentences in which there is one difficult word that she has guessed in her oral reading. Have her work independently, using the method described in item I, to determine correctness of the difficult words.

K. Teach the student that there are a number of types of context clues. The student does not have to categorize them; however, working with several different kinds of context clues will enable her to become more adept in their use. For example:

1. Definition context clues:

   The word *mongrel* sometimes refers to a *dog* of mixed breeds.

2. Synonym context clues:

   The team was *gleeful* and the coach was also *jubilant* because they had won the game.

3. Contrasting words:

   He was *antisocial,* but she was *friendly.*

4. Common sayings or expressions:

   It was *dark* as *pitch.*

L. Use commercially prepared materials designed to improve use of context clues.

11

Voicing-Lip Movements, Finger Pointing, and Head Movements

RECOGNIZED BY

When reading silently, the student voices words or reads with visible lip movements; when reading orally or silently, the student points to words with his finger or moves his head while reading.

DISCUSSION

A student who continually voices words or moves his lips while reading silently is not likely to gain any speed until he can be taught that it is not necessary to pronounce each word as it is read. Many people unconsciously pronounce words to themselves even though they do not actually move their lips. Often voicing and lip movement can be detected by watching for visible signs that are apparent when someone speaks. Other students may voice words and yet show no visible signs of doing so. One way to determine whether students are voicing words is to ask them. Very slow, silent reading is also a sign that a student may be voicing words. That in itself, however, is not enough evidence to support such a diagnosis. Remember that voicing or lip movement is often an indication that a student is reading material that is too difficult for him. By giving him material that is considerably easier and then noting whether the voicing and lip movement continues or stops, you can determine whether they are caused by habit or indicate that the student has been reading at or near his frustration level.

Finger pointing and head movements can also reduce a student's reading speed and interfere with comprehension. All of these behaviors are normal for beginning and severely remedial readers. Usually, they disappear as reading ability improves. When these habits continue in spite of the student's improving reading ability, they can usually be extinguished rather easily. Occasionally, teachers will *temporarily* encourage a student to finger point to remediate another problem, such as excessive omissions (see Chapter 5, item D).

RECOMMENDATIONS

For students with a habit of lip movements and/or voicing of words:

A. As strange as the technique may seem, a most effective way to alleviate these problems is to ask the student to hum a familiar tune as he reads. While doing this, the student can neither subconsciously nor consciously voice the words he is reading. The student may at first find it distracting and complain about a lack of comprehension. However, if he continues, the student will soon find that his reading speed is not only considerably faster in most cases, but that his comprehension has also improved. The methods that follow are also effective but will usually not work as well as the method just described.

B. As the student reads, have him hold his mouth shut with the teeth firmly together. Tell the student to hold his tongue against the roof of his mouth.

C. Have the student place a finger against his lips when reading silently.

D. Have the student place a small piece of paper between his lips when reading silently.

E. Discuss with the student the importance of forming mental images when reading silently. Explain that it is not necessary to say each word.

F. Temporarily reduce the amount of oral reading.

G. Have the student pace his reading with his hands. Make sure the rate he uses is faster than his normal speaking rate. This technique may not be effective with children in first, second, or third grade.

H. Use controlled reading devices that require reading at a rate too fast for voicing words. Such devices may not be effective with children in first, second, or third grade.

For students with a habit of finger pointing:

I. If you suspect a vision problem, have the student's eyes checked by an appropriate professional.

J. Have the student use a marker *temporarily*.

K. Provide practice in phrase reading.

L. Provide practice in reading from charts and the chalkboard.

M. Have the student use both hands to hold the book.

N. Use material with large, clear print.

For students with a habit of head movements:

O. Have the student place his elbows on the table and his index fingers against his temples.

P. Demonstrate how to use the eyes to scan a page while the head remains stationary.

III

DECODING ABILITIES

12

Basic Sight Words Not Known

RECOGNIZED BY

The student is unable to read some or all of the basic sight words, those words of high utility that make up from 50% to 70% of the words in most reading material. The percentage is, of course, higher in materials written at a lower reading level.

DISCUSSION

There are several lists of the common or basic sight words. One is provided in Appendix D. Since these words appear frequently, it is important that students recognize them instantly. If students do not have these words in their sight vocabulary, or cannot recognize them instantly, they cannot become fluent readers. Students often confuse certain basic sight words, especially those with similar beginnings, e.g., *when, where,* and *what;* or *this, that,* and *those.*

If you observe your students when they read orally, you can determine if they are usually pronouncing basic sight words accurately. With some experience you will have little difficulty recognizing which words are basic sight words. (Just by glancing at the words listed in Appendix D, you will see that most of the words you would think of as most common do in fact appear on the basic sight word list.)

A first-grader is generally expected to master about one-third of the basic sight word list by the end of the year, a second-grader is expected to master another third, and a third-grader should master the final third of the list by the end of the school year. Mastery means that the student can pronounce the basic sight words instantly on viewing them. Also, the student should pronounce the words correctly *each time* they appear. If a student mispronounces or even hesitates on the pronunciation of a basic sight word, or if the student pronounces the word correctly only some of the time, then the student has *not* mastered this basic sight word.

Many children older than third-graders and most illiterate adults have significant problems with basic sight words. These individuals, along with primary-age children who are not progressing satisfactorily, need systematic and thorough instruction on basic sight words.

A test of the basic sight words often is given by showing the student four or five words and asking her to circle or underline the words you pronounce. The ability to distinguish a word from a choice of four or five words is not, however, the same as the ability to pronounce the word in print. You frequently will find that older students can score 100% on a basic sight word test if it is given in this manner, but may not be able to pronounce many of the same words when they are asked to read them.

When testing for students' knowledge of basic sight words, the words should be presented for approximately one-half to one second each. If you give more time than this, then, to some extent, the test becomes a measure of word-analysis skills rather than of knowledge of sight words. You can have the student read words from a list; however, it is difficult to control the time each word is exposed to the student. If you do have the student read basic sight words from a list, remember to count any word wrong at which the student pauses for more than about one second. Having students read the basic sight words from a list is a quick way to check those students whom you think, but are not quite sure, know most of the words. The *Quick Check for Basic Sight Words,* which appears in Appendix C, may be used for this purpose.

The best way to test basic sight words is to use flash cards with a tape recorder. Specific instructions for doing this are presented along with the lists of basic sight words and phrases that appear in Appendix D. This procedure should be used to test both the individual basic sight words and the basic sight word phrases. Each sight-word test takes approximately six minutes to administer and score.

When the testing is completed, you can examine the prepared lists and determine specifically which basic sight words and phrases the student has not mastered. These can then be taught without having to misuse instructional time teaching words or phrases that are already known.

RECOMMENDATIONS

The suggestions listed in items A through J and the games and exercises will be helpful in teaching the words. Most students will learn basic sight words quickly and easily when they are simply shown the word, hear it used in a sentence, repeat it, and practice reading it. Immediate reinforcement (lots of practice) is essential for the students to *master* the new words. The best way to provide this is to have students read over and over simple student- or teacher-constructed sentences that contain the new words and to do lots of reading in easy books.

The suggestions listed in items A through F and the games and exercises can be used to have students learn and practice the sight word *phrases* as well as the individual words. Many teachers will have students practice the phrases after a set number, say 20, of the words have been mastered. The sight word phrases that appear on the list in Appendix D are compiled so that each word from the isolated words list is presented in a phrase without adding a lot of new

words for the student to master. In addition, a comprehensive list of prepositional phrases is provided in Appendix M. You may wish to have students practice reading these phrases after all the basic sight words have been learned. A
list of basic sight word *sentences* is provided in Appendix N. These sentences are
derived from the basic sight word phrases presented in Appendix D.

The language-experience approach and the various oral reading procedures
presented in Chapter 29 are also effective. In using these methods, you will not
be focusing on any particular basic sight word. However, since the words appear so often, most will be learned because they are used repeatedly, either in
the stories that the student writes using the language-experience approach or
in the passages she reads during oral reading.

When teaching children individually or in small groups, introduce the words
a few at a time. The number of words to be learned per week will vary from
student to student. Success, however, is critical. *It is better to learn fewer words
well.* The students should see mastery as a challenging goal. Often the students themselves can best determine the number of new words to be learned at
a time. If in doubt, begin with five words.

When presenting sight words, always be sure that the student is looking *at
the word,* not at you. If possible, you should try to spend a few minutes with the
student individually when presenting the words for the first time.

A. The following dialogue presents a thorough approach to the initial
teaching of basic sight words. Usually not all of the steps noted are
necessary.

Teacher:	(Hold up a flash card.) "Look at this word. The word is *the.*" (Use it in a sentence.) "I am *the* teacher. Say the word."
Student:	"The."
Teacher:	"Good. Now say it five times."
Student:	"The, the, the, the, the."
Teacher:	"Outstanding. Now say it really loud."
Student:	"The."
Teacher:	"No, that's not loud enough. Let me hear you say it really loud."
Student:	"The."
Teacher:	"Here, I'll show you. THE!"
Student:	(chuckle) "THE!"
Teacher:	"Fantastic! Now let me hear you whisper it."
Student:	(whispering) "The."
Teacher:	"Excellent. Now close your eyes. Can you see the word on your eyelids?"
Student:	"Yup."
Teacher:	"Spell it."
Student:	"t-h-e."
Teacher:	"Good. Now describe the word. What does it look like?"
Student:	"Well, it's kinda small."

Teacher:	"How are you going to remember it?"
Student:	"Uh, it has two letters that stick up."
Teacher:	"Terrific!"

Present each new word using the "overlearning" procedure: 1, 2; 1, 2, 3; 1, 2, 3, 4; 1, 2, 3, 4, 5. For example, *the, to; the, to, and; the, to, and, he;* etc. If, after all the new words have been presented, the student still has difficulty pronouncing them quickly, the following steps may be taken:

1. Have the student trace the word, write it on paper, or use chalk or magic slates.
2. Have the student repeat the word each time it is written.
3. Have the student write the word without looking at the flash card; then compare the two.

B. Create "study buddies." Match learners in the classroom with fellow students who have mastered the words. Take time to teach the "tutors" how to reinforce new words. Provide a reward to both tutor and learner once the learner has attained the goal.

C. Provide reinforcement games for students to use on their own or with their study buddies. (See suggestions under "Games and Exercises" later in this chapter.)

D. Pass out a few basic sight words on cards to students. Each student in turn goes to the board and writes her word. The other students participating should try to say it aloud. After it is pronounced correctly, have them write it in a notebook. On some days have students select words from their notebooks and write them on the chalkboard. Then ask various members of the group to say these words.

E. Provide charts, graphs, and other devices for students to display their progress. These serve as excellent motivators, especially since students are competing with themselves rather than with one another.

F. Have the student write troublesome words on cards. Use the cards to form sentences. Also, provide sentences with the sight words omitted. Have the student fill in the blanks with the appropriate word from her cards.

G. For students who have particular difficulty with certain words, try cutting letters from fine sandpaper or velvet so that the student can "feel" the word as she pronounces it. For certain students it is helpful to put a thin layer of salt or fine sand in a shoe box lid and let them practice writing the word in the salt or sand.

H. Place a piece of paper over a piece of screen wire such as the wire used for screen doors. It is a good idea to cover the edges of the screen wire with bookbinding tape, so the rough edges do not cut anyone. Writing on the paper over the screen with a crayon will leave a series of raised dots. Have the student write basic sight words in this manner, then have her trace over the words, saying them as they are traced.

I. Use the sight words that cause difficulty in sentences. Underline the words that cause difficulty as in the following examples:

1. I <u>thought</u> it was you.
2. I could not go even <u>though</u> I have time.
3. She ran right <u>through</u> the stop sign.

A list of basic sight word sentences, derived from the sight word phrases, is provided in Appendix N.

J. Have the student read the entire sentence, look at the beginning and end of the word, and then try to pronounce it on the basis of its context and configuration.

GAMES AND EXERCISES

(See also "Games and Exercises" in Chapter 13, General Sight Vocabulary Not Up to Grade Level. Many of the games and exercises listed there are appropriate for improving knowledge of basic sight words.)

Dominoes

Purpose: To provide practice in word discrimination

Materials: Flash cards, divided in half by a line, with a different word on each side of the line. (See examples.) Make sure that the words are repeated several times on different cards.

the	what	and	the
a	and	go	a

Procedure:

After mixing the cards, the game proceeds the same as dominoes. The student pronounces the word as she matches it.

Word Order

Purpose: To provide practice on basic sight words, general sight words, or in recognition of phonic elements

Materials: Dittoed sheets of words arranged in the same manner as the following example:

A. why _____	B. c _____
what _____	d _____
when _____	g _____
where _____	b _____
which _____	f _____

C. cat _____	D. sound _____
mule _____	frog _____
cage _____	wolf _____
pill _____	rabbit _____
duck _____	pass _____

Procedure:

Play a recording or read words or sounds to the students who have the dittoed
sheets. Each set of words should, however, concentrate on practice in only one area.
The directions for the preceding sets would be similar to the following example:

Set A: Number the words in the order in which they are read.

Set B: Number the letters that correspond with the same beginning
sound that you hear in the following words (in the order they
are given): book, food, good, can, dog.

Set C: Put numeral *1* in front of the word with a long /a/ sound.
Put *2* in front of the word with a short /u/ sound.
Put *3* in front of the word with a short /a/ sound.
Put *4* in front of the word with a long /u/ sound.
Put *5* in front of the word with a short /i/ sound.

Set D: Number the words, in the order they are given, that have ending letter sounds. Give the following sounds: /f/, /t/, /g/, /d/, /s/.

Passport

Purpose: To provide practice on the basic sight words or general sight words

Materials: Use either group-size (6″ × 3″) or individual-size cards (3″ × 1 ½″).
One set is given to the group of students and one is kept by the
captain, who is usually a student who knows the words well.

Procedure:

Each student is given one or several words (passports). In order to get aboard
the boat, she must show her passports to the captain. When the captain calls
the port (the word or words) from her deck of cards, the person who has a card
matching the captain's must show it to her to get off the boat.

Variation in Procedure:

The same game can be played with the sounds of the consonants and vowels. In this case, the captain has word cards, and the student who has a letter matching the sound of the first letter in the word called by the captain shows her passport (letter) and is allowed to leave the boat.

Word in the Box

Purpose: To provide review and reinforcement of words that present problems to students

Materials: A large box
             Word cards with words on them that have given the students trouble in their reading

Procedure:

The students sit in a circle around the box. You either read or play a tape recording of a story. Before hearing the story, each student is given a card on which there is a word from the story. When that word is read in the story, the student says "_____ goes in the box" and throws the word in the box. The student then is given another word, so she may continue in the game.

Word Football

Purpose: To provide practice on recognizing basic sight words or general sight words

Materials: A large sheet of drawing paper
             A small replica of a football
             Word cards

Procedure:

Draw a football field on a large piece of paper. The game begins at the 50-yard line, where the football is placed. The word cards are placed faceup on the table, and two students, or two teams, take turns reading them. If a student reads a word correctly, she moves the ball 10 yards toward the opponent's goal. If she reads the word incorrectly, it is considered a fumble, and the ball goes 10 yards toward her own goal. Each time the ball crosses into the end zone, six points are scored. The scoring side then gets to read one more word to try for the extra point.

Word Checkers

Purpose: To provide practice in word recognition or phonic sounds

Materials: Checkerboard
             Small squares of paper with sight words or phonic sounds on them

Procedure:

You or the student covers the black squares with the words. The game is played the same as regular checkers, but the player must say the word that appears on the square before a checker is placed on that space.

Variation in Procedure:

Phonic sounds may be used instead of words.

Pack of Trouble

Purpose: To discover which children do not know certain words and to provide special help in such cases

Materials: Word cards using the vocabulary currently being studied
Blank cards on which you can print words

Procedure:

You flash word cards to individual students and ask them to pronounce the words as quickly as possible. Whenever a student misses a word, she is given that word and makes a copy of it to keep. The student then can give the original back to you. Each student develops her own pack of trouble, which she can use for study with another individual or with a small group. As soon as the student masters a word, she may give it back to you. The idea is, of course, for students to keep their pack of trouble as small as possible.

Climbing the Word Ladder

Purpose: To provide practice on basic sight words, on general sight words, or on sight phrases

Materials: A number of card packs of 10 words. On the cards can be basic sight words, other sight words, or sight phrases
A small ladder that will hold 10 cards. The rungs of the ladder may be made from wood ¾" round and the vertical poles from wood of 1" × 2". See illustration following.

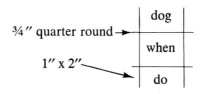

Procedure:

Each student receives a pack of cards and tries to try to climb the ladder with them. Cards are laid on each rung of the ladder. The student then tries to climb it by saying the words. After the student has mastered her own words, she exchanges packs and begins again with new words.

Hands Up (Words)

Purpose: To provide practice on recognition of basic sight words or general sight words

Materials: Group-size cards (6″ × 3″)

Procedure:

Quickly flash a word card around the group, allowing each student to see it. The student whose turn it is to pronounce the word then has a chance to do so. If the student pronounces the word correctly, she is given the word card. If the student does not pronounce the word correctly, then she is required to raise her hand. When the next card is flashed, the second student has a chance to say it. If, however, the student who has her hand up can pronounce the word before the second student, she gets the card and may put her hand down. The second student then receives a chance at another word. If she misses that word, then that student must hold up her hand, and so on. The object is to get the most cards. There may also be a number of children with their hands up at any one time. If this is the case, the one who pronounces the word first gets the card.

Surprise Words

Purpose: To reinforce knowledge of the basic sight words or general sight words

Materials: Word cards to fit pocket chart
A pocket chart

Procedure:

Fill the pocket chart with words that are currently being studied. Turn the cards so only the backs are showing. The children take turns coming up to the chart and taking a surprise word. If they can pronounce the word, they get to keep it; if they cannot, they must leave it in the chart. The student with the most words at the end of a certain time period wins the game.

Gamble for Words

Purpose: To provide practice on either basic sight words or general sight words

Materials: Pocket chart
Cards with either the basic sight words or any sight word on them
A die

Procedure:

Place the words to be worked on in a pocket chart or on the shelves of a pegboard unit. One student then rolls a die. She may pick up the same number of cards from the chart as the number indicated on the die. She must, however, be able to say each word as she picks it up. The turn then passes to another student. The object is to see who can get the most words. This game may be played using either a student vs. student approach or a team vs. team approach. You may set a time limit for the game or limit the game to a certain number of refills of the pocket chart.

Word Match

Purpose: To provide practice on word recognition

Materials: A pack of word cards in which every card has a word on it that is duplicated; that is, there should be two cards for each word to be used. The number of cards will depend on the number of players involved.

Procedure:

The players are each dealt four cards, which are placed faceup in front of each player. Five cards are then placed faceup in the middle of the table. The remainder of the pack is placed facedown in the middle of the table. If the first player has a card that matches any of the five faceup cards in the middle of the table, she picks it up, pronounces the word, and keeps the pair, placing them facedown in front of her. The student may continue playing until she can make no more pairs. The student then draws to fill her hand to four cards and replaces the five faceup cards on the table. If, in this process, cards that match are drawn and placed on the table, they are left for the individual who has the next turn. Play continues to the first player on the left. If a player can match a card in the middle of the table but cannot pronounce the word, she must place her card on the middle and leave it. If the following player can pronounce the word, she receives the pair. The winner is the person with the most cards when all of the cards are paired.

Rolling for Words

Purpose: To teach and provide practice on basic sight words

Materials: Three colors of construction paper
A die
Three small boxes

Procedure:

Cut the colored construction paper into 1″ squares. Print a basic sight word on each square. Put the squares into separate boxes according to the color of the paper. The players throw the die to see who starts the game. The student with the highest number starts by selecting as many words from any one box as the number on the die. If she fails to say any one of the words, she loses all the words from that turn. After being told the missed word by the teacher, the student returns the words to the appropriate box. Play continues to the first player's left. The winner is the one with the most words when all three boxes are empty, and the game ends.

Finding Rhyming Words

Purpose: To teach and reinforce basic sight words

Materials: Flash cards of basic sight words from which rhyming words can be made
A pocket chart

Procedure:

Place the flash cards in the pocket chart. You then say, "I want a word that rhymes with fat." Students take turns looking for a word to rhyme with the one you give. If the student cannot find the word, she is given a word to hold by you or by another student who knows it. The winners are those students who are holding no words at the end of the game.

Finding Phrases

Purpose: To reinforce knowledge of the basic sight words

Materials: Pocket chart
Basic sight word cards 3″ × 8 ½″

Procedure:

Place the words in the pocket chart to make four or five phrases (for example, *is in* and *wants to go*). Then say a sentence such as, "The boy wants to go." Students take turns going to the pocket chart and placing their hands on the phrase from the sentence and reading it. If a student fails to read it correctly, she must take the cards from that phrase to be studied. The object is to have no cards at the end of the game.

The Password

Purpose: To provide practice on especially difficult basic sight words

Materials: Straight or safety pins
3″ × 8 ½″ cards

Procedure:

Take a group of students who are having trouble with the same basic sight words. Write one of the basic sight words on each card, and go over the words thoroughly with the students. Then pin one card on each student. Throughout the day, whenever one student must deal with another or whenever you wish to get a response from that student, call the basic sight word written on the student's card rather than her name before that student is to respond. This can be done daily with different groups of words and students.

Concentration

Purpose: To develop the ability to recognize basic sight words

Materials: Basic sight word flash cards in which each card has a duplicate

Procedure:

Find 10 to 12 cards and their duplicate cards (total of 20 to 24). Shuffle the cards and lay them facedown on the table. The first student turns up a card and says the word. She then turns up another card trying to find the duplicate of the first one turned up. If the second card is not a duplicate of the first or if the student does not know the word, she turns them facedown, and the next student takes her turn. If a student is able to turn up one card, say the word, and then turn up the duplicate of that card, she gets to keep the pair. As play continues, students will, of course, find it easier to find matching pairs. The person with the most pairs at the end of the game wins. (Note: Be sure to have each student *pronounce* each word as it is turned over. This is where the practice and learning takes place. Often, in a game of concentration, the students are interested only in matching pairs quickly and will prefer not to say each word.)

13

General Sight Vocabulary Not Up to Grade Level

RECOGNIZED BY

The student fails to instantly recognize words thought to be common for or below grade level. (Failure is not limited to basic sight words.)

DISCUSSION

In advancing from grade to grade, the student should increase his sight vocabulary at each grade level. A student's sight vocabulary is not up to grade level unless he can correctly pronounce 95% of the words in a book at his grade level. The student who has not developed an adequate number of sight words is greatly handicapped since he must analyze many more words than a normal reader. This student is more likely to encounter reading material at his frustration level.

You should not determine whether a book is at a certain grade level from the publisher's recommendation unless that recommendation is based on one of the better readability formulas. Unfortunately, even many of the popular basal readers are prepared with stories at a variety of levels. That is, you cannot be sure that all stories in a basal reader that is designated at, say, a fourth-grade level, are actually written at that level.

RECOMMENDATIONS

The first, and most important, recommendation to help a student increase the size of his sight vocabulary is to have the student read widely on many subjects. If the student has adequate word-attack skills and is pronouncing the words correctly, then he will automatically learn many new sight words by seeing them a number of times. However, if the student does not have adequate word-attack skills for his grade level, then the appropriate procedures in Chapters 14 through 19 should be used as needed to improve the student's ability with phonics, structural analysis, or context clues. The various methods described in Chapter 29 will also improve the student's overall sight vocabulary.

A. Have the student read as widely as possible on his independent or low instructional level. In doing so, he will learn new words from their context.

B. Have the student start a card file of new words. Write the word (or have the student write the word) and the definition on the front of the card. On the back, write the word in its proper context in a sentence. (Never write just the word and the dictionary definition alone.)

C. Some basal readers have lists of new words introduced in the book. Sometimes these are at the end of each chapter. Determine the appropriate grade level at which to begin (where the student can pronounce approximately 95% of the words in these lists) and read stories from the basal reader to him. Discuss the meanings of new words as you come to them. Following this, have the student read the stories. Give him help when it is needed. (Remember that students will *not* learn to read merely by being read to; they must have substantial *practice* in the act of reading.)

D. Build on the student's background of experience as much as possible. Use discussions, demonstrations, films, filmstrips, records, tape recordings, or anything that will build his listening-speaking vocabulary. This will make it easier for the student to acquire new words through context clues.

E. Use picture word cards on which the unknown word appears under a picture illustrating that word. When making these, it is important to use the word in a sentence as well as by itself. Have the students work in pairs or small groups to learn these new words from the word cards. Have the students work cooperatively to build a file of pictures representing scenes, action events, and so forth in stories. Before the students begin to read the new stories, discuss these picture files with them. Pictures may also be put in scrapbooks, and pages may be divided into sections (represented by letters) on numbered pages. You can then make a tape recording to go along with the scrapbook. The script for the tape recording might read as follows:

On page three of the scrapbook in picture A, you see a picture of a waterfall. In the story you are going to read today, a man goes over a waterfall in a boat. The boat probably looks like the one in picture B. The men have been camping in the woods and probably look like the men in picture C.

Put the students at listening stations and have them prepare for reading a story by listening to these tapes and looking at the scrapbooks.

F. Have the students pantomime certain words such as *write, hear,* and *walk.* Make sure the students see the word immediately before, during, and after the pantomime.

G. Allow the student to preread material silently before asking him to read it orally. Encourage the student to ask you for assistance with difficult words during the silent reading phase. Remember, if the student asks for help on more than 10% of the words, the material is too difficult and should be replaced with easier material.

H. Teach the *word-attack strategy* described in Chapter 19.

GAMES AND EXERCISES

Sight Words in Context

Purpose: To provide practice on sight words and context clues

Materials: Pocket chart
             Group-size word cards
             Tape recorder

Procedure:

Place eight to 10 words in the bottom pockets of the pocket chart. These should be new words on which you wish to provide practice. Play a tape recording of a short story that uses the words in the bottom rows of the pocket chart. Say the word and at the same time ring a bell or sound a buzzer. At the signal, the student picks the correct card from the eight to 10 choices in the bottom rows and places it in the top row of the pocket chart. Be sure to pause briefly after the word to give the student a chance to look for it. You will need to allow for longer pauses at the beginning of the story when there are more words at the bottom of the pocket chart. The cards should be placed in order from left to right beginning with row one. When the top row is full, the cards begin the left-to-right sequence in row two and so on until all cards have been transferred from the bottom to the top of the chart. After all the words are transferred from the bottom to the top of the chart, you can check the words with the students in the following manner: "In row one, the first word is _____ , the next word is _____ ," etc. This makes the exercise self-correctional when it is programmed on the tape along with the rest of the exercise.

Variation in Procedure:

Instead of saying the word as a bell or buzzer rings, ring the buzzer and let the student find the word from context.

Zingo

Purpose: To provide practice in the recognition of the basic sight words or general sight words

Materials: A number of word cards (7″ × 7″) with 25 squares, each of which has a different sight word on it
             A list of each of the sight words
             A number of kernels of corn, buttons, or beans

Procedure:

This game is played like bingo. Read a word from the word list and ask the students to hunt for that word on their word (zingo) cards. When they find the word pronounced, they place a kernel of corn or some other marker on it. The first student to get five spaces filled in any direction is the winner. After a student has won, he should pronounce the words covered by the markers. This will ensure that the students not only recognize words by sight but that they also can say them.

Construct your word list so that you can allow various individuals to win if you so desire, e.g., zingo card 3 may win by saying words 2, 8, 10, 12, and 15. Although this is a prearranged game, it will enable you to allow the students who need motivation to win.

Racetrack

Purpose: To provide practice in recognition of basic sight words or general sight words

Materials: A large sheet of drawing paper
Two duplicate sets of individual-size word cards (3″ × 1½″)
Two toy automobiles

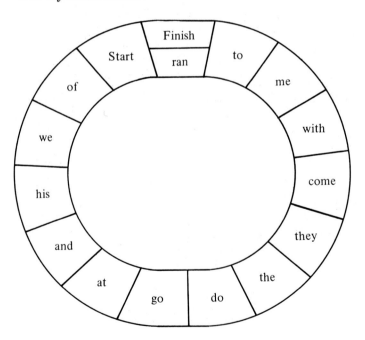

Procedure:

Draw an oval track on the drawing paper to resemble a racetrack. Be sure to put in a start and finish line. Divide the track into sections in which there are printed drill words. Each of the two players has a toy automobile, placed on the starting line of the track. Each player has a set of small word cards that are duplicates of those of the opposing player and are the same as the words on the racetrack. Each player places his pile of cards faceup. One player then reads the word on his top card. If the word is the same as the one in the first space of the racetrack, he moves his auto to that space. If it is not the same, he may not move. His card is placed on the bottom of the deck, and the other player takes a turn. The winner is the first player to go around the racetrack to the finish line. Be sure cards are shuffled well before each game.

Treasure Hunt

Purpose: To provide practice on the basic sight words or general sight words

Materials: Sight word cards with a word on one side and a direction on the back such as "Go to a word that starts with *c*," or "Go to a word that starts with *w*."

Procedure:

A number of word cards are placed on the top of the students' desks with sight words showing. To begin the hunt, give two or three people different cards with the directions faceup. The students immediately start to hunt for words with the beginning letters as indicated. When they find a word that starts with one of the letters, they say it. They may then turn the card over and get directions for the next step in the treasure hunt. The last card should have a picture of a treasure chest on the back of it instead of directions to look further. You will need to arrange the card sets, so each student goes through the same number of steps.

Donkey

Purpose: To provide practice on basic sight words or general sight words

Materials: Make a deck of cards using one new word causing difficulty on each. You may use any number of players. In the deck you should include three to five cards with the word *donkey* written on them.

Procedure:

Deal all cards to the players facedown. The players then take turns turning up a card, pronouncing it, and placing it in a pool in the middle of the table. When the *donkey* card appears, the player drawing it says "donkey" and throws it in the center of the table. All the players try to grab the *donkey* card. The one who gets it may keep it and all cards that have been thrown into the pool. The winner of the game is the player who ends up with all of the cards or the most cards when all *donkey* cards have been drawn.

The Head Chair

Purpose: To provide practice in recognizing basic sight words or general
             sight words

Materials: Group-size word cards (6″ × 3″)

Procedure:

Arrange students' chairs in a circle and mark one as the head chair. Begin play
by flashing a card to the person in the head chair. If the student says the word
correctly, he stays in his chair. If the student misses the word, he goes to the
end chair; and all the students from this student to the end move over one
chair. Continue around the circle from the head chair to the end chair. The
object is to try to end up in the head chair.

Variation in Procedure:

If you are working with a relatively small group, have all of the chairs facing
you. This will enable all of the students to see all of the words.

Cops and Robbers

Purpose: To provide practice in recognizing basic sight words or general
             sight words

Materials: Tagboard
             Word cards

Procedure:

On a piece of tagboard construct an irregular course of dots and then connect
the dots with lines. At points along the course place hideouts, dried-up water
holes, deserts, etc. The game is played with two students—one a bank robber,
one a police officer. The bank robber will place his marker on the course as far
from the officer's marker as possible. The game begins with each player turning over a word card from a pack placed facedown on the table. The student
reads the word on the card and then moves the number of dots denoted by a
number appearing in one of the corners of the word card. The robber tries to
avoid the officer. The game ends when the robber is captured (i.e., when the
police officer catches up with the robber). A more difficult game can be made by
increasing the number of moves allowed according to the difficulty of the word
given.

Team Sight Word Race

Purpose: To provide drill on basic sight words or general sight words

Materials: A group-size (6″ × 3″) set of basic sight word cards or sight words
             on which you want to provide practice

Procedure:

The students are divided into two teams. Each team member takes a turn attempting to pronounce a word turned up from a pile of sight words. If one team member misses, the opposite team then receives a chance to pronounce that word, in addition to the team member's regular turn. Score is kept on the number of words each team pronounces correctly. Do not have the members sit down when they miss a word, but have each team member go to the back of the line after each try, whether successful or not. This enables all members of each team to gain equal practice and does not eliminate those people who need practice most.

Variation in Procedure:

Instead of using single or isolated words, use phrase cards or sentence cards in which the word being emphasized is underlined. Allow the students to make the cards with a final check by you. You can use a number of smaller teams and have several races going at one time.

Stand Up

Purpose: To provide practice in recognizing the basic sight words or general sight words

Materials: Group-size word cards (6″ × 3″)

Procedure:

The students are seated in a group around you. One student stands behind the chair of another student who is sitting with his chair facing you. You then flash a card. If the student who was standing pronounces the word before the student in the chair, then the student who was sitting must stand up behind someone else.

Word Hunt

Purpose: To provide practice on the basic sight words or general sight words

Materials: Blindfolds
Group-size word cards (6″ × 3″)

Procedure:

Have several students cover their eyes. The rest of the group hides the cards where they can be found easily. When all the cards are hidden, the students who are "it" are given a signal to immediately take off their blindfolds and begin hunting for the cards. A student may pick up a card if he knows the word on it. No cards may be picked up unless the word is known. The student who finds the most words is the winner.

Seven Up

Purpose: To provide practice on word recognition and word meaning

Materials: Group-size word cards (6″ × 3″). Be sure there are seven times as many cards as students playing.

Procedure:

The students sit in a circle, with flash cards in a pile facedown in the center of the group. Each student takes a turn by turning over a card and reading it. If the student reads it correctly, he keeps it. When a student has seven correct cards, he stands up. The game continues until all the students are standing. The students then sit down and see how fast they can make a sentence with some or all of their seven cards. Be sure both nouns and verbs are included in the stack. As soon as a student has made a sentence, he stands. This play continues until all the students who can make sentences of their words have done so.

Noun Label

Purpose: To teach nouns to non-English-speaking students and to improve the vocabulary of those students who are deficient in their vocabulary development. It may, of course, be used in the early stages of reading in the regular developmental program.

Materials: Group-size word cards (6″ × 3″) with the names of common nouns written on them
8 ½″ × 11″ tagboard sheets with a picture of one of the common nouns on the top half of the sheet.

Procedure:

The pictures on the tagboard sheets are placed on the tray of the chalkboard. The students are then given words that correspond to the pictures. They come up to the chalkboard and place their words under the appropriate pictures. See the example on page 63.

Erase Relay

Purpose: To provide practice in recognizing newly learned words

Materials: A list of words on which you wish to provide practice

Procedure:

Write on the chalkboard two columns of words that are approximately equal in difficulty. Write as many words on the board as there are students in the relay. The students then choose sides or are numbered 1, 2, 1, 2, and so on, and stand

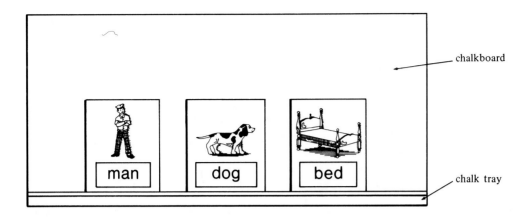

in two lines at right angles to the chalkboard. At the signal, the first student in each line points at the first word in his respective column of words and pronounces that word. If the student pronounces it correctly, he is allowed to erase the word. The game is won by the side that erases all the words first.

Variation in Procedure:

Do the same exercise using such sounds as long vowels, short vowels, consonants, consonant blends, prefixes, suffixes, and word parts.

Words and Pictures

Purpose: To learn and review the common nouns

Materials: Envelopes
Make word cards that are divided as shown on the next page. On one side the word should appear, and on the other side there should be a picture representing that word. After the cards are completed, cut them into two pieces, each with a different pattern along the cut edge; however, both sides should be approximately the same size. Put about 10 of these word cards and pictures (20 pieces) inside each envelope and pass them out to the students.

Procedure:

The students should be told to first line up their words in a column. After this is done, they will pronounce the first word and check to see if it is right by putting the picture representing that word beside it. The cut edges will, of course, match if the student knows the word. If the student does not know the word, he may continue to match the word and pictures until the edges do fit. Thus, the game will be self-correcting. Pass the envelopes around, and let each student do each set.

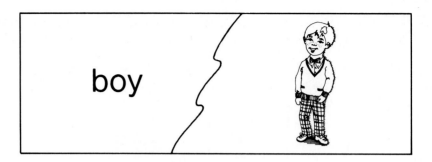

What is It? What Does It Mean?

Purpose: To provide practice on the recognition and definitions of sight words encountered in daily reading lessons

Materials: Use lists of words that are new to the students in various reading groups. The words should be divided to indicate that word two came from the lesson being studied by group two, etc.

Procedure:

This game should be used after you have introduced the words to the students in their reading groups. Divide the students into teams, so students from different reading groups will be working together. If possible, use these same teams in school work other than reading. This way, students are not singled out by their reading groups but are working together in group activities. (If regular reading groups are not used in the classroom, this will obviously not be a problem and you may modify the directions that follow accordingly.) At the time of the game, section off the two teams and start by writing a word on the board for the first student in team A. If he is in reading group three, the word would be from the story on which group three is working. In other words, each member on the team is given a word from his reading group's story. The student is to pronounce the word and use it in a sentence. If the student only pronounces it, he gets one point. If the student does not know how to pronounce it but can explain what it means or what it is, he gets three points. If the student can do both, he gets five points. If the student cannot do either, he receives no points. A word is then put on the board for a student on team B, and so forth. A score is kept on the board, so everyone can see it. The team with the most points at the end of a designated amount of time is the winner.

Word Golf

Purpose: To provide practice on the basic sight words or general sight words

Materials: Nine packs of word cards. Each pack should have 10 sight words in it.
A player and a scorekeeper

Procedure:

The player takes the first pack, shuffles the cards, and places them facedown in front of him. He takes a card from the top of the pack, turns it faceup, and reads it. If he misses a word, the scorekeeper makes one mark on the scoring sheet. The number incorrect for the first pack is the player's score for the first hole. The student continues in this manner through the nine packs, trying to receive as low a score as possible.

What Word Am I?

Purpose: To provide practice with sight words

Materials: Two duplicate sets of cards with sight words printed on them

Procedure:

Divide the class into two groups. Each student has a word card pinned on his back. The duplicates of the cards are spread out on a table. The object of the game is to see which group can guess all their words first. The students take turns going to the table, picking up a word card, and asking, "Am I _____ ?", saying the word on the card. If the student chooses the card that matches the word on his back and pronounces it correctly, he keeps the card. If the student selects a card that doesn't match, he puts the card down on the table and takes his seat. The game continues until one group guesses all its words.

Jumping the Fence

Purpose: To provide practice on the basic sight words or general sight words

Materials: Flash cards with sight words on them
             White tape

Procedure:

Place the flash cards in a row leading to the fence (white tape on the floor). A student who reads a word correctly jumps over the card and advances toward the fence. He may jump the fence when he reaches it. If he misses a word, he sits down and another student has a turn.

Baseball

Purpose: To provide practice with the basic sight words, general sight words, or phonic sounds

Materials   Flash cards with basic sight words, general sight words, or phonic sounds on them

Procedure:

The four corners of the classroom may serve as bases and home plate. Two teams of players participate. One student goes to home plate. The pitcher then holds up a flash card. The student pronounces the word, defines it if possible, and uses it in a sentence. If the student is correct, he advances to first base. This continues until the bases are loaded. Runs are scored as the students cross home plate. An out occurs when a student misses a word. There are three outs per team. The team with the most runs wins the game.

Variation in Procedure:

The flash cards may be vowel or consonant sounds, and the student must give a word that has the same beginning or ending sound on the card.

Flinch*

Purpose: This game is adaptable and may be varied to reinforce many reading skills, but it is especially valuable in developing vocabulary in the content areas. This game works well with two to four players and may be played with as many as six.

Materials: The deck is composed of 52 cards numbered from 0–12. In each deck there will be four cards numbered 0, four numbered 1, four numbered 2, and so on. On another part of the card there will be a word. Use terms or words peculiar to the unit and any other words in the basal text that are new or difficult.

Procedure:

The dealer shuffles and deals out all of the cards one at a time. Each player stacks the cards facedown on the table in front of him. The first player to the left of the dealer draws the top card from his pile and pronounces the word. If the player pronounces the word incorrectly, his opponents tell him the word, which is then placed on the bottom of the original stack to be redrawn at a later time. If the player pronounces the word correctly, he tries to find a place to play the card. Zero cards (treated as wild cards) play on any opponent's discard pile. Number 1 cards are played to start card piles in the middle of a table. Any other number card plays only if it is an adjacent number to one showing on an opponent's discard pile or to the top card of a pile in the center, e.g., a 7 card would play on either a 6 or 8 card. If a player pronounces the word correctly, but cannot play the card either on an opponent's discard pile or on a center pile, he places it faceup beside his original stack. This is his discard pile. A player continues to draw from his original pile, to pronounce the word, and to play the card. His turn ends when he must play on his discard pile. Play rotates to the left. Should a player fail to see a play, any opponent may call it. Then each player, in turn, gives the person overlooking his play an extra card, which is placed on the bottom of his original stack. The game ends when one player disposes of all of the cards in his original stack.

_____

*Invented by Mrs. Alice Hays of Imperial, Nebraska.

The Witch

Purpose: To provide practice with sight words. This game works well with four players if 20 cards are used.

Materials: Use a deck containing about 20 cards with one additional card that has a witch on it. Print one set of words on half of the cards. Duplicate the first set of words on the other half of the cards.

Procedure:

One person deals out all the cards; players pick them up and look at them. Beginning with the person at the dealer's left, the players take turns drawing cards—each player draws from the person on his right. As students form pairs, they pronounce the words and place their on the table. Play continues until all cards are matched. The player left with the witch is the loser and receives a *w*. The next time he loses, he is a *wi*, and so on. The object is to try to avoid losing enough times to spell *witch*.

Word-Object Hunt

Purpose: To teach or reinforce words used as nouns

Materials: A number of flash cards with the names of various objects written on them

Procedure:

Each student is given about 12 cards that he spreads out before him. You then say, "I went to the grocery store to buy b _____ ." Any student may raise his hand if he has an object that starts with *b* and would normally be bought at a grocery store. You then verify the answer, and all students get a chance to look at the word. The game may be varied by not giving the beginning letter and by using the names of objects bought in various stores.

Silly Sentences

Purpose: To teach or reinforce sight words

Materials: Plain cardboard flash cards or flash cards with flannel backing and a flannel board

Procedure:

Lay out sentences in mixed-up order either on a table or on a flannel board. Have students take turns coming up and unscrambling the sentences and reading them after they are placed in a sensible order. Make sure all students get a chance to read each logically ordered sentence.

Tape-Recorded Object Search

Purpose: To teach or reinforce sight words

Materials: Tape recorder
              Cassettes
              Envelopes
              Sight word cards

Procedure:

Tape-record a message that says, "Lay all of your cards out in front of you in two rows. There are eight cards. Place four cards in the top row and four cards in the bottom row. Turn the tape recorder off until you have done this. (Allow a four-second pause.) "Listen carefully. We need a scale to weigh the package. Pick up the word *scale*." (Allow about five seconds per word.) "The word *scale* has a number four on the back of it. Check to see if you got it right." When playing this game, make sure each card is numbered 1–8, so they can easily be checked. Place a tape cassette and eight cards in each envelope. Number the envelopes and give students sheets with corresponding numbers on them, so they can check off each envelope after it has been completed.

Matching Nouns and Verbs

Purpose: To teach or reinforce sight words

Materials: Envelopes
            Sight word cards

Procedure:

In each envelope place about 10 nouns and 10 verbs, such as the following examples:

birds   fly
brooms   sweep
people   talk

Instruct students to match the noun with the proper verb. Number the correct pairs with matching numbers, so the students can check the pairs on their own. Number the envelopes and give students sheets with corresponding numbers, so they can check off each envelope after they complete it.

Matching Noun Pictures with Words

Purpose: To teach various noun sight words

Materials: Pictures cut from catalogs and other sources
            Small cards
            Envelopes

Procedure:

Place about 15 or 20 pictures in each envelope and the name of the object in the picture on a small card. On the back of the card and matching picture write the same number. Also number each envelope. Pass out envelopes to students and instruct them to match the pictures with their written names. When they are done, they can look at the numbers on the back of each card and pictures to make sure they have matched them correctly. Give students a sheet of paper with as many numbers on it as you have envelopes. When they complete each envelope, they should check it off their numbered sheet.

14

Phonics Difficulties: Consonants

RECOGNIZED BY

The student is unable to give the correct sounds and variant sounds of the consonants (see Appendix K), the student is unable to use consonants to decode, or both.

DISCUSSION

Before beginning a program of help in phonics, you will find it helpful to administer a phonics test such as the *El Paso Phonics Survey* found in Appendix E. If a student is deficient in nearly all areas, e.g., initial consonants, consonant clusters, etc., you may wish to start from the beginning with the teaching of phonics. In this case you will find that, for most students, work with the phonogram list as described in Appendix L will enable the student to quickly learn a great many initial consonants, consonant blends, and consonant digraphs in a relatively short time.

RECOMMENDATIONS

Many of the recommendations listed below provide effective ways to teach students to recognize and pronounce consonants in isolation or in single words. However, for phonics instruction to be effective, students must transfer their knowledge of consonant letter-sounds to the act of decoding. The best way to help students do this is to first provide direct instruction, then give the student substantial practice in the act of reading. As each consonant sound is taught, you should provide short, easy sentences and/or stories for the students to read. You may create these sentences or stories yourself, have the students assist you in their development through language-experience activities (see Chapter 29), or use commercial materials that have been designed for this purpose. The students may need to read these sentences and stories over and over to master their phonics skills. The use of contextual material is essential because you want students to rely on context clues as they are learning phonics. You also want to be sure that students understand that the purpose of your instruction is to aid them in decoding so that they can obtain *meaning* from printed words.

There are many methods of teaching phonic elements. One typical procedure for teaching a consonant letter-sound follows:

1. Develop awareness of hearing the sound:

   a. Say, "Listen to these words. Each of them begins with the *b* sound. Circle the *b* on each word on your paper as you hear the sound. *Ball, bat, base, banana, etc.*"

2. Develop awareness of seeing the sound:

   a. Tell the student to circle all of the words in a passage that begin with *b*.

3. Provide practice in saying words with the *b* sound:

   a. Pronounce each word and have the students pronounce it after you: "*big, bad, baseball, basket, beach, etc.*"

4. Provide practice in blending the *b* sound with common word families or phonograms:

   a. Teach or use several phonograms with which students are already familiar, such as *ake* and *and*. Put the *b* in one column, the phonogram in a second column, and the two combined in a third column as follows:

b	ake	bake
b	and	band
b	at	bat
b	ig	big
b	ike	bike

   etc.

   Instruct the students to say *b* (either the letter name or the sound /b/), then the phonogram (the sound represented by the letters in the phonogram, such as /āk/), and then the word formed by the two, *bake*.

5. Ask the students to help you make a list of some words that begin with *b*. Ask the students to say each word with you as you write it. You may then have the students themselves write the same words (on paper, small chalkboards, or magic slates) and say them as they write them.

6. Provide practice in reading *b* words. Present sentences, paragraphs, or stories that have a number of *b* words in them for the students to read. If the students are able to read only a few words, then you can use illustrations if necessary instead of the other words.

The following activities will also assist students in learning the consonant sounds:

A. If the student does not know a great many of the initial consonants, consonant clusters, vowels, vowel teams, and special letter combinations, use the phonogram list as described in Appendix L.

B. Construct flash cards on which the consonant is shown along with a picture illustrating a word that uses that consonant, e.g., *b* in *ball*, and *c* in *cat*. On the opposite side of the flash card print the letter only. This can be used as the student progresses in ability. See example following:

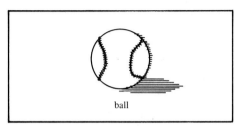

ball

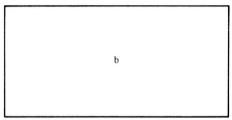

b

Front of Card   Back of Card

C. Put the consonant letters on 3″ × 3″ cards. Divide these cards into groups of 10 each. Lay out separate groups of letters, so the student can see all 10 at once. As you call the sounds of letters, or as they are played from a tape recording, have the student pick up the correct card to match the sound of the letter. As there are fewer words to observe—that is, after some have already been picked up—you will need to speed up the rate at which you pronounce the remaining words. The following timing seems to work well: pronounce the first word, wait 7 seconds; pronounce the second word and wait 7 seconds again; then 6, 6, 5, 5, 4, 4, and 3 seconds. Many students are unable to manipulate the cards in less time than this.

D. Tape-record words and have the students write the letter that stands for the beginning, ending, or both beginning and ending sounds of these words. See the following example:
Directions: As you hear a word called on the tape, write the letter that begins the word. (Tape script says, "Number one is *come,* number two is *dog,*" and so on.)

1. c
2. d
3.
4.
5.

E. Use the same system as in item D. Instead of having the students write letters they hear, have them pick up the card that matches the beginning or ending letter they hear in the words.

F. Put various consonant letters on the board and have the students make lists of the words that begin with these letters.

G. Record the consonant letters with their sounds and let the students hear these as many times as is necessary. They should, however, have a chart they can follow to see the letters as they hear the sound.

H. Use commercial charts that are available for teaching consonants. Records that give the proper pronunciation of the consonant sounds are also available.

I. Use commercially prepared games designed to teach consonants and consonant usage.

GAMES AND EXERCISES
Phonic Rummy

Purpose: To provide practice in various phonic elements. This game works well with two to four players when using 36 cards, or up to six players when using 48 or 52 cards.

Materials: A deck of cards with phonic elements that you wish to teach. On each card will appear one phonic element and four words that use that particular phonic element. One of the four words will be underlined. The deck may consist of 36, 40, 44, 48, or 52 cards. For each phonic element there will be four cards, each of which has a different word underlined. A deck of 36 cards would involve 9 phonic elements; 40 cards would involve 10 phonic elements. See the following example of the cards:

i	*ay*	*gr*
did	stay	green
pit	<u>may</u>	<u>grass</u>
if	play	grow
<u>fish</u>	clay	grab

Procedure:

The dealer shuffles the cards and deals eight cards facedown to each player. The rest of the cards are placed facedown in the center of the table. The first player to the left of the dealer calls for a word using a certain phonic element on which she wishes to build. (See the examples.) For example, the student might say, "I want Sam to give me *fish* from the *i* group" and would pronounce the short /i/ sound. If Sam had that card, she would give it to the caller. The player (caller) then continues to call for certain cards from specific people. If the person called upon does not have the card, the player takes a card from the center pile, and the next player to the left takes her turn. When a player completes a "book" (i.e., she has all four cards from a certain phonic element), she lays it down. Players can only lay down books when it is their turn to draw. The object is to get the most books before someone empties her hand.

Think

Purpose: To provide practice with initial vowels, consonants, and initial consonant blends. This game works well with four players.

Materials: Enough small cards so that each letter of the alphabet and each initial blend can be printed on a separate card. There may be more than one card for each vowel.

Procedure:

Place the cards facedown on the table. The players take turns selecting a card and naming a word that begins with the same letter or blend. If someone cannot name a word within five seconds, she puts the card back. The winner is the person who has the greatest number of cards after the entire pile has been drawn.

Checkers

Purpose: To provide practice on various vowel or consonant sounds, and to improve auditory discrimination

Materials: Cards with phonic elements, such as consonant sounds, vowel digraphs, and diphthongs on them
Large squares of paper in two contrasting colors

Procedure:

Draw a checkerboard on the floor or place sheets of construction paper on the floor in a checkerboard pattern. Divide the students into two groups and place each group back to back on the two middle rows. Each group must not have more students in it than there are squares across one row of the checkerboard. Each student stands on a square and holds one card with a sound on it. You call the words (these may be prerecorded on the tape recorder) that have the sounds that correspond with the sounds on the cards the students hold. When a student hears a word that has her sound in it, she may move one square toward the outer part of the checkerboard. The object of the game is for one side to have all its players reach the king row first. If a student misses a sound, or moves when she should not, then her side has to move a player back one space. There may be times when several students will move at once depending, of course, on the words chosen by you.

Variation in Procedure:

Play the same game, but ask comprehension questions over a reading assignment that all the students have read.

Word Trail

Purpose: To provide practice on consonants, consonant blends, vowels, digraphs, and diphthongs

Materials: A piece of tagboard
A list of phonic elements to be taught
A die

Procedure:

Draw a margin (approximately 2″) around the sheet of tagboard. Divide the margin into spaces large enough for inserting the phonic elements for practice. On the corners and in several spaces between corners, insert penalties and rewards such as, "Take another turn" or "Move back three spaces." The players then take turns rolling the die and moving their markers (perhaps pieces of corn) along the spaces, saying each phonic element as they move. If they cannot say a certain phonic element, they must stop on the space behind it and wait for another turn. The first player around the word trail is the winner.

Any Card

Purpose: To provide practice with consonants, consonant digraphs, consonant blends, and rhyming sounds. This game can be played with two to four players.

Materials: A deck of 36–52 cards with words such as the following:

pan	fun	sock	mill	call	harm
man	bun	knock	still	fall	charm
can	run	shock	kill	ball	farm

Also include four cards with *any card* written on them.

Procedure:

A player deals out five cards. The player to the left of the dealer plays any one of her cards and names it. The next player plays a card that either rhymes or begins with the same letter as the first card. For example, if *sun* has been played, *bun* (rhyming with *sun*) or *sock* (with the same first letter) could be played. If a student cannot play, she draws from the pile in the center until she can play or has drawn three times. If the student has the card with *any card* written on it, she may play this card and name any appropriate word. The first player who runs out of cards wins the game.

I'm Thinking of a Word

Purpose: To provide practice in auditory discrimination and the recognition of beginning, ending, or both beginning and ending sounds

Materials: Pocket chart
Cards with words that begin with various consonants
Cards with words that end with various consonants

Procedure:

Fill the pocket chart with about 10 cards, each of which has a different beginning sound. The first student says, "I'm thinking of a word that begins like /d/." (The student says the *d* sound.) The student draws a card, trying to get the word beginning with that sound. She gets to keep the card as long as she matches a sound and word. She may thus take all of the cards from the pocket chart. If the student gives a sound and draws a word that does not begin with that sound, play then passes to the next student. If the student gets all of the cards, another student then follows the same procedure. The same procedure can also be used with ending sounds.

Variation in Procedure:

There are many possible variations of this game. You may have students come to the front and say, "I'm thinking . . . ," and call on someone to guess the word. Another game might have a student put letters in the pocket chart and say, "My word is *dog*." The other students then have to find a *d* or *g* depending on whether you are working with beginning or ending sounds. The students also may play the same game and be required to find both the beginning and ending sounds.

Catch the Stick

Purpose: To improve auditory discrimination and to improve the students' ability to make the connection between sounds and letters

Materials: A number of group-size cards (6″ × 3″) with the beginning consonant sounds on them
A yardstick

Procedure:

Seat the students in as small a circle as possible for the number of students you wish to have play the game. Ten to 12 students are optimum. The students are all given a different beginning consonant sound on a group-size card. One student stands in the center of the circle and holds a yardstick in an upright position with one end on the floor and the top end held in place by the tip of her finger. The student in the center then pronounces a word that begins with a consonant. At the same time the student pronounces the word, she takes the tip of her finger off the top of the yardstick. The student who has the beginning letter of the word named by the student in the center of the circle must catch the yardstick before it falls on the floor. If the student who had the consonant letter catches the stick, she returns to her seat and the person in the center must say another word. However, if she does not catch the stick, then she must change places with the student in the center and give her card to the student she is replacing.

Blending Wheel

Purpose: To provide practice on blending beginning consonants, consonant blends, and/or beginning consonant digraphs

Materials: Two cardboard circles, one of which is approximately 2″ smaller in diameter (convenient sizes are 8″ and 10″)

Procedure:

Fasten the two circles together with a paper fastener as shown in the following illustration. The outside circle should have word roots or major parts of a word on it, and the inside circle should have a specific consonant, consonant blend, or consonant digraph on which you wish to provide practice. Have the student rotate one of the circles and practice blending the root or word part with the consonant, consonant blend, or consonant digraph.

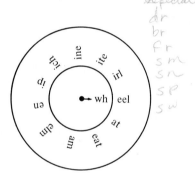

especially – Vicente
dr
br
fr
sm
sn
sp
sw

Word Puzzles

Purpose: To provide practice in recognizing blend sounds and to provide practice in blending

Materials: Envelopes
Word cards

Procedure:

Cut out a few word cards of equal size. Print a word containing a blend that has been taught, e.g., *gl*ad, *st*and, on each card. Cut each word in two between the blend and the remainder of the word. Place about 8–10 of these in each envelope and pass out the envelopes to the students. The students then assemble the blends and word parts to make words. After you check them, have students exchange the envelopes so that each student eventually assembles the words in each envelope.

Phonics Posters

Purpose: To develop an awareness of related sounds

Materials: Tagboard
             Old magazines or old textbooks

Procedure:

At the top of a piece of tagboard, place a letter or combination of letters. Have the students find pictures of objects in magazines or old readers that start with the sound or sounds displayed in the heading. These object pictures should be cut out and mounted on the tagboard to provide practice for individuals who need special help.

Poet Play

Purpose: To help students develop an awareness of sound similarities through the use of rhyming words

Materials: Pocket chart
             Word cards
             Envelopes

Procedure:

Give the students envelopes containing a number of word cards. Place a master word in the pocket chart and have the students locate in their envelopes a word that rhymes with the one posted. Number the envelopes and allow the students to exchange them after each round, so they will become familiar with a great many words and their sound similarities.

Stand-Up

Purpose: To provide practice in discriminating between like and unlike sounds

Procedure:

When there is extra time before lunch or dismissal, you might use this game. It is both interesting and beneficial. You call, "All those whose names start like *meat* may stand up and get their coats." Repeat as many times as needed to dismiss the students. As a variation, use letters that are in the middle or end of students' names. The students also might use this same method to choose groups or sides in other games.

Rhyme Time

Purpose: To discover which students are having auditory discrimination problems and to provide practice through the use of related phonic sounds

Materials: Tagboard
              Word cards

Procedure:

Write sentences on the tagboard. On small word cards print a variety of words that will rhyme with selected words given in the sentences. Have the students locate and match their cards with the rhyming words in the sentences. Place each set of cards in an envelope and number the envelopes, so the students can keep a record of the sets on which they have worked. See the example following:

1. The <u>dog</u> bit the mailperson. (log, hog, etc.)
2. The candy tasted <u>sweet</u>. (treat, beat)
3. <u>Look</u> out the window. (took, book)
4. The wall had a large <u>crack</u>. (back, sack)
5. She cut down the apple <u>tree</u>. (see, flee)

Making and Exchanging Picture Dictionaries

Purpose: To learn initial consonant sounds

Materials: Old notebooks or paper to be bound together
              Crayons and/or paints
              Magazines and other materials containing pictures

Procedure:

Have students cut out or draw pictures representing various initial consonant sounds. Under the picture write the letter or letters of the initial sounds and the word that stands for the picture. Also under each picture use the word in a sentence. After the students have finished their books, have them exchange dictionaries, so each student learns to read every other student's dictionary.

Hard and Soft *C* and *G*

Purpose: To teach the rules for hard and soft *c* and *g*

Materials: Rule chart with pockets and flash cards with various *c* or *g* words
              on them

Procedure:

Construct a large chart about 8½″ × 11″ like the chart that follows. The bottom half should contain two large pockets marked as shown. The top half should contain the rule for soft and hard *c* and *g*. Students are then given a number of flash cards with soft and hard *g* words on them. They put each card into the appropriate pocket according to the rule stated on the chart. Students may check their own work if the words *hard* or *soft* are written on the back of each flash card. (Do the same for *c*.)

G followed by *e, i,* or *y* usually has a soft sound.

If *g* is followed by any other letter, it usually has a hard sound.

Hard *g*	Soft *g*
(*g*ame)	(*g*entle)

15

Phonics Difficulties: Vowels

RECOGNIZED BY

The student is unable to give the correct sounds and variant sounds of the vowels, as well as vowel teams and special letter combinations, such as *al, ur,* etc. To check the vowel sounds, use the *El Paso Phonics Survey* in Appendix E. A test for checking students' knowledge of vowel rules and syllabication principles is in Appendix F. (Keep in mind that you cannot accurately assess students' knowledge of vowel rules until they have mastered the vowel sounds.)

DISCUSSION

In the past there were many rules that students who were learning phonics supposedly had to learn as an aid to decoding. However, research studies over many years have shown that some of the rules formerly taught have little utility in reading programs. Rules that appear to be worthwhile to teach to *some* students are:

1. If there is only one vowel letter and it appears at the end of a word, the letter usually has a long sound. Note that this is only true for one-syllable words.
2. A single vowel in a syllable usually has a short sound if it is not the last letter in a syllable or is not followed by *r*.
3. A vowel followed by *r* usually has a sound that is neither long nor short.
4. When *y* is preceded by a consonant in a one-syllable word, the *y* usually has the sound of long *i;*. But in words of two or more syllables, the final *y* usually has the sound of long *e*. Some people hear it as short *i*.
5. In words ending in vowel-consonant-*e*, the *e* is silent, and the vowel may be either long or short. Try the long sound first.
6. In *ai, ay, ea, ee,* and *oa*, the first vowel is usually long and the second is silent.
7. The vowel pair *ow* may have either the long *o* sound as in *low* or the *ou* sound as in *owl*.
8. In *au, aw, ou, oi,* and *oy*, the vowels usually blend or form a diphthong.

B 9. The *oo* sound is either long as in *moon* or short as in *book*.

RLI 10. If *a* is the only vowel in a syllable and it is followed by *l* or *w,* then the *a* will usually be neither long nor short, but will have the *awe* sound heard in *ball* and *awl*.

These rules certainly do not cover all the rules or exceptions; however, learning too many rules often proves almost as fruitless as knowing none. The vowel rules are the *least* consistent phonics generalizations in English. Furthermore, a remedial reader who has completed the primary grades (first, second, and third) will often find it difficult to learn by using rules.

You should not attempt to give a great deal of remediation until you are fairly sure what areas of phonics are causing difficulty for the student. The *El Paso Phonics Survey* will help to determine where the student is weak. This test will not only help determine whether the student knows the sounds and rules, but will also show whether he is able to apply them in analyzing a word.

RECOMMENDATIONS

A. It is helpful to teach the long and short vowel sounds in words that have the vowel-consonant-final *e* configuration for long vowel sounds and words that have the CVC configuration for the short vowel sounds. Remember, however, that as the student progresses into multisyllable words, the vowel-consonant-final *e* rule does not apply to as high a percentage of words. Later, students should probably be taught that when they encounter the vowel-consonant-final *e,* they should try the long vowel first and then the short sound for the first vowel. The procedure for teaching the long and short vowel sounds, as well as words for that purpose, is given in Appendix L. It will be briefly reviewed here.

1. If you wish to teach the long and short vowel sounds for *a,* choose the following words:

   mat   hat   rat   fat

   Discuss the sound represented by short *a*. Then present the previously listed words. If the student cannot pronounce them, help him to do so. Then present the following words:

   mate   hate   rate   fate

   Discuss the fact that when the *e* is added, the first vowel takes on its long sound and when it is removed it takes on its short sound. Review the long sound as you did the short vowel sound. Then present other words, such as those following, from Appendix L. Cover up the final *e* in each word and ask the student to pronounce the word. Then expose the final *e* and ask him to say the word with the long sound.

   pale   gale

Use the words in Appendix L to teach each of the short and long vowel sounds in the same manner. The advantage of this method of teaching the vowel sounds is that students learn these two fundamental rules at the same time.

B. Construct flash cards in which the vowel is shown along with both the word and a picture illustrating a word that uses that vowel, e.g., short *a* in *hat,* long *a* in *rake.* On the opposite side print only the vowel letter, marked long or short, to be used as the student progresses in ability. When using this method with an entire class, you can substitute 2″ × 2″ slides or transparencies for the overhead projector for flash cards. An example follows:

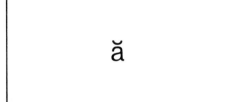

Front of Card   Back of Card

C. Have the students circle or underline the words that have vowels with the same sound as the first word in the line. See the following examples:

1. Long—lone, dog, of, to
2. Rat—car, bear, happy, same
3. Line—with, win, wild, is
4. Treat—tread, same, easy, well

D. Record the vowel letters with their sounds and variant sounds and play them to the students as many times as necessary to learn them. They should, however, have a chart they can follow to see the letter as they hear the sound.

E. Put the vowel letters on cards (3″ × 3″). Use the breve (˘) and the macron (−) to indicate the short and long sounds. Divide these cards into groups of 10 each. Lay out separate groups of letters, so the student can see 10 at once. As you call the sounds of the vowel letters, or as they are played from a tape recording, have the student pick up the correct card to match the sound of the letter. (See directions under item C for "Phonics Difficulties: Consonants," Chapter 14.)

F. Use the same system as in item E. Instead of having the students match letters they hear, have them write the letter matching the letter sound (phoneme) they hear in words.

G. Use commercial charts that are available for teaching vowels. Records to accompany the sounds are also available.

H. Use commercially prepared games designed for teaching the vowels and vowel usage.

GAMES AND EXERCISES

Game Board for Sorting Vowel Sounds

Purpose: To learn to hear various vowel sounds

Materials: Pictures or words with various vowel sounds in them
Construct a board as follows:

	A	E	I	O	U
Long					
Short					
R = Controlled					

Procedure:

Have students sort pictures or words into the correct intersecting squares (pictures must be used with beginning readers) according to the sound in the name of the object in the picture. For example, *hen* would go under the square under the *e* column and the row across from *short*. The pictures from some commercially sold games such as *Vowel Lotto* work well with this game board.

Vowel Tic-Tac-Toe

Purpose: To learn vowel sounds

Materials: Flash cards with the following written on them:

Short *a*	Long *a*	R-controlled *a*
Short *e*	Long *e*	R-controlled *e*
Short *i*	Long *i*	R-controlled *i*
Short *o*	Long *o*	R-controlled *o*
Short *u*	Long *u*	R-controlled *u*

Procedure:

Have the two students who are playing tic-tac-toe draw a vowel card. Then, instead of marking each square with *X* or *O*, the student writes words that have the sound on his card. If, for example, one student gets short *o* and the other gets long *a*, then each person must write a word with that sound when it is his turn to play instead of making the traditional *X* or *O*. An example of a partially finished game is shown:

cake		
	hot	
make	pot	

Variation in Procedure:

This is also a good learning device if the two participants have to draw a new card before each move. When playing the game this way, use two different colors of chalk or pencil to help remember which words belong to each player.

Sorting Pictures According to Matching Vowel Sounds

Purpose: To teach short and long vowel sounds

Materials: Construct a large chart using all 10 of the short and long vowel sounds on pictures placed on pockets as shown. On the top half of the chart, glue a large envelope in place. Find many pictures representing various short and long vowel sounds and place them in the large envelope.

Procedure:

Construct the chart similar to the example.

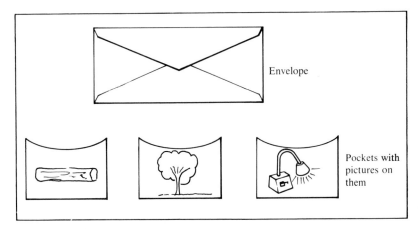

NOTE: This illustration shows only three pictures, a log, tree, and light. There should, of course, be 10 pictures, each representing a short or long vowel sound.

Have students take pictures from the large envelope and say the word related to the picture. Remind them to listen for the vowel sound they hear in that word. Then have them find the corresponding vowel sound from the picture on the pockets below and place the picture from the large envelope in the proper pocket. This activity can be made self-checking by numbering the pockets and the backs of the pictures from the large envelope to correspond with the small pocket it should go in. After students have placed all of the pictures from the large envelope in the small pockets, they can turn the pictures over to see if they match the numbers on the small pockets.

Sorting Vowel Sounds

Purpose: To learn to hear various vowel sounds

Materials: Ten shoe boxes for each group
             About 100 word cards, each using the sound of only one vowel

Procedure:

You or a team captain draws a card. Students read it and listen for a specific vowel sound. They then analyze the word and place it into the correctly marked short or long *a, e, i, o,* or *u* shoe box.

Vowel Relay

Purpose: To give practice in blending and learning sight words

Materials: Flash cards with various sounds (graphemes) such as the following:

Long *a*	Short *a*	R-controlled *a*	L-controlled *a*
Long *e*	Short *e*	R-controlled *e*	W-controlled *a*
Long *i*	Short *i*	R-controlled *i*	W-controlled *o*
Long *o*	Short *o*	R-controlled *o*	W-controlled *e*
Long *u*	Short *u*	R-controlled *u*	

Procedure:

Divide the students into two groups and the chalkboard into two parts. Each group lines up in front of its half of the chalkboard. The pile of cards is divided in half and placed in the chalk tray below each of the two divisions of the chalkboard. When you say "Go," the two front players each move up and turn over a card. Each player must write a word using his designated vowel sound in a period of 10 seconds. However, new players cannot move up until you again say "Go" in 10 seconds. If the student cannot think of a word, he draws a line. The next player moves up and turns over another card when you say "Go." The team that has all of its cards turned over with the most correct words is the winner.

NOTE: Much of the material listed under "Games and Exercises" in Chapter 14 can be adapted for teaching the vowel sounds.

16

Phonics Difficulties: Blends, Digraphs, or Diphthongs

RECOGNIZED BY

The student is unable to give the correct sounds of the blends, digraphs, or diphthongs (See Appendix K), the student is unable to use these phonic elements to decode, or both.

DISCUSSION

As with the consonant and vowel sounds, it is important that the student know the blends, digraphs, and diphthong sounds to analyze certain words. The *El Paso Phonics Survey* in Appendix E will help you determine which areas are causing the most difficulty for the student. It also will help you to determine if the student possesses a knowledge of the blends, digraphs, or diphthong sounds but does not use her knowledge. Administer the test before beginning a program of help in this area.

RECOMMENDATIONS

A. As with the initial consonant sounds, if a student does not know a number of consonant blends, use the phonogram list as explained in Appendix L. You are likely to find that the student learns most of these in a relatively short time. You can then retest the student and teach those that are still not known.

B. For teaching vowel digraphs and diphthongs, use the phonogram list to find words with the digraphs or diphthongs not known. Use the tape recorder to provide practice on those combinations, as explained in Appendix L. For example, give students who do not know the *ai* sounds words such as *aid, braid, laid, maid,* and *paid,* and *ail, hail, nail, pail, quail,* etc.

C. Construct flash cards in which the blend, digraph, or diphthong is shown along with a picture that illustrates a word using that letter combination. See Appendix K for suggested words. On the opposite side of the card, print only the blend, digraph, or diphthong, to be used as the student progresses in ability. When using this method with an entire class, you can substitute 2″ × 2″ slides or transparencies for the overhead projector for the flash cards. (See illustration of card under item B, Phonics Difficulties: Vowels, Chapter 15.)

D. Record the letter combinations with their sounds and let the students hear these as many times as necessary to learn them. They should, however, have a chart they can follow to see the letter combinations as they hear the sounds. Ask each student to point to the letters as she hears them on the tape.

E. Put diphthongs, digraphs, and blends on 3″ × 3″ cards. Divide these cards into groups of 10 each. Lay out separate groups of diphthongs, digraphs, and blends and allow the student to see all 10 at once. As you call the sounds of these various letter combinations, or as they are played from a tape recording, have the student pick up the correct card to match the sound of the letter combinations. (See directions under item C, Phonics Difficulties: Consonants, Chapter 14.)

F. Use the same system described in item E, only tape-record words and have the student pick up the letter combinations she hears in these words.

G. Use commercial charts that are available for teaching various letter combinations. Recordings to accompany these sounds are also available.

H. Use commercially prepared games that the students can play individually or in groups.

GAMES AND EXERCISES

See "Games and Exercises," Chapter 14, and "Games and Exercises," Chapter 15. Much of the material listed in these two sections can be adapted to the teaching of blends, digraphs, and diphthongs.

17

Structural Analysis Difficulties

RECOGNIZED BY

The student is unable to pronounce multisyllabic words.

DISCUSSION

Structural analysis, often referred to as *morphology,* is concerned with the study of meaning-bearing units such as root words, prefixes, suffixes, possessives, plurals, accent rules, and syllables. As a decoding skill it is analogous to phonics but is used to decode words of more than one syllable. In using structural analysis, the reader first identifies the separate units or parts of a word, pronounces the units, then blends them together. (In using phonics, the reader goes through the same process, but identifies, separates, and blends *phonemes,* or individual sounds, to decode one-syllable words.)

Structural analysis begins when the student is able to recognize the root word in words with *s, ed,* or similar endings, e.g., *run* in *runs* and *look* in *looked.* From this beginning the student should learn to recognize the parts that make up compound words, such as *tooth* and *ache* in *toothache,* and *green* and *house* in *greenhouse.* He should also begin to recognize common roots, suffixes, and prefixes. Most authorities in the field of reading believe it is not good, however, to look for little words within bigger words since the smaller words may not have their usual pronunciation. (For example, the words *go, over,* and *me* are not helpful in decoding the word *government.*)

One of the best ways to determine if a student is having difficulty with structural analysis is to ask him to read orally. While the student reads orally, you can note the types of errors he makes. The student with structural analysis difficulties will often decode basic sight words and most one-syllable words successfully but fail to pronounce accurately words of more than one syllable. This is a common and serious problem among students with reading difficulties. Such students are usually unable to read material with a readability level above grade 3. As the difficulty of the material increases, the student's ability to read it decreases.

Fortunately, structural analysis difficulties can be overcome if several conditions are present. First, the student must master the prerequisite decoding skills (basic sight vocabulary and phonics) required to read up to about the third grade level. (See Chapters 12–16.) Second, the teacher must provide adequate direct instruction. Third, the student must receive sufficient practice decoding multisyllable words both in isolation and in context.

Students are often taught five or six syllabication rules to assist them in dividing long words. (A syllabication test is found in Appendix F.) This approach is helpful to some, but not all, students. It is unnecessary for any student to memorize the syllabication principles if he is able to divide multisyllable words into pronounceable units. An alternative method for teaching students to divide words is presented in the recommendations that follow.

RECOMMENDATIONS

A. Teach the students to apply the following five-step strategy to decode multisyllabic words: (This strategy is similar to the word-attack strategy presented in Chapter 19.)

WHEN YOU COME TO A HARD WORD

1. Look for prefixes or suffixes.
2. Look for a base or root word that you know.
3. Read to the end of the sentence. Think of a word with those parts (from steps 1 and 2) that makes sense.
4. Try other sounds, syllables, and accents until you form a word that makes sense.
5. If you still cannot figure the word out, skip it, ask someone, or use the dictionary.

To teach the strategy you should model its use, then provide the students with guided and independent practice as follows:

1. Present the steps, using a written chart that students can remember and refer to.
2. Choose a difficult word and put it into a sentence.
3. Demonstrate how you would use the steps, one at a time, to figure out the hard word.
4. Use enough examples to show how a student may use a different number of steps each time to get the correct pronunciation (always go through the steps in order).
5. Provide students with sentences that they may use to apply the steps as you provide guidance.
6. Reassure students that the strategy works and encourage them to read a lot until the strategy becomes automatic.

Listed below are 10 sentences that you may use to teach and give students practice in the five-step strategy. They are difficult because most include more than one long word. If they seem too difficult for your students at first, prepare more sentences like numbers 1 and 2.

1. The amplifier made the music louder.
2. Sara is a kind, compassionate person.
3. The archaeologist studied the bones of the dinosaur and the other artifacts found near the caves.
4. The twelve contributors contributed five hundred dollars to the charity.
5. That delicatessen has delicious potato salad.
6. After the explosion there was an evacuation of the building.
7. The horizontal lines on the television screen make it impossible to see the picture.
8. The intricate puzzle is very frustrating.
9. The hurricane did substantial damage to our neighborhood.
10. The barometric pressure is falling rapidly.

B. Make lists of the common word endings and have the students underline these endings and pronounce their sounds.

C. Use multiple-choice questions that require the student to put the proper endings on words. (See examples following.)

1. The boy was (looked, looks, looking) in the window.
2. That is (John, John's, Johns) ball and bat.
3. The boys came (early, earlier, earliest) than the girls.

D. Make lists or flash cards of the common roots, prefixes, and suffixes. Use these in forming new words. You may have students practice these sounds, but do not require memorization of the meanings of affixes. (See Appendix O for a list of suffixes and prefixes.)

E. Make lists or flash cards of common letter combinations such as *tion* and *ult*. Practice with these may be helpful; however, avoid listing letter combinations that have sounds that may vary according to the word in which they are used. Make lists on transparencies for the overhead projector or on large pieces of cardboard.

F. Make lists of and discuss compound words as the student encounters them in his reading lessons.

G. Make lists of all the words that can be made from certain roots. For example:

1. work—works, working, worked
2. carry—carrying, carrier, carried, carries
3. faith—faithful, faithless
4. lodge—lodger, lodging, lodged, lodgement

H. Write a number of words on the board with prefixes that mean the same thing, e.g., *imperfect, unedited, irreplaceable.* Have the students add to the list. Underline roots or prefixes and discuss them.

I. Teach the student the following syllabication principles and work through a number of words to enable him to become proficient at dividing words into syllables. The syllabication principles that follow tend to be consistent and help students to identify pronounceable units in words.

1. When two consonants stand between two vowels, the word is usually divided between the consonants, e.g., *dag-ger* and *cir-cus.*
2. When a word ends in a consonant and *le,* the consonant usually begins the last syllable, e.g., *ca-ble.*
3. Compound words are usually divided between the word parts and between syllables within these parts, e.g., *tooth-ache, mas-ter-mind.*
4. Prefixes and suffixes usually form separate syllables. Examples: *dis-own, north-ward.* Use Appendix O as a study aid to help students recognize prefixes and suffixes.

GAMES AND EXERCISES

Prefix and Suffix Baseball

Purpose: To provide practice in recognizing prefixes, suffixes, and their meanings

Materials: Make cards with a prefix such as *un* _____ or a suffix such as _____ *ly* on them. Be sure to include the line to indicate whether it is a prefix or a suffix.

Procedure:

This game is not to be used until considerable work has been done with prefixes and suffixes (collectively called *affixes.*) Native English-speaking students have less trouble with the game than non-native speakers since they already have a large vocabulary and only need to realize that these words contain prefixes and suffixes.

Each of the two teams chooses a pitcher who will "pitch" a word to the "batter." The batter will think of a word to go with the prefix or suffix and then pronounce it. If the student does this much but cannot use it in a sentence, he has hit a single. If the student can think of a word, pronounce it, and use it in a sentence, he hits a double. After the students become more adept at the game, you may wish to confine the hits to singles to slow down the game.

Caution: Remember that only a few suffix and prefix meanings are consistent enough to warrant memorizing their meanings.

Dig Up the Root

Purpose: To develop recognition of word roots and attached affixes

Materials: Pocket chart
Word cards

Procedure:

Divide the pocket chart into two columns. On the left-hand side, list a number of root words. In an adjacent column, randomly list words composed of the root words plus an affix. Have the students match the root word in the first column with the root and its affix in the second column.

1. finish   undecided
2. reach   finishing
3. determine   replace
4. decided   nationality
5. place   reached
6. nation   predetermine

Prefix and Suffix Chart

Purpose: To teach the meanings and uses of suffixes and prefixes

Materials: Chart similar to the following example

Procedure:

Construct a chart like the following and have the students fill in the blank spaces. Place an X in the spaces that are not applicable.

Prefix	Prefix Meaning	Root	Whole Word	Suffix	Suffix Meaning
un	—	do	undo	x	x
x	x	soft	softly	—	in a way
x	x	play	playful	ful	—
—	from	port	—	x	x
pre	—	—	—	x	x
x	x	care	—	—	without
re	—	gain	—	x	x

Spinning for Suffixes (for small groups of two to five students)

Purpose: To give practice in recognizing and attaching suffixes. This game will also help the student to learn the meanings of certain suffixes.

Materials: A heavy piece of cardboard or a piece of plywood cut in a circle about 2–3 feet in diameter. Around the edge of the board, write a few suffixes, so they occupy the same positions as the numbers on the face of a clock. (You don't need 12 suffixes. See example.)

Extra overlays of paper to attach to the face of the circle. These overlays will enable you to readily change the suffixes with which you are working.

A pointer in the center of the circle that can be spun

A number of word cards that can be used with each overlay. For example, for the suffixes *ed, ing,* and *tion* on the overlay, you might use the word *direct* on a word card.

A shoebox

Procedure:

Pass out an equal number of word cards to each member of the group. You or a student then spins the pointer, which stops on a certain suffix. You call on each member of the group, and ask them to take their top card and try to attach the suffix at which the pointer stopped. The students may be asked to spell and pronounce the word, and then define what it means. When a student has done this correctly, he puts his card in a box. The student who has all his cards in the box first is the winner.

Variation in Procedure:

Make overlays that contain prefixes to fit on the face of the circle and play the game in the same manner as with the suffixes.

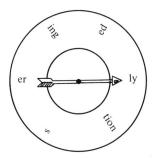

Endings

Purpose: To provide practice in structural analysis

Materials: A number of cards with suffixes or word endings printed on them

Procedure:

Divide the class into two equal teams. On the chalkboard, list a number of familiar root words such as *run, sleep, help, rain, ask,* and *splash.* In a circle on the floor place cards of suffixes such as *ed, d, ing,* and *y.* In the center of the circle, a blindfolded team member is turned around. The student points to a card and the blindfold is removed. He goes to the chalkboard, chooses a word, and adds the ending to it, writing the new word on the board. He then pronounces the word. If the word is written correctly, he scores a point. If the word is pronounced correctly, he scores another point. If the word is written incorrectly, the next member of the rival team gets a chance to write and pronounce the word. If he writes it correctly, the rival team scores a point. The first team to receive 25 points wins.

18

Contractions Not Known

RECOGNIZED BY

The student is unable to pronounce contractions when she encounters them in print. For comprehension and writing purposes, it is also useful to know what two words each contraction stands for and to be able to make contractions from various words. A test for students' knowledge of contractions may be found in Appendix G.

DISCUSSION

For some students a part of poor oral reading is the student's lack of knowledge of contractions. This is usually a minor reading problem.

When testing for student's knowledge of contractions, you should show the student the contraction and ask her to pronounce it. If she can pronounce the word, it will suffice for decoding purposes. (For example, for decoding purposes the student must pronounce *can't,* but she does not necessarily need to know it means *cannot.*) You may wish to have the student tell what two words the contraction stands for, so you know if she understands the meaning of the contraction and will be able to use it in her written work. Refer to the list of contractions "Contractions Commonly Taught in Six Sets of Well-known Basal Readers" on page 100 from the Scope and Sequence of Reading Skills presented in Appendix J.

RECOMMENDATIONS

A. For any contraction not known, write the two words it stands for and then the contraction on the chalkboard. Have students make up sentences using both the contracted and noncontracted form. See the example.

let us   let's

1. Let us go with Mother and Father.
2. Let's go with Mother and Father.

B. Give students a matching exercise by placing a few contractions on slips of paper in an envelope. Number each contraction. In the same

*Contractions Commonly Taught in Six Sets
of Well-known Basal Readers*

anybody'd	I'd	weren't
aren't	I'll	we'd
can't	I'm	we'll
couldn't	I've	we're
didn't	let's	we've
doesn't	she'd	what's
don't	she'll	where's
hadn't	she's	who'd
hasn't	that's	who'll
haven't	there'll	won't
here's	there's	wouldn't
he'd	they'd	you'd
he'll	they'll	you'll
he's	they're	you're
isn't	they've	you've
it's	wasn't	

envelope place slips that name the two words each contraction stands for and write the matching number of the contraction on the back. Students should then try to match the contractions with the correct words by placing them side by side as illustrated in the example.

After the student has completed the exercise, she can turn the cards in the right-hand column over to see if the numbers on the back match the numbers on the slips in the left-hand column.

C. Give students paragraphs to read in which several words could be contracted. Underline these words. Instruct students to change these words to a contraction as they read. See the following example.

Frank said to Jim, "*We have* only two days before *you are* going to leave." "Yes," said Jim, "*I am* waiting to go, and *I have* already packed my suitcase."

After doing this type of exercise, discuss why contractions are used and which form, long or short, sounds more natural in common speech.

D. Conduct contraction races between two students. Tell the students two words and see who can call out the contraction first. Also give contractions and have students call out the words that are contracted.

E. Give students newspaper articles and have them underline all contractions and words that could have been contracted.

F. As students talk, call attention to the contractions they use by writing them down. Discuss why they used the contracted form.

19

Inadequate Ability to Use Context Clues

RECOGNIZED BY

The student is unable to derive meaning or pronunciation of a word from the way it is used in a sentence.

DISCUSSION

The use of context clues can be one of the student's greatest helps in determining the pronunciation and meaning of unfamiliar words. It is not a difficult reading skill to teach; however many teachers incorrectly assume that all students will learn to use context clues on their own. Capable readers usually do, but disabled readers often need a considerable amount of instruction and a great deal of practice to learn this skill.

A test for determining if a student is able to use context clues effectively is found in Appendix H. When using this test, it is important that the student read at his independent level or at an easy instructional level. Do not expect students who are reading at a difficult instructional level or at their frustration level to be able to use context clues effectively. (An explanation of each of these three levels is found in the section entitled "Definition of Terms" at the beginning of this book.)

You can also determine if a student is having difficulty using context clues by listening to him read orally from material on which he will make 5 to 10 errors per page. While the student reads, note whether miscalled words are logical replacements; that is, does the student rely on context clues when other decoding skills are inadequate? You may also question the student about the meaning of certain words where that meaning is evident from the context.

Bear in mind that students' difficulties with context clues may be reflected in two opposite behaviors. Many students fail to use context clues adequately and appear to read word-by-word. A common example of this type of problem is the student who reads the sentence *The boy went into the house* as *The . . . boy . . . went . . . into . . . the . . . horse.* This student apparently overrelied on graphic information at the expense of meaning clues, thus substituting the word *horse* for *house*. The two words are similar in appearance but quite dissimilar in meaning. At the other extreme are students who overrely on context. These students may appear to be reading fluently, but what they read may not be what was written. Such a student might read the sentence given above as *The boy went into the garage.* While the first type of problem is more common and often more difficult to remediate, both forms of context-clue difficulties are detrimental to reading ability.

RECOMMENDATIONS

A. The best way to teach students to use context clues when they are reading independently is to teach them the following *word-attack strategy:*

WHEN YOU COME TO A WORD YOU DON'T KNOW:

1. Say the beginning sound.
2. Read the rest of the sentence. THINK.
3. Say the parts that you know. GUESS.
4. Ask someone or skip it and go on.

The first step, applying initial letter-sound associations, is the one most students will do automatically. This is fortunate because beginning sounds are often the most helpful clue in decoding an unknown word. The second step requires the student to use context clues before applying additional phonics or structural analysis. Most often the combination of initial letter sounds and context will result in correct identification of the unknown word. Step 2 requires the student to read to the end of the sentence to take advantage of the context clues that may come after the unknown word. (Words that come *after* are often more helpful than those that come *before* unknown words.) If the student still has not decoded the word, step 3 has him use other word-analysis clues, such as ending sounds, vowel sounds, and structural analysis. The student is encouraged to guess, if necessary, so as not to spend too much time trying to decode a single unknown word. The last step encourages the student to ask for help or continue reading if all else fails. It is quite possible that context clues picked up in reading further will permit the student to identify the unknown word.

If students must resort to step 4 often, they should be given easier material to read. Similarly, if students encounter more than one unknown word in a single sentence, the strategy is likely to break down, indicating that the material is too difficult.

To teach the strategy, you should use the following steps:

1. Present the steps, using a written chart that students can remember and refer to.
2. Model use of the steps yourself with sample sentences.
3. Reassure students that the strategy works.
4. Provide students with sentences that they may use to apply the steps as you provide guidance.
5. Ensure that students use the steps as they practice in the act of reading.

At the end of this paragraph is a list of sentences that you may use to teach and give students practice in the four-step strategy. The numbers after each sentence indicate which steps are likely to assist students. It is not possible to determine exactly which steps will help students. Some students will recognize unknown words at sight. Others will use only one or two steps. Some may not succeed at all. You will need to provide other examples for students based on their specific needs.

1. The *light* is red. (1, 2)
2. I will *take* you there. (1, 2)
3. I cannot *remember* your name. (1, 2, 3)
4. I like *chocolate* cake. (1, 2, 3)
5. The *cat* is my pet. (1, 2)
6. The *hamster* is my pet. (1, 2, 3)
7. The *armadillo* is my pet. (1, 2, 3, 4?)

B. Encourage practice in the act of reading. Such practice is essential for students to learn to read for meaning. Provide time, appropriate materials, the proper setting, and encouragement for sustained silent reading.

C. Show the student that it is possible to derive the meaning of words from their context. Provide specific examples.

1. The careless boy did his work in a *haphazard* manner.
2. He felt that although his work was *imperfect,* it was still good.
3. When he tried to *insert* the letter in the mailbox, the mailbox was too full.
4. They called in a *mediator* to help settle the problems between labor and management.

D. Have students preread material silently before reading orally. Discuss troublesome vocabulary.

E. Set purposes for reading. Stress accuracy in reading, not speed.

F. Use short, easy selections. Have students stop frequently to explain what they have read in their own words.

G. Use high-interest material, including student-authored language-experience stories.

H. Have students scan for important words. Have them guess the content and then read to see if the guess was accurate.

I. Construct sentences or short paragraphs, omitting selected words that students should be able to determine by their context. In place of each key word, insert an initial consonant and then *x*s for the rest of the letters in the words. See the example below:

> When Jack <u>ix</u> in a hurry, he always <u>rxxx</u> home from school.

When students have become proficient at this, advance to the next step, which is to replace key words with *x*s for each letter.

> When Jack <u>xx</u> in a hurry, he always <u>xxxx</u> home from school.

After students are able to get most of the omitted words by replacing the letters with *x*s, then leave blank lines to replace the entire omitted words.

> When Jack _____ in a hurry he always _____ home from school.

J. Use multiple-choice questions in which the student fills in blanks: e.g., "Jack _____ a black pony (rock, rode, rod)." Using words that look alike also will give the student practice in phonic and structural analysis.

K. Make tape recordings in which key words are omitted. Give the student a copy of the script and have him fill in the blank spaces as the tape is played.

L. Create a series of sentences using words that are spelled alike but may have different pronunciations or meanings, e.g., *read, lead.* Have the student read sentences using these words in proper context.

> He *read* the book.
> He will *read* the story.
> It was made out of *lead.*
> He had the *lead* in the play.

IV

COMPREHENSION ABILITIES

20

Vocabulary Inadequate

RECOGNIZED BY

The student does not understand the meaning of words commonly understood by students of this age level. The student's weakness may be reflected in poor performance on tests of vocabulary knowledge. Inadequate vocabulary causes reduced reading comprehension.

DISCUSSION

A strong relationship exists between vocabulary knowledge and comprehension. Authorities have differing notions of what it means to know a word. Part of the problem is that one may know a word at five different levels or stages. These stages are listed below from lowest to highest level of vocabulary knowledge.

1. A student has no recognition of a word. Indeed, she may have never seen it before.
2. A student has heard of the word (that is, recognizes that it is a word), but has no knowledge of its meaning.
3. A student recognizes the word in context and has a vague understanding of its meaning.
4. A student knows well the meaning of the word in the context in which it appears.
5. A student knows the multiple meanings of the word (if they exist), and can actually use the word in thinking, speaking, or writing.

Knowledge at level 2 is usually required for a student to decode a difficult word, while knowledge at levels 3 or 4 is required for the student to comprehend what she reads. Thus, one of the important reasons that teachers teach vocabulary is to enable students to understand written material. Adequate decoding ability alone will not enable a student to understand material in either a narrative or subject-matter book.

The most common method of testing students' knowledge of words or overall vocabulary is the use of standardized achievement tests. The most widely used format is the multiple-choice measure in which the student chooses, from among several choices, a short definition or a synonym for a target word. Such tests usually measure vocabulary knowledge at level 3, rather than the student's full continuum of word knowledge. If you use such a test, examine the student's raw scores to see if they are above that which could have been made by chance guessing. A number of standardized reading achievement tests will allow a student who may essentially not read at all to score well into the norms and to have a vocabulary achievement score well above her actual vocabulary ability. Some students do poorly on standardized tests of vocabulary knowledge because they lack sufficient decoding ability. If a student does much better on an individually administered oral vocabulary test, you may then assume that a lack of proper word-attack skills is contributing to her low score on the standardized test.

Another method of testing students' knowledge of vocabulary is to ask them the meaning of several words that appear in their textbooks (at their grade level). This will give you a general feel for their vocabulary knowledge; however, it will not allow you to compare the vocabulary achievement of your students with those in the country as a whole. If you are a teacher in a school with a large group of students from a low socioeconomic level, this method of testing vocabulary knowledge within the class may give you "tunnel vision," since students with only a normal vocabulary may appear very good in comparison to other students in the class.

RECOMMENDATIONS

Since the meanings of many words can be learned through context and repeated exposure, it is not necessary to teach every new word. Only a very small percentage of the total meaning vocabulary of adults is achieved through specific vocabulary instruction or through the use of the dictionary. Unfortunately, research has shown that students in remedial reading programs usually get little practice in the act of reading. For students with a limited English vocabulary, much practice in oral language is essential. For students who come from an English-speaking background, the single best way of increasing their vocabulary is to encourage them to read widely about a number of subjects. The importance of this cannot be overemphasized.

Direct instruction is also very important. The most effective instructional activities tap into students' prior knowledge and involve the students actively in learning new vocabulary. Often it is best for students to practice these strategies while working in small cooperative groups, so that students can learn from each other as well as from the teacher.

A thorough discussion of the meaning of only a few words is more worthwhile than having students look up several words in the dictionary, write the definitions of the words, and then use them in sentences. Eldon E. Ekwall and an elementary principal once checked students' knowledge of 20 words that they had just completed writing the meaning of and using in a sentence during a one-hour period. The average number of words known by each student was 2 out of the 20, or 10% of the words. And, this was immediately after completing the lesson! This indicates that a little more time spent in discussing each word and making sure that it was well known by each student would be much more productive than attempting to introduce many words, in a less thorough manner. In addition, the "look it up, write the definition, use it in a sentence" approach tends to be boring for most students.

You will find that the following recommendations are motivating and effective for most students, all the more so when the teacher participates in or directs the activities.

A. Students of all grades can benefit from the use of **semantic feature analysis.** To use this technique, pick a theme somewhat familiar to a number of students, such as *speech communication*. First, discuss various ways in which we communicate through speech and list them; for example, *seminar, congress, forum, debate, dialogue, conversation, symposium, lecture, homily, testimony, caucus, interview, sermon,* and *hearing* (used as a noun). If students are at an age where they are familiar with the use of a thesaurus, they can quickly find synonyms for words first mentioned.

After the list has been completed, discuss characteristics of several of the items on it. Commenting on the list in the preceding paragraph, students may note such characteristics as one-way, two-way, no control over who speaks, one person controls who speaks, anyone can speak, formal, and informal. After a logical set of characteristics has been developed, construct a matrix (on an overhead transparency or on the chalkboard), such as the one on page 116.

When the matrix is complete, ask students to decide whether to place a plus (+) or a minus (−) in each blank space of the matrix, depending on the characteristic of the item in the column. For example, for *seminar* one would be likely to place a plus in the blanks for two-way, one person controls who speaks, anyone can speak, and, perhaps, informal. On the other hand, a minus would be likely to appear after one-way, no control over who speaks, and formal.

Semantic feature analysis provides students with a much better understanding of terms than definitions from a dictionary. Encourage students to discuss the merits of placing a plus or a minus after various items. Also allow them to place both a plus and a minus in certain blanks. For example, a *seminar* might be formal or informal, depending on who is conducting it as well as on its purpose.

After students have completed marking each item with a plus or a minus, have them ask each other questions such as, "Jim, what is the difference between a *debate* and a *dialogue?*" This will, of course, make students more active participants, and they will be much less likely to forget the meanings of various words. The discussion following the completion of the matrix should be considered an essential part of the use of this technique for vocabulary development.

Semantic Feature Analysis
for
Speech Communication

	One-Way	Two-Way	No Control Over Who Speaks	One Person Controls Who Speaks	Anyone Can Speak	Formal	Informal
Seminar	----	----	----	----	----	----	----
Congress	----	----	----	----	----	----	----
Forum	----	----	----	----	----	----	----
Debate	----	----	----	----	----	----	----
Dialogue	----	----	----	----	----	----	----
Conversation	----	----	----	----	----	----	----
Symposium	----	----	----	----	----	----	----
Lecture	----	----	----	----	----	----	----
Homily	----	----	----	----	----	----	----
Testimony	----	----	----	----	----	----	----
Caucus	----	----	----	----	----	----	----
Interview	----	----	----	----	----	----	----
Sermon	----	----	----	----	----	----	----
Hearing	----	----	----	----	----	----	----

B. **Semantic word maps** also can be fun and challenging to students. Using semantic word maps together with a dictionary and a thesaurus will enable students to learn words that are not in the listening-speaking vocabularies of the students involved in making the map. In using this technique, first pick a topic familiar to students, such as *house*. Then ask them simply to list a number of things that come to mind when hearing this word. Examples might include *stone, wood, ice, concrete, electricity, dishwasher, carpenter, mason, skins,* and *concrete*.

After a fairly comprehensive list has been developed, ask students if they see logical categories into which they could fit each of the items. For example, logical categories for this list might be as follows: *equipment* (electricity, dishwasher, garbage disposal), *building materials* (stone, wood, ice, concrete, skins), and *workers* (painter, carpenter, mason).

Show the development of the semantic map as shown in the illustration.

Semantic Map for Houses

stone _____
wood _____
ice _____
concrete _____
skins _____

painter _____
carpenter _____
mason _____

Workers

Building materials

HOUSES

Equipment

electricity _____
dishwasher _____
garbage disposal _____

In doing a topic as common as a house, there would, of course, be more categories than those shown in the example. After the map has been developed, draw lines beside each word in the various categories, as shown. Then have students use a thesaurus to find a word or, preferably, more than one word, that could possibly be a synonym of each listed word. Also, depending on the ages of the students involved, you may wish to use words that are synonyms of the roots of words used in each category. Place these words in the blanks. Examples of words that might be used in the illustration would be *painter* (tint, dye, pigment, stain); *carpenter* (cabinetmaker, builder, producer); *mason* (bricklayer, plasterer, cement worker); *electricity* (current, juice, power); *dishwasher* (cleaner, cleanse, filter, purify); *garbage disposal* (dirt, filth, muck, slime); *stone* (boulder, gravel, pebble, rock); *wood* (forest, lumber); *ice* (freeze, chill, refrigerate); and *concrete* (cement).

C. The **four-square strategy** will help students use prior knowledge to increase vocabulary.[*] First, select about four important words from an assignment students are about to read and have the students fold four papers into quarters. Have the students write the first word in square one, e.g., *salubrious.*

Use the word in appropriate context so that the students will have some clues to its meaning, e.g., *Joggers lead a <u>salubrious</u> lifestyle by engaging in regular exercise.* Ask, "Is there anything you do that you believe is *salubrious*?" Label these student examples as *salubrious.*

Have students write in the second square something they personally find to be *salubrious.* In the third square, have students write a nonexample—something that is not *salubrious,* e.g., smoking. Finally, in the fourth square, have students write a definition of the word in their own words. See the completed example.

salubrious	surfing
1	2
4	3
any aspect of life that is healthful	smog

D. The **context redefinition** strategy[**] encourages students to predict word meanings, then use oncoming context to confirm their predictions. This is a strategy that is used unconsciously by all good readers and consists of five steps.

---

[*]Source: Eeds, M., & Cockrun, W. A. (1985). Teaching word meanings by expanding schemata vs. dictionary work vs. reading in context. *Journal of Reading, 28,* 492–497.

[**]Source: Bean, T. W. (1981). Comprehension Strategies: What Makes Them Tick? In E. K. Dishner, T. W. Bean, & J. E. Readence (Eds.), *Reading in the content areas: Improving classroom instruction,* (pp. 188–191). Dubuque, IA: Kendall-Hunt.

1. *Select* about four key words from a story or text chapter (try to pick at least one that students may know).
2. *List* these on the chalkboard or overhead projector with a blank space for the students' predictions.
3. Have students *predict* what they think each word means, write their predictions verbatim, then vote on the most plausible prediction.
4. Have students read to *verify* their predictions.
5. After reading, have the students edit or *redefine* their initial predictions to reflect contextual meaning. (Students can copy these definitions in their own glossaries.)

An example of context redefinition follows.

Write a definition or synonym for the two words that follow:

1. eggrails: _____
2. mushburgers: _____

Now read the following selection to see if you need to modify your initial hypotheses:

She preferred a surfboard with *eggrails* for slow, sloppy waves. A board with rounded edges was ideally suited to this afternoon's conditions. The wind was blowing straight onshore, creating bumpy *mushburgers*.[*]

E. Whenever new words come up in lessons, stop and discuss them in sufficient detail so that all students develop a concept of their meaning.

F. When reading stories or books aloud to students, stop occasionally to discuss the meanings of new or unfamiliar words. With practice, teachers can learn to do this without spoiling the flow of the story. For example, when reading books to younger children, vocabulary can be discussed while you are showing the students the illustrations in the book.

G. Appoint a vocabulary committee to preview each new lesson and to identify all words for which they do not know the meaning. Use these words as a guide to the new vocabulary in addition to the vocabulary given in the textbook. You might also have members of this committee find out the meanings of these words and introduce them to the rest of the class. Of course, it is a good idea to rotate membership on this committee.

H. Develop picture files for each unit in the students' textbook. Use the pictures to show the meaning of new words and concepts. These pictures may be placed on a bulletin board or shown and discussed as you introduce each new unit.

---

[*]Source: Cunningham, J. W., Cunningham, P. M., & Arthur, V. (1981). *Middle and secondary school reading*. New York: Longman.

I. Place pictures on the bulletin board and have students try to find as many words as possible to describe the pictures. If students are old enough to use a thesaurus, allow them to do so. Place the words under the picture and discuss them regularly.

J. Brainstorm other words for common words used most often, e.g., *said*. With the assistance of the students, prepare charts with lists of synonyms for the overused words. These charts may be hung in the classroom where they can be easily seen by students. Then, when students write creative stories, encourage the students to use alternatives to the overused words. Similarly, model the use of these words when speaking to the students and encourage the students to use them in their conversations.

K. Encourage students to raise their hands whenever someone uses an unfamiliar word. Praise students for asking what a word means and indicate that such students usually have large vocabularies.

L. Develop word awareness by showing students how they often skip words for which they do not know the meaning. Promote awareness of new words by getting students to look for new words that they or other students may not know the meaning of. Write the new word on the chalkboard along with the name of the student who found it.

> Carlos' new word—idealism
> Frank's new word—afterthought

Discuss these words daily until most students know them. Keep adding new words to the bottom of the list and erase the ones from the top after they have been discussed several times.

M. Encourage students to use vocabulary cards. As students read assignments or any other reading material, have them search for new words. When a new word is found, the student writes it on a vocabulary card. Then she copies the sentence in which it was used and underlines the word. (Encourage the use of context to derive meaning.) After the student completes her reading, she locates the new word in the dictionary and writes its meaning on the card. File the new vocabulary cards in a shoe box and review them periodically.

N. Help students become aware of new words by having contests: who can find the most words that other students do not understand? Limit the contest to a particular book and one day.

O. Discuss the use of figurative language and have students look for idiomatic expressions, such as "Our teacher was a bear today," "She was as quiet as a mouse," or "He lost his cool."

P. Provide a wide background of experiences for students. This can be done, to a certain extent, by taking students on field trips, showing videotapes, films, and filmstrips, and discussing a wide range of topics in the classroom. After returning from field trips, using audiovisual materials, or engaging in class discussion, identify and discuss any new words and concepts. Also, encourage students to write down any unfamiliar words as they listen to the narration of a videotape, film, or filmstrip. After viewing, list the students' words on the chalkboard or overhead projector and discuss them. In presenting each word, discuss its meaning with the class and use it in a sentence. Then have several members of the class use the word in sentences they make up. Follow that procedure with all unknown words. Finally, have students write a summary of the field trip, videotape, film, filmstrip, or class discussion, and use all of the new words that were presented.

Q. Encourage students to use the dictionary to derive a word's meaning. Although only a small percentage of one's total meaning vocabulary comes from the use of the dictionary, all students should learn how to use the dictionary in order to derive word meaning, as well as the accompanying skills such as understanding a word's first, second, and third meaning.

R. Encourage students to use books marketed for the purpose of building vocabularies. These are constantly being updated, and new ones appear on the market each year. To find them, look under the subject of *vocabulary development* at a local bookstore. These books present many words, and most teachers can learn much about the teaching of vocabulary by using them.

S. Teach students to use affixes as clues to word meanings. Although research indicates that the study of prefixes and suffixes is somewhat questionable, a knowledge of affixes is highly useful in understanding words in subject areas such as science, where a student might encounter such prefixes as *bio-, sub-,* and the like.

T. Teach students how to use a thesaurus and constantly encourage them to use it in their writing.

U. Many commercial materials have been designed for vocabulary development, including a number of computer software programs.

V. A good sourcebook on the teaching of vocabulary is Johnson, D. D., & Pearson, P. D. (1984). *Teaching reading vocabulary (2nd ed.).* New York: CBS, College Publishing.

GAMES AND EXERCISES

Matching Words and Definitions

Purpose: To enrich vocabulary

Materials: Envelopes that contain slips of paper with numbered words printed on them. The envelopes should also contain a larger second set of slips with a definition of each word, numbered on the back to match the first set.

Procedure:

Have students each take an envelope and empty it on their desks. They should then place the word slips in a column in numerical order, e.g.,
1. candid
2. slipshod

Students try to match the definition slips with the words. Students can check the accuracy of their work when they have finished by checking to see if the numbers match. Number each envelope and give students a number sheet corresponding to each envelope. Have them check off each number as they complete the words in each envelope. Thus, each student will be sure to do each envelope.

Homonym Concentration

Purpose: To enlarge vocabulary

Materials: Set of word cards (about 8–10) with a corresponding set of homonym cards (total of 16–20)

Procedure:

Play the game the same as "Concentration." Shuffle the cards and place them facedown in rows on a table or on a "Concentration" board with squares on it. Two students play. One begins by turning over a card. Then she tries to find its homonym by turning over another card. If the words are not homonyms, she turns both cards facedown, and the next student takes her turn. Whenever a student turns over a pair of homonyms, she gets to keep the cards. The student with the most cards at the end of the game is the winner. (This same exercise may be done with antonyms and synonyms.)

Phrase It Another Way

Purpose: To enrich vocabulary

Materials: Phrase cards or phrases written on the chalkboard

Procedure:

On the chalkboard each day place a new phrase that the students or you commonly use in daily conversation and activities. Opposite the phrase, write another way of saying the commonly used phrase. Each day you and the students concentrate on using the phrase in a new way. You may wish to place the phrases on chart paper and display them as the number grows.

Old phrase	*Phrasing it another way*
is done	is completed
runs fast	is a rapid runner
couldn't get it	was deprived of it

Drawing New Words

Purpose: To build vocabulary and improve dictionary skills

Materials: A number of 3″ x 5″ cards with new vocabulary words written in a sentence (underline the new word)
Dictionary

Procedure:

The cards are shuffled and placed facedown on the table. Students then take turns picking up a card, reading the sentence, and defining the underlined word. Another student looks up the word in the dictionary to see if the definition was correct.

New Word for the Day

Purpose: To enrich vocabulary

Materials: Word cards for new and old words

Procedure:

Decide on a new word that can be substituted for one that is commonly used each day (see example). Place the old and new word in a chart holder. During the day both you and the students should use the new word instead of the old word. Discuss how doing this type of activity will enlarge vocabularies and make students' speech sound more mature.

Old word	*New word*
talk	discuss
hate	dislike
do better	improve

21

Comprehension Inadequate

RECOGNIZED BY

The student cannot answer questions about subject matter he has read or cannot retell what he has read.

DISCUSSION

Definitions

The term *reading comprehension* has several different definitions. While most experts agree that reading comprehension is the meaning gained from what is written on the page, they often disagree about the source of the meaning. Currently the three most common models are the *bottom-up, top-down,* and *interactive* models. The bottom-up model emphasizes the material being read and is often described as text-driven. Proponents of this model believe that the material being read is more important to the process of reading than the person who reads the material. The top-down model emphasizes the reader and is often described as concept-driven. Proponents of this model suggest that the reader is more important to the process of reading than the material being read. This is because readers usually have some prior knowledge (or *schema*) about the topic. Using prior knowledge, the reader makes predictions about the meaning of the material. In other words, the reader's prior knowledge can be a powerful influence on his comprehension of the text.

The interactive model was developed to describe the reading process as both concept- and text-driven, a process in which the reader relates information stored in his head with new information in the text. Most experts subscribe to the interactive model, believing that comprehension is a process of constructing meaning by interacting with the text. Many of the suggestions presented in the recommendations section stress interactive *strategies* as the most effective way to correct and teach comprehension.

Factors That Affect Comprehension

Several factors about the reader affect his comprehension of the reading material. Other factors that affect a student's comprehension are related to the material he reads. Some factors that affect comprehension in terms of the reader are

1. *The knowledge the reader brings to the subject.* This means that what a student knows about a particular subject is directly related to how much he will understand about that subject when he reads. This is, of course, a major tenet of the interactive model.

2. *The reader's interest in the subject.* A student will understand more of what he reads if he is particularly interested in the subject. This interest is often a reflection of the student's prior knowledge of the subject.

3. *The reader's purpose for reading.* A student who has a purpose for reading is more likely to understand more of what he reads than a student reading the same material who has no purpose for reading. For example, if a student wishes to learn how to operate a computer to play a particular game, he will be more likely to understand more of what is read than a student of equal ability who has no desire to operate the computer or to play a particular game on that computer.

4. *The reader's ability to decode words rapidly.* If the student must stop to puzzle over new words, he cannot be expected to comprehend well. The whole process of reading, when many of the words are not easily decoded, becomes mind-boggling. The student must give so much attention to the decoding of new words that attending to comprehension to any degree is difficult. Teachers often experience a similar problem when they are reading a book out loud to a group of students. The demands of oral reading, watching the students in the group, showing the pictures, and so on may cause the teacher to have little or no comprehension of the story being read.

Some factors that affect comprehension in terms of the material being read are

1. *The number of unfamiliar words.* Unfamiliar words are usually considered to be those that are not on a particular word list according to a readability formula. This means that the more words on a higher grade level, the more difficult the material is likely to be to comprehend.

2. *The length of the sentences.* Research has consistently shown that longer and more complex sentences within a passage are more difficult to comprehend than shorter, simpler sentences.

3. *The syntax.* Syntax is the way words are put together. Some writers use syntax in ways that make material more difficult to comprehend.

Methods for Teaching Comprehension

Teaching students how to comprehend what they read can be a challenging task. Certain reading methods have contributed to the problem. Comprehension is often *tested* but seldom *taught*. In fact, the only instruction some students receive in comprehension skills is in the form of questions over a paragraph or story. While this questioning may help some students to develop a strategy for comprehending on their own, it does not teach students how to comprehend.

Perhaps the study of metacognition has added to our understanding of what educators must do to help students learn to comprehend more than any other approach. Cognition is the process of thinking, and metacognition is the process of understanding *how* a person thinks or the process of monitoring one's thinking. Practical methods of using metacognition to improve reading comprehension will be discussed in the first section under "Recommendations."

Comprehension Subskills

Studies on the nature of comprehension have shown that although reading specialists often refer to comprehension subskills, they cannot really prove these subskills exist. Reading specialists definitely know that comprehension involves both a word or vocabulary factor and a group of skills that might be referred to as "other comprehension skills." Even though they cannot prove that these other comprehension skills exist, many teachers find them useful for teaching purposes. These skills include the ability to

1. Recognize main ideas
2. Recognize important details
3. Develop mental images
4. Predict outcomes
5. Follow directions
6. Recognize an author's organization
7. Do critical reading

Assessing Comprehension Ability

Teachers can often tell if students are having difficulty comprehending by observing their written work, their ability to answer questions, and their participation in discussions about material read. If you suspect that a student has comprehension difficulties that are not related to decoding problems, you might have the student read a passage silently, then retell the contents of the passage to you. Often it is best to have such a student read both narrative and expository selections to see if he is able to comprehend both types of material. You may use a section from a library book, literature, or reading textbook for the narrative material and a section from a science or social studies book for the expository passage. If the student is unable to retell the contents of the selection with adequate comprehension, you may assume that student will benefit from the recommendations in this chapter.

There are several commonly used methods for more systematic assessments of students' ability to comprehend. One of the most widely used methods is the standardized test. Some standardized tests in the field of reading are divided into two main sections—reading vocabulary and reading comprehension. Perhaps this is a misnomer, since an adequate reading vocabulary is essential for reading comprehension. Thus, reading vocabulary is actually one of the subskills of reading comprehension. Because vocabulary is such an important subskill of comprehension, procedures for dealing with vocabulary were presented in the previous chapter. When using standardized tests to assess reading ability, you should note if an individual's score is higher than what he could have achieved by simply guessing. Some standardized tests have no provision for enabling teachers to measure the reading ability of students with extremely limited reading ability, e.g., by guessing, a student may be able to achieve a score that is one to three levels above that at which he is actually reading. Also remember that standardized reading tests are designed, for the most part, to measure the reading ability of a group rather than that of an individual.

Another method of assessing reading comprehension ability is to have students read passages from their basal reader or from other material at their grade level. After reading, the students should be asked questions that test their ability to remember facts, make inferences, get main ideas, and understand the vocabulary. The major drawback with this approach is that it is difficult for the teacher to construct meaningful questions. Some questions that may appear relatively easy are seldom understood when they are used with a number of different students. At the same time and for no apparent reason, some questions are almost always answered correctly. When using this method to check comprehension, consider the student to be comprehending on a level equivalent to that at which the material is written if the student can answer at least 75% of the questions correctly.

A third approach to measuring comprehension is the use of commercial reading inventories. Although some studies have shown that the questions on some of these are sometimes irrelevant or could be answered without reading the passages over which they were constructed, in most cases, the teacher can be assured that the questions are appropriate.

Another approach that is very useful in determining how well a student comprehends, as well as how his reading ability matches the level of the material he is reading, is the cloze procedure. A detailed description of how to use the cloze procedure is presented in Appendix I.

RECOMMENDATIONS
Strategic/Metacognitive Procedures

A. Use the semantic mapping technique

   Definition: A semantic map is a diagram of relationships and ideas within a reading selection.

Steps: 1. The teacher selects a key word or idea from the upcoming reading selection.
2. During whole-class discussion, students brainstorm to come up with as many ideas as possible related to the key word or concept. These ideas are recorded on a chart or board.
3. As a class, these words and ideas are categorized.
4. The categories are recorded in a graphic form (map) that shows the relationship of the categories to the main idea (key word) at the core of the map.
5. The class reads the selection.
6. New terms and ideas are added to the map after the reading selection has been read and discussed by the class. Previous categories may be changed or eliminated as the class decides.

Example:

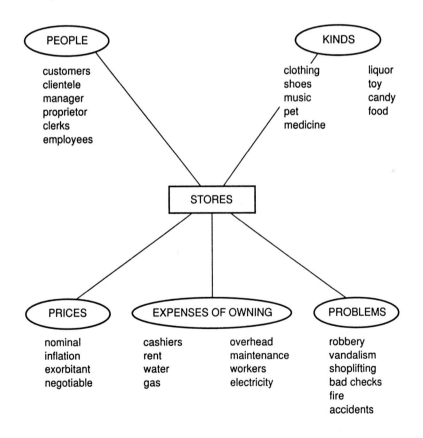

PEOPLE		KINDS	
customers		clothing	liquor
clientele		shoes	toy
manager		music	candy
proprietor		pet	food
clerks		medicine	
employees			

STORES

PRICES	EXPENSES OF OWNING		PROBLEMS
nominal	cashiers	overhead	robbery
inflation	rent	maintenance	vandalism
exorbitant	water	workers	shoplifting
negotiable	gas	electricity	bad checks
			fire
			accidents

Summary: Semantic mapping has been encouraged for three primary reasons. They are:

    1. development of critical thinking
    2. increased reasoning ability
    3. improvement of memory

B. Use the K-W-L technique[*]

Definition: K-W-L is a logical, three-step procedure named for the three basic cognitive steps required: What I *K*now (K), what I *W*ant to learn (W), what I did *L*earn (L). This reading comprehension strategy was developed by Donna Ogle.[**]

Steps:
1. The teacher selects a key concept from the upcoming reading selection.
2. The class brainstorms and lists ideas they already know (step K) about this key concept. These ideas are recorded on a chart or board.
3. As a class, these ideas are categorized.
4. The teacher encourages students to think of questions they wish to know from the reading selection (step W). This may begin as early as step 2. The questions are recorded.
5. The class reads the selection.
6. After reading, the class discusses and records ideas they learned (step L). This may be done in the third column of the K-W-L chart.

Example:

K	*W*	*L*
What I Know about spiders	*What I Want to know about spiders*	*What I Learned about spiders*
1. _____	1. _____	1. _____
2. _____	2. _____	2. _____
3. _____	3. _____	3. _____
4. _____		4. _____
5. _____		5. _____

Summary: With the K-W-L reading strategy, students are in charge of their learning and actively pursue knowledge. As a result, students learn to use their prior knowledge, locate key concepts in the reading, and remember to recall information.

---

[*]Appreciation is extended to Cathy Langmoreland, Reading Specialist, Fremont, California Unified School District, for the description of the semantic mapping and K-W-L techniques.
[**]Ogle, D. M. (1986). K-W-L: A teaching model that develops active reading of expository text. *Reading Teacher, 39,* 564–570.

C. Research suggests that an important metacognitive skill for students to develop is that of rereading something that does not seem to make sense when read the first time. In the beginning stages, ask students to read one sentence at a time and then ask themselves, "Do I know what the author is saying?" If the answer to this is yes, instruct the students to keep on reading. On the other hand, if the answer is no, instruct the students to reread that sentence. Continue to practice this skill until the students have developed the ability to monitor their thought processes while reading.

D. One of the most effective methods to teach students to monitor their thought processes is to develop a code to mark their reactions to each paragraph. The code system will vary somewhat according to the grade level of the students involved. To develop the system, give a group of students a paragraph that is rather difficult for even the better readers. Before having them read the paragraph, tell them that you are about to have them read something that you believe will be rather difficult for them. Ask them to be aware of what happens to them as they read. Point out that most students have some sort of strategy for deriving meaning when a passage is somewhat difficult, so they should think about these strategies as they read. Following their reading, use the overhead projector or the chalkboard to record their responses. Assign each logical response a code. Responses typical of middle- or upper elementary-grade students would be

RRS	I had to reread a sentence because I lost what the author was saying.
RRP	I had to reread the whole paragraph and then I understood.
CGVI	I couldn't get a visual image.
GVI	I got a visual image of what the author was talking about.
DKWM	I didn't know a word meaning.
UCGWM	I didn't know the meaning of a word, but I figured it out from the way it was used in the sentence. (Used context to get word meaning.)
DU	I didn't understand what was there.
UJF	I understood just fine.

Other responses you might expect to get less often are

W	I am wondering why I have to read this?
UEC	The student used "expanded context." The students will, of course, not be likely to refer to this as using expanded context but rather something on the order of

"I saw the word in the paragraph above [or in the title, etc.] and went back to read it there to see if I could figure out what it means."

CITQ   Can I think of a question over this material? Once students have begun to use metacognitive techniques, they are likely to begin to give answers similar to this one.

BNR   I was bothered by noise in the room or from an airplane flying overhead.

VI   Very interesting

Once a set of responses somewhat similar to those above is elicited, place them on something more permanent, such as a piece of chart paper or a bulletin board, so that they are in full view of all students at all times when using this technique. Use a paper cutter to cut a number of strips of paper about 1″ wide and 11″ long from sheets of 8 ½″ × 11″ paper. Ask students to align the bottom of the strip of paper with the bottom of the page of the material they are to read. Then ask students to use these codes to mark each paragraph you have assigned. The material might be in their basal reader, their science or social studies text, or any other material that you feel is appropriate for their grade level.

In doing this activity, be flexible in determining the code students are to use. For example, in the original development of the code, students may not list all of the things they believed happened to them as they read. In this case allow for more to be added or for some, seldom used, to be removed.

This procedure will enable the good comprehenders to teach the poor comprehenders their procedures for coping with difficult material. Although the procedure may appear complicated, students catch on quickly and are highly motivated to participate in this activity.

E. Young students should be counseled on the importance of getting meaning from reading. Young readers, low achievers, and disabled readers all seem to share the characteristic of believing that fast, fluent oral reading is their ultimate goal. Do not take it for granted that some students know that comprehension of the material read is the most important purpose for reading. For younger students, it will also be helpful to discuss the vocabulary of reading: what is a *sound, paragraph,* or *sentence?* Studies have shown that many students, as late as first grade, do not know the difference between a letter, a word, and a sentence.

F. Stress the necessity for the student to be able to recognize words for which he does not know the meaning while he reads. Instruct the student to attempt to determine the meaning of unknown words from their context. If the student is unable to derive the meaning of the word from context, then urge the student to use the dictionary. Most people become somewhat "expert" at omitting or ignoring words for which they do not know the meaning. Simply being aware of this habit will be most helpful in breaking it. Think back to a time when you looked up a word in the dictionary. You then may have noticed that same word several times in the very near future. Chances are that you had encountered the same word many times in the past but had simply ignored it. Once you knew the meaning of the word, you became much more aware of how often it appeared in materials that you were reading.

G. Stress the need for students to change their reading speeds depending upon the kind of materials they read. Many students read everything at the same rate. You could show students that a story problem in a math book would not be read at the same rate as a newspaper story about a familiar subject. (See Chapter 23 for additional suggestions for helping students adjust their rate of reading.)

H. Teach students to predict what may lie ahead as they read. In instructing students to do this, you may wish to have them read up to a certain point in a story or passage. Then discuss what they think the author will write next, based on what they have already read.

I. Instruct students to anticipate what questions the author or teacher might ask about a story or passage after it has been read. To do this, have students read a paragraph and then discuss what they think the author or you might ask them about the material. Practice this until students are proficient in this skill. Show students the difference between main ideas or overall comprehension of a passage and the comprehension or learning of only minor facts or details.

J. Use some type of marker for words that you think students will find difficult to understand. For example, you might put an asterisk before words that you feel will be difficult for students or an X before words that you believe they will not know. This will help them to be more aware of new words.

K. Talk to students about how stories progress from page to page to show a sequence of events and make students aware of the headings in social studies and science books. Discuss the reason authors use headings and how they may be used to improve the students' understanding of the material they read.

L. Place all of the sentences of a paragraph on the board or on an overhead projector and discuss their importance to the overall understanding of the paragraph. You may wish to have students place the sentences in order according to their importance in the paragraph, e.g., putting the most important sentence first, the next most important sentence second, and so on.

M. Teach students to learn to distinguish when text does or does not make sense to them. You may wish to provide practice in this skill by rewriting a passage and adding sentences within the text that contribute nothing to its meaning. Then have students read the material and attempt to locate those sentences that do not contribute to the overall comprehension of the material. This will help students monitor their comprehension in the future.

N. Tell students to think about the material they read, so when they complete the assignment, they will be able to explain the material to other students. This too will help students monitor their comprehension as they read.

O. Ask students to pretend they are the teacher while they read. Have them attempt to think of as many questions as they can about each paragraph.

P. Linda B. Gambrell[*] urges teachers to make use of think-time in questioning. She suggests that teachers allow students 5 seconds to think about a question both before and after they answer it to improve the quality of the answers they give. Teachers often observe that the same few students seem to want to answer any question the teacher asks, often before the asking has been completed. Teachers who are patient and allow think-time will get more responses from students who otherwise might not participate.

Q. Students' ability to monitor their comprehension as they read may be enhanced by using story frames such as those suggested by Gerald F. Fowler.[**] Fowler suggests that story frames be introduced shortly after students have read a selection. Five types of story frames are presented here. Note that all five types may not be appropriate for all types of stories; however, you will find that several can often be used in many stories. It is suggested that you first introduce students to one of the simpler types of story frames, such as the one in Figure 1, after students have completed reading a story. Answers to the questions posed by the story frames may then be solicited from the entire class. After students become more adept at using each type of story frame, they may then be given to students prior to reading a story as an advance organizer to help them monitor their comprehension as they read.

---

[*]Gambrell, L. B. (1980). Think-time: Implications for reading instruction. *Reading Teacher, 34,* 143–146.

[**]Reprinted with permission of Gerald L. Fowler and the International Reading Association from Fowler, G. L. (1982). Developing comprehension skills in primary students through the use of story frames. *Reading Teacher, 36,* 176–179.

You may have to modify these story frames to fit the story you are working on. For example, you may start with "This story begins when" and then add "and then." Following this you may add words that appropriately follow the sequence of events for the story such as, "next," "following that," and "the problem is solved when."

Figure 1
Story summary with one character included

Our story is about _____
_____. _____ is an important character in our story. ___
tried to _____
The story ends when _____
_____.

Figure 2
Important idea or plot

In this story the problems starts when _____. After that,
_____.
Next, _____
_____. Then, _____
_____. The problem is finally solved when _____
_____. The story ends_____
_____.

Figure 3
Setting

This story takes place _____
_____. I know this because the author uses the words "_____

_____." Other clues that show when the story takes place are
_____.

Figure 4
Character analysis

_____ is an important character in our story. ___ is important because
_____. Once, he/she
_____. Another time,
_____. I think that
_____ is _____
(character's name)   (character trait)
because _____.

Figure 5
Character comparison

_____ and _____ are two characters in our story. _____
(character's name)
is _____ while
(trait)
_____ is _____
(other character)   (trait)
For instance, _____ tries to _____.
_____ learns a lesson when _____
_____.

Procedures for Improving Overall Comprehension

A. Set a purpose for reading before students begin to read. Have them skim the material and make predictions about the nature of the material and what they may expect to get from it. These predictions may be made from captions under pictures, the actual pictures, or from any headings that may appear in the story or article.

B. Teach students to find material that is not too difficult for them by counting about 100 words of the material they are about to read. Tell them when they read these 100 words, they should not find more than one or two words they do not know. This refers to material the students would be reading without having any type of review of the words and content before they begin reading. Research in this area shows that students cannot be expected to comprehend well unless they have rapid word recognition of the material.

C. Having students combine sentences can also be an effective aid to the improvement of overall comprehension. Use the basal reader or a literature selection to find various sentences that can be combined. In using this method, you may wish to call students' attention to the use of words such as *and, but, therefore, however, neither, either, which, that,* etc. You may also wish to develop, with students' help, a permanent list of these words. They can then be placed on chart paper or a bulletin board and kept in a place where all students can readily refer to them.

In doing this exercise, you may also wish to indicate which sentences should be combined by placing a number after each sentence and then giving students a sheet indicating which sentences should be combined. For example, the sheet may appear as follows:

¶1: 1 & 2
¶3: 1, 2, & 3, etc.

You may also wish to have them use words from certain sentences to form their sentence (sometimes called *embedding*). In this case, you may wish to indicate which words are to be embedded using a coding system such as this.

¶1: 1, 2 (cute), 3 (angry)
¶1: 4, 5, & 6

Example of original paragraph

Fred had a pet coyote. It was very cute. It sometimes got very angry. When Fred went to school it sometimes followed him. When the coyote followed Fred he sometimes had to take it back home. Then Fred was late for school.

Example of combined paragraph

Fred had a pet coyote that was very cute, but sometimes it got very angry. Sometimes Fred's coyote would follow him to school and then he would have to take it back home, which made Fred late for school.

D. One method of making students familiar with the new words and content of the material they are about to read is to make an audiovisual presentation of the vocabulary and concepts. For example, if the students are about to begin a unit on weather in their science book, the teacher might find or have the students find various pictures that represent concepts and the vocabulary that students are likely to encounter. In a unit on weather, new words might be *barometer, hygrometer,* and *thermometer.* After finding pictures of these instruments, the students can paste them on sheets of paper and place them in a review notebook. The words listed above might be found in three different sections of a page. The sections would be labeled *A, B,* and *C,* and in each section one of the words listed above would appear along with a picture of that instrument. See the following picture.

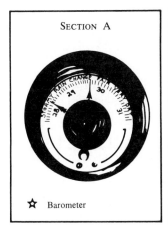

SECTION A

☆ Barometer

SECTION B

☐ Hygrometer

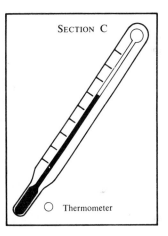

SECTION C

○ Thermometer

The teacher or advanced students would then write and record a narrative to go along with the material in the notebook. Before students begin reading, they would go to a listening station with the notebook and audio tape to prepare them for the concepts and vocabulary of that unit in the textbook. The script for a unit on weather might be as follows: "Look on page one in section A where you will find a picture of a barometer. The word *barometer* is written by the star. Note the spelling of this word b-a-r-o-m-e-t-e-r. A barometer is used to predict what the weather will be like in the future. When a barometer shows a high reading, the weather is likely to be fair. And when the barometer shows a low reading, we might expect wind and maybe rain or snow. Now look in section B where . . . . "

E. Students who read word-by-word or who do not use proper phrasing are not likely to comprehend as well as students who do use proper phrasing. One way to improve a student's ability to phrase is to give him material and indicate where he might phrase properly, as in the following sentence:

Tom's dog/was very little/but he could/run as fast/as most dogs/much larger/than he.

F. Another method of getting students to phrase properly is to have them read dialogue or use materials such as *Plays for Echo Reading* published by Harcourt Brace Jovanovich. (For additional recommendations to help students who read word-by-word or do not use proper phrasing, see Chapters 2 and 3.)

G. Constantly make the point to students that reading can be a source of information to help them with hobbies and any other subjects they would like to know more about. Refer them to various source books, encyclopedias, etc.

Ability to Recognize Main Ideas

A. You should work with students to help them find the main idea and supporting details of a story. You may list the main idea as well as the supporting details as shown in the following paragraph.

A little bird sang a song day after day. The old man had heard it so many times that he knew the tune by heart. Even the students who played nearby could sing it.

Main Idea: A little bird sang his song day after day.
Supporting Details: The old man had heard it many times.
                      The old man knew it by heart.
                      Even the students who played nearby could sing it.

Another way of bringing out the main idea of a paragraph and of showing the supporting details is to draw the paragraph as a diagram. In doing this type of exercise, you will note that most paragraphs could be classified using one of five to perhaps as many as ten different forms. It is suggested that you let students develop the forms based on the information in each paragraph. After it is discovered that most paragraphs take one of five to ten forms that are essentially the same, you may then wish to have students name or classify the various types of forms. For example, the paragraph concerning various brands of soap could be labeled the *Sales Pitch*. It is more meaningful to students to let them develop the various forms and then name them than it is to tell them in the beginning that there are X normally used types that have names previously given to them.

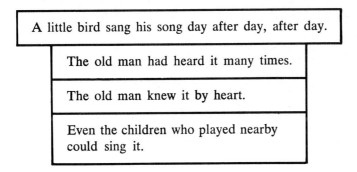

Other paragraphs may have two main ideas.

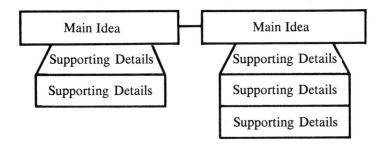

Other types of paragraphs may look like the following.

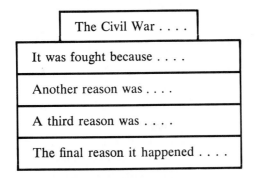

Many people eat too much . . . .

Many people drink too much . . . .

Many people watch TV too much . . . .

But on the other hand there are the people who . . . .

Even some of these do not . . . .

Some do not even . . . .

Sometimes there are those who . . . .

I will run for public office again if . . . .

Senator Brown must . . . .

Governor Turner should . . . .

My health . . . .

If I run I am sure . . . .

The first reader introduces . . . .

The second reader introduces . . . .

The third reader discusses . . . .

All of the readers in the series are deeply concerned with . . . .

Once upon a time . . . .

Therefore children, you should . . . .

When drawing paragraph diagrams with the students, do not expect to find complete agreement on how they should look. Keep in mind that the important thing is to get the students to think about paragraph structure. When using this system, you may want to have the students suggest names for certain common structure patterns, for example, *the logical conclusion, the sales pitch,* and *the conditional.* However, do not try this technique in the early stages of pattern development, as the students will try to fit new structures into old forms.

B. Read the introduction or title to the story or a chapter and then anticipate with the students what the author is going to say.

C. Select appropriate titles for paragraphs, chapters, or short selections. You might also have the students select the best title from several listed.

D. After the students read a paragraph, have them tell in their own words what the author has said.

E. Many writers use subheadings to help students organize the text. Turn these subheadings into questions and then have students read specifically to answer those questions.

F. Use a series of three pictures, one of which represents the main idea of a paragraph. Have the students pick the picture that best represents the main idea. Or you could have the students illustrate a paragraph and put the pictures on cards, e.g., one paragraph and three pictures on a card.

G. Have the students underline the sentences in paragraphs that best represent the main idea. Make sure there is a sentence that best represents the main idea, and also make sure the paragraph has a main idea.

H. Find stories in the newspaper with charts or photos and remove the original captions from each of them. Give these to students and have them read each story and then write their own captions. Compare the students' captions with those of the original stories. Discuss reasons for differences and if captions written by the students are appropriate.

I. Have each student write a paragraph and place an identifying number at the top of the paper. Then pass the paragraph to another student who reads it and writes the main idea or a caption for it on the back of the paper. Then read the various paragraphs and discuss the appropriateness of each caption or main idea sentence.

J. Have students write paragraphs with one sentence being the main idea of that paragraph. Pass these paragraphs around and have other students try to identify the sentence that the writer of the paragraph thought best represented the main idea.

Ability to Recognize Important Details

A. Discuss with the students the important details in several paragraphs. Students often focus on minor dates and details that are not really important. Perhaps the kind of testing often used encourages this type of reading.

B. Help the students to find the main idea, then ask them to find significant details that describe or elaborate on the idea.

C. Ask the students to write down all the details from a selection. Have them classify the details from their list as (1) important, (2) helpful, but not essential, and (3) unnecessary.

D. Have the students answer questions or complete sentences that require a knowledge of the important details.

E. Have the students draw a series of pictures to illustrate details, for example, in the description of a scene.

F. Write three or four paragraphs about a picture and then have students read each of the paragraphs to see which one best describes the picture. The picture may be placed at the top of an 8½″ × 11″ piece of paper with each of the paragraphs arranged below it.

G. Have students read stories in newspapers and magazine articles and then have them attempt to answer the following: Who? What? When? Where? and Why?

Ability to Develop Mental Images

A. One research study indicated that the principal differences between younger students who comprehended well and those who did not were that the good comprehenders were able to develop mental images or visualize as they read, and they reread when they did not comprehend. Based on this information, the teacher should strive to help students develop mental images. Teach the student to be aware of mental images he is forming as he reads. Have the student read a sentence or two and then ask if he was able to actually see the scene or the action described in what he read. If the student cannot do this, then read the same sentence and tell the student what you saw in your "mind's eye" as you read. Ask the student to read the same material and attempt to get approximately the same mental image. In beginning to develop this skill, be sure to use reading passages that contain information with which the student is already somewhat familiar. Keep in mind that the mental image a student is able to get will depend on his background or experience.

B. For students to visualize a certain setting or image effectively, they must have actually or vicariously experienced it. Review the setting of a story with students before they begin. You could also supplement their information with a film or filmstrip or have students bring pictures from books and magazines.

C. As a student reads a selection, you might stop him from time to time and ask him to describe images gained from the reading. Also, the student might be asked questions combining the images from the passage and his own images. Two examples of questions are *What color coat do you think the person is wearing?* and *Was it a big tiger or a little tiger?*

D. Discuss figures of speech such as *big as a bear, black as pitch,* or *as cold as a polar bear in the Yukon.* Help the students to see that figurative language can either add meaning to a story or, in some cases, be misleading. Ask the students to listen for and collect various figures of speech.

E. Ask the students to draw pictures of certain settings they have read about. Compare and discuss.

Ability to Predict Outcomes

A. Show a series of pictures from a story and ask the students to tell, either in writing or orally, what they think the story will be about.

B. Read to a certain point in a story and then ask the students to tell or write their own versions of the ending.

C. Ask the students to read the chapter titles of a book and predict what the story will be about. Read the story and compare versions.

D. Encourage the students to make logical predictions and be ready to revise their preconceived ideas in the light of new information.

Ability to Follow Directions

A. Make students aware of key words that indicate a series of instructions, such as *first, second, then,* and *finally.* Discuss the fact that, in this case, there were actually four steps, although the writer only used the terms *first* and *second.* As students read directions, have them reinforce this knowledge by having them make lists of words that were used to indicate steps.

B. Write directions for paper folding, etc., which the students can do at their seats. Have the students read and perform these directions step by step.

C. Write directions for recess activities on the chalkboard. Try to get the students in the habit of following these directions without oral explanation.

D. Ask the students to write directions for playing a game. Have them read their directions and analyze whether they could learn to play the game from a certain student's written directions.

E. Encourage the students to read written directions such as those in workbooks and certain arithmetic problems without your help.

F. Write directions for certain designs to be drawn on a certain size of paper. For example the following directions may be given.

1. Make an X on your paper halfway between the top and bottom edges and ½″ from the left-hand side.
2. Make a Y on the same horizontal plane as the X, but ½″ from the right-hand side of the paper.
3. Make a Z directly below the Y ½″ from the bottom edge of the paper.
4. Draw a line to connect the X and Y.
5. Draw another line to connect the Y and the Z.

After these are completed, have students examine their pictures in relation to one drawn correctly and shown on the overhead projector or on the chalkboard. Discuss reasons for some common mistakes.

Ability to Recognize the Author's Organization

A. Discuss the fact that all authors have some form or organization in mind when writing. Look over chapter titles and discuss other possibilities for organization. Do the same with shorter selections including paragraphs.

B. Discuss the author's use of pictures, graphs, charts, and diagrams to clarify certain concepts.

C. Discuss the use of introductory material, headings, study questions, and summaries.

D. Explain the value of "signal" words and phrases in showing organizational patterns.

E. Make the students aware of "signal words" and "signal phrases" in selections: *to begin with, next, not long after, then, finally, several factors were responsible for, these led to, which further complicated it by.*

F. Write down a sequence of events from a story the students have read and ask them to number the events in the order in which they happened. Explain before they read the story what they will be expected to do.

G. Write each of the sentences from a paragraph on a separate (small) piece of paper in mixed-up order. Ask the students to arrange these sentences in a logical sequence to form a paragraph that makes sense.

H. Cut up comic strips or pictures of sequential events and have the students assemble them in their correct order.

Ability to Do Critical Reading (A higher-level reading skill)

A. Discuss the use of "colored" or "loaded" words and have students search through editorials or transcripts of speeches of political candidates for these words. Some examples of these words are *left-wing, reactionary, rightist, playboy*, and *extremist*.

B. Examine advertisements for cigarettes to see how they are designed to appeal to various age groups. Note statements that are made about such products and examine if these statements have merit.

C. Examine advertisements for various products in men's and women's magazines to see how they are designed to appeal to different audiences.

D. Find accounts of a political event as reported by two or more newspapers or magazines. Note ways in which the information differs.

E. Examine political cartoons and discuss if they are designed to show the candidate in a positive or negative way.

F. Examine various advertisements to see how they attempt to get the buyer to infer information about the product, which, in reality, may be quite meaningless. For example, a claim for X brand of aspirin may say, "Nine out of ten doctors surveyed recommended the ingredients in X brand." What this may mean is that nine out of ten doctors recommend that people take aspirin at some time!

G. Analyze editorials to determine if the writer of the editorial used biased statements or if the writer wished the reader to make certain inferences. Also discuss why a certain writer may be biased in certain areas.

H. Write or have students write paragraphs. Then have the students write statements about the paragraphs, based on the information in those paragraphs, which may or may not be true. Discuss various statements and determine if they are true or if statements made about those paragraphs could logically be inferred.

I. Read reports of interviews with political candidates and note if a candidate had taken certain stands on issues before, or if the candidate's views on a subject tended to change to take advantage of a situation.

GAMES AND EXERCISES

Story Division

Purpose: To provide practice in comprehension and oral reading skills for students who lack self-confidence

Materials: A basal reader or other story selection for each student

Procedure:

You first divide a story, such as the following, into parts.

1. Toddle was Pam's pet turtle.
   He liked to crawl.
   He got out of his pan of water and crawled all around the house.
2. Toddle bumped into things.
   Bang! Bang! Down they went.
   Mother did not like this.
3. She said, "Please, Pam, put Toddle back into the water, and do make him stay there."

Each student studies one part of the story and reads it orally. After a whole story is read, the students are given a comprehension check.

This type of procedure gives the students confidence because they know the part they will be required to read and they can practice reading it silently before reading it orally.

A Matching Board

Purpose: To provide practice on the various components of comprehension

Materials: A piece of ½" plywood the same size as a sheet of ditto paper
             Shoestrings

Procedure:

Drill two columns of holes 1½" apart down the center of the piece of plywood as shown. Make holes the entire length of the board, spacing them the same vertical distance as four spaces on a typewriter. The holes should be just large enough to let the shoestrings pass through them quite easily. Attach shoestrings through the holes in the left column. Tie a knot on the back side, so they will not be pulled through. Make sure each string in the left column is long enough to thread through any hole in the right column.

Ditto various exercises such as sentence completion, missing words from the context of a sentence, word opposites, sentence opposites, etc. Make each set of opposites four vertical typewriter line spaces, so they will correspond with the holes on the board. Use a tack or clear tape at the top and bottom of each column of questions and answers to hold the dittoed material in place. Use these boards with individual students to provide practice in areas in which they need help. Various kinds of exercises are illustrated on the following pages.

Main Ideas

Purpose: To improve students' ability to concentrate and locate the main idea in a selection

Materials: Basal readers, library books, science or social studies textbooks

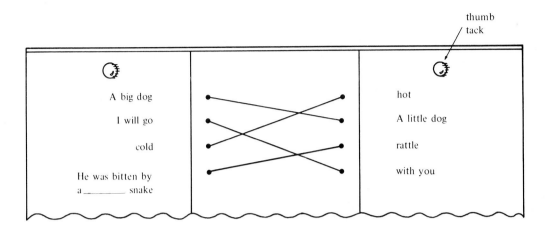

Procedure:

Before giving the students a reading assignment, show them a list of true-false questions concerning the material on the reading assignment. Construct the questions so they test for the main ideas of paragraphs from the reading material. This test will give the students an idea of what they are expected to gather from the assignment, and it will improve their ability to recognize main ideas in future reading. Make sure students understand that the questions test for main ideas and not for details.

Directions: Some of the statements below are true and some are false. Write *T* after the true statements and *F* after those that are not true.

1. Carlos did not really want to race his car. _____
2. The weather was just right for racing. _____
3. Someone had been fooling around with Carlos's car. _____
4. Most of Carlos's friends felt that he could win the race if he wanted to. _____

Picture Puzzle

Purpose: To help students recognize, evaluate, and describe various situations

Materials: Pictures clipped from magazines or old discarded readers mounted on tagboard
Word cards
Flannel board

Procedure:

Display a picture on a flannel board. Allow the students to select from a large number of word cards the ones they feel best describe the given picture. Place these word cards on the flannel board with the picture and discuss their appropriateness to the situation.

Variation in Procedure:

Use the same procedure as above, except substitute sentence strips for the individual word cards or make sentences from the individual cards.

Riddles

Purpose: To provide practice in the comprehension of descriptive details

Materials: Tagboard

Procedure:

Write a series of short stories describing a particular object or animal. Have the students read the story and decide what the object or animal is. In the bottom corner, under a flap of paper, place the correct answer. The students may check their answers after they have made their decisions. See the example.

My home is in the country.
I live on a farm.
The farmer's children take care of me.
They give me grain and water.
I give them eggs.
I am a good friend of yours.
What animal am I?

Answer
is here

What Do You See?

Purpose: To develop picture-word description relationships

Materials: Pictures cut from magazines
Tagboard
Flannel board

Procedure:

Place pictures of objects on a flannel board. On tagboard write some questions about the pictures and some questions that will act as distracters. Have the students answer the questions about the pictures posted.

Do you see a frog?

Do you see a hopping rabbit?

Do you see a fat pig?

Do you see a door?

Do you see an open window?

Do you see a red ball?

The Wizard

Purpose: To provide practice in reading for specific questions

Materials: A basal reader or literature selection for each student

Procedure:

One student is chosen as the Wizard. The student asks a question relating to the reading lesson and calls on a classmate to answer. If that student answers correctly, he is the Wizard, and he makes up the next question. Those students who do not answer a question correctly have another chance to be the Wizard with further play.

Classification Game

Purpose: To develop the ability to classify related words

Materials: Pocket chart
Word cards
Envelopes

Procedure:

Divide the pocket chart into four columns. In the first three columns in each row, place three related word cards. Leave the fourth column blank and have the students select a word card from their envelopes that belongs in the same class as the other three words in that row.

car	boat	airplane	_____
ball	top	doll	_____
Susan	Bill	Lassie	_____

walk   gallop   skip   _____
red   blue   green   _____

Variation in Procedure:

Instead of filling in the missing word as described above, use four words in which one word does not fit the category represented by the other three words. Have students find and remove the "misfit."

As I See It

Purpose: To provide students with an opportunity to express the visual images they gain from reading or hearing a story

Materials: A story (preferably one with vividly described scenes)
            Drawing paper and paints or colors

Procedure:

After the students have heard or read a story, have them illustrate various scenes as they perceived them. After drawing the scenes, mix the illustrations up in a box and have one student stand in front of the room and pull out pictures. After he has chosen a picture, he will try to reconstruct the story on a bulletin board from the many pictures that are in the box. Discuss various differences in drawings and discuss why some students interpreted things differently. At times you will want to reread parts of the story to see if material was interpreted incorrectly.

Furnish the Empty Room

Purpose: To develop the ability to recognize appropriate visual images

Materials: Flannel board
            Pictures of specific objects cut from magazines or old books

Procedure:

At the top of the flannel board, place printed subject headings such as *kitchen* or *playroom*. Have the students select object pictures that are appropriate to the given headings. See an illustration on the next page.

My Image

Purpose: To encourage the building of sensory images

Materials: Various materials to create sounds that are very familiar, somewhat familiar, and less familiar to students

Procedure:

Have the students close their eyes and listen as you or another student makes a noise. Have the students open their eyes and write words or phrases that

describe the noise. Then have them draw pictures to represent the noise. Encourage them to use a varied vocabulary in their descriptions.

That Makes Sense

Purpose: To develop the ability to associate objects with their sources and to develop the ability to logically complete a given idea

Materials: Pocket chart
Word cards
Envelopes

Procedure:

A series of incomplete statements is placed on the pocket chart. Word cards containing the appropriate missing words or phrases are provided for the students. From these they will select the correct answer and place it in the pocket chart next to the incomplete idea. See the illustration on the next page.

Ordered Phrases

Purpose: To provide practice in skimming and in determining sequence (comprehension)

Materials: Cards with phrases copied from a story, book, or basal reader

Procedure:

Have the students read the passage and place the phrases on the cards in columns in the order that the phrases occurred on the page.

You should also write the number order on the back of the cards. Such numbering will enable a student to correct his own work.

A dress is made from	in the ground
Fish usually	flour
Cocoa is made from	fly
Oil can come from	seeds
Cabbage grows	beans
Parrots can	on the ground
Strawberries have	swim in water
Cakes are made from	whales
Potatoes grow	wool

Sentence Puzzles

Purpose: To help students see a sequence of ideas

Materials: Envelopes
Paragraphs or short stories that are written in a logical order

Procedure:

Cut up the stories or paragraphs into sentences and paste each sentence on a small rectangular piece of paper. Place one story or paragraph in each envelope. Pass these envelopes out to the students and have them assemble the stories in a logical order. Number the envelopes and have the students keep a record of the stories or paragraphs (by envelope number) they have assembled. The students continue to exchange these envelopes until all have had a turn at each envelope. In some cases you may want to have stories or paragraphs graded according to the reading level of a particular group. In such a case reading group B will do only those envelopes marked 1-B, 2-B, and so forth.

It Does—It Doesn't

Purpose: To help students classify words according to descriptive specifications

Materials: Pocket chart
Envelopes
Word cards

Procedure:

Divide the pocket chart into two columns. Place a statement and its opposite next to each other at the top of the chart. Provide each student with an envelope of word cards containing current vocabulary words. Have the students classify the words found in their envelopes according to the given statements. Use a great variety of statements and word cards that will require careful thought. Vocabulary and classification sentences will vary with grade levels.

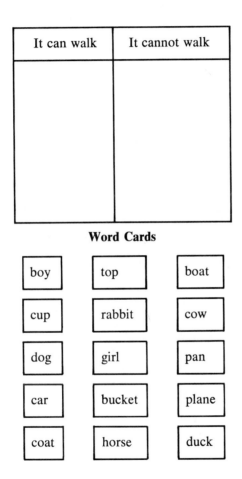

It can walk	It cannot walk

Word Cards

boy   top   boat

cup   rabbit   cow

dog   girl   pan

car   bucket   plane

coat   horse   duck

What Did It Say?

Purpose: To develop phrase recognition and the ability to follow directions

Materials: Flash cards

Procedure:

Write specific directions on individual flash cards. As the cards are flashed before the class, call on certain students to respond. Examples of directions are
1. Close the door.
2. Give a pencil to a brown-eyed boy.
3. Stand up. Turn three circles. Touch the desk behind yours.
4. Draw a circle inside of a triangle on the board.

Story Pantomime

Purpose: To provide practice in reading for information and following directions

Materials: Cards on which are printed directions for acting out certain activities

Procedure:

The cards are passed out to all the students in the class. One student is selected to act out each set. The other students watch critically for the complete acting of every detail in the directions.

Example: Pretend you are washing dishes. Stop up the sink, open the doors under the sink, and get the soap. Put the soap in the sink, turn the faucet on, test the water, put the dishes in the water, and then wash and rinse three dishes. Put the dishes in the dish rack to dry. A story pantomime might also include such things as

drawing water from a well

making the bed

rocking the baby

picking flowers for a bouquet

singing a hymn

winding the clock

watering the flowers

ironing

picking and eating apples

playing baseball

Good Words—Bad Words

Purpose: To provide practice in critical reading, especially concerning the purpose the author had in mind when the material was written

Materials: Various written or tape-recorded advertisements

Procedure:

Have the students locate and circle or make a list of words they can classify as either "good" words or "bad" words. Good words might include such words as *freedom, well-being, number-one rating,* and *delicious.* Bad words might include words such as *disease, cracks, peels,* and *odor.* Discuss how the use of these words influences our thinking about a certain product. Carry this exercise into the study of characters in books about whom the author wishes to convey a good or bad impression.

V

STUDY SKILLS ABILITIES

22

Low Rate of Speed

RECOGNIZED BY

The student is unable to read as many words per minute as would be normal for a student of her age on a certain kind of reading material. Low rate of speed usually applies to silent, rather than oral, reading.

DISCUSSION

You can determine if certain students are slow readers by giving a timed reading exercise to an entire class. The various reading speeds listed in words per minute can be graphed or charted to determine which students are considerably below average on a particular kind of material for their class. When giving timed exercises, choose several pages that are normal reading material in story reading. You should not use pages containing questions, lists, etc. Timed exercises from two to five minutes should be sufficient. You seldom need to worry about achieving a very rapid reading rate in the elementary grades. Therefore, the suggestions listed under items A, B, and C are more appropriate for junior- or senior-high-level students. Activities to increase speed of reading should be used only with students who have strong decoding skills and who comprehend adequately when reading slowly. Students should be expected to read with accuracy before attempts are made to increase their reading speed.

RECOMMENDATIONS

A. Have the students pace their reading with their hands. They should attempt to move across the page slightly faster than their comfortable reading speed normally allows. It should, however, be emphasized that the hand paces the eyes and the reading speed, not the opposite.

B. Focus on speed by using material that can be read fast. Give timed reading exercises followed by comprehension questions. Let the student keep her own chart on speed and comprehension. See Appendix S for sample chart.

C. For older students, assign or let them pick short paperback novels that are meant to be read rapidly. Use these in conjunction with hand pacing to practice for speed.

Timed Stories

Purpose: To encourage rapid reading while still focusing on improving comprehension

Materails: A number of envelopes with short stories in them, along with sets of questions about each story

Procedure:

Before doing this, you should have given speed reading tests to your class and grouped them accordingly, i.e., one group that reads from 75–100 words per minute, one group that reads from 100–125 words per minute, and so on. Cut a number of short stories from old basal readers or another source. Put one of these stories, along with approximately 10 comprehension questions, in an envelope. Develop norms for each story; for example, a certain story for the 100–125 wpm group may be labeled an eight-minute story. Label the envelopes under headings such as *Dog Stories, Family Life Stories,* and *Science Stories.* Let the students choose the stories they want to read. From the labeling, the students will know that they should read the story in a certain number of minutes. This technique is a change from the timed test in which each student is reading the same subject matter. It also avoids having the faster readers wait for the slower readers; when they finish a story, they can get an envelope and begin another one. Have the students keep a record of the stories they have read and their percent of comprehension on each story.

23

Inability to Adjust Reading Rate

RECOGNIZED BY

The student reads at the same rate regardless of the *type* of material he is reading. This applies to silent, rather than oral, reading.

DISCUSSION

Many people are in the habit of reading all kinds of material at one speed. They read a newspaper or novel as though it were a science book or a set of directions. This is a habit that can be overcome easily if the student is shown how varying his reading rate can save time and improve comprehension. To determine whether a student is reading all kinds of material at the same speed, give him a speed test on several kinds of material. The first material should be of the type found in novels or in a newspaper. Then give another speed test on material that would require more careful reading, such as the expository writing in a science book. If the student reads all of the material at approximately the same rate, he is having problems adjusting his reading rate to the difficulty of the material.

To determine reading rate, find the total number of words in the passage and the length of time, in seconds, that the student takes to read that passage. Divide the number of words by the number of seconds. Multiply the resulting figure by 60. The result will be *words per minute*.

RECOMMENDATIONS

A. Discuss various types of reading material and show the students how rates should vary on these materials. You may wish to construct a chart to explain this idea.

How We Read Different Kinds of Materials

Skim	*Fast*
1. Telephone book	1. Novels
2. Newspaper (when looking for one thing)	2. Newspaper (when reading normally)

Medium	*Slow*
1. Our history assignments	1. Procedures for experiments in science
2. A magazine article of high interest	2. Our mathematics book
	3. A computer manual

B. Time an entire class on a reading passage from a novel, and then time the class on a reading passage from a mathematics or science book, preferably one that explains a process. Compare the average amount of time taken to read each passage or the number of words read in a certain amount of time. Emphasize that comprehension is necessary in both cases.

C. Check the students' comprehension on easy and difficult material when each is read fast and when each is read slowly. Determine proper reading speeds for adequate comprehension of each type of material.

D. Much of the material in science and social studies is presented with a number of boldfaced headings within the chapters. The student should study this material in the following manner:

1. Turn the first boldfaced heading into a question; for example, the heading may state **The New World**. The student might then make a question of this by asking himself, "Where was the New World?"
2. The student then reads to answer that question.
3. When the student has read down to the next boldfaced heading, he should stop and try to answer the question he has just posed. If he cannot answer it, he should read the material again. If he can answer it, he should proceed to the next boldfaced heading and do the same with it.

E. Discuss when it may not be necessary to read every word, such as in a descriptive passage of scenery in a novel or details in newspaper articles. Have students underline only those parts that would be necessary for adequate comprehension. Then have students exchange articles or pages of a novel and read only the parts that other students have underlined. Discuss information derived by various students by reading only the underlined material. Ask the students who underlined the material to comment on the adequacy of the second reader's comprehension.

F. If the reader's rate is much too slow, then discuss when it is desirable to skim. If the reader cannot do this, then see the suggestions under "Inability to Skim or Scan," Chapter 25.

24

High Rate of Reading at the Expense of Accuracy

RECOGNIZED BY

The student reads quickly but with poor recall. Often such a student completes reading assignments before the rest of the class, yet lacks comprehension of what she has read.

DISCUSSION

Reading at a high rate of speed is desirable at times. There are, however, certain types of reading material that should be read more carefully than others. For example, mathematics, science, and other content reading materials often require slow, careful reading. Many students are not able to adjust their reading rate downward as the reading material becomes difficult. This situation is especially true of the student who constantly reads novels or the newspaper and then must read material in school that requires considerable concentration.

You occasionally may find a student in the lower elementary grades who reads at a rate that impairs her accuracy. The problem is more prevalent, however, with older students who have become accustomed to reading material that requires little concentration.

RECOMMENDATIONS

A. Demonstrate and then discuss the various reading speeds that are desirable for certain types of material. You may show students how you read different types of material by preparing overhead transparencies of selections that are triple-spaced. Use a pointer to indicate the speed at which your eyes move over the material and stop to explain to students why you are reading at the chosen speed and what thinking is going on in your mind as you are reading. Take time to thoroughly discuss this and to answer students' questions. Do not be concerned about telling students the *best* way to read different materials. Explain to students that they may think about other things while they are reading and that is fine. What is important is that you model the process of strategic reading. Once students see that their teacher actively thinks while reading, they will begin to do the same thing.

B. Have the students react to each paragraph using a code similar to that suggested on ideas for using metacognition, shown in item D in Chapter 21.

C. Ask the students to use techniques in which they are required to react to each boldfaced heading. (See item D in Chapter 23.)

D. From material found in a reading passage, ask oral and written questions that require accurate answers. Let the students know ahead of time that they will be required to answer questions about the reading passage.

E. Give students worksheets that contain reading passages and questions about subject matter in the reading passages. Ask them to underline the answers to questions as they read them.

F. Give the students study-guide questions over material they are to read. Many books contain questions over a unit or chapter at the end of that unit or chapter. Encourage the students to read these questions before they begin reading the material in the chapter or unit.

25

Inability to Skim or Scan

RECOGNIZED BY

The student is unable to get a general understanding of reading material through rapid, superficial reading (skimming) or to find specific information or answer specific questions about material that is read quickly (scanning).

DISCUSSION

Skimming and scanning are reading strategies to accomplish specific objectives. Skimming requires more comprehension than scanning but less than normal reading. It can be an effective way for students to preview reading material that they may later read more carefully. One of the causes of the inability to skim is that the students have not felt a need for this skill. People who actually need to learn to skim, and who are shown how to do so, soon become adept at this skill. To determine if a student is able to skim, select material you wish the student to read and skim it yourself. Note how long it takes you to get the gist of the material and add some additional time for the student to do this, depending on the age and reading ability of the student and the difficulty of the material. Next, tell the student that you would like him to look at a reading selection quickly, then tell you what it is about. The best way to judge a student's ability at this task is to compare his performance to that of other students when skimming the same material.

To scan effectively the student must know what he is looking for and how to use key words to find specific material or answers to specific questions. Scanning is usually more rapid than skimming and requires less comprehension. To assess students' scanning ability, list 5–10 facts, dates, sentences, or the like that appear in a lesson and then ask students to find the material within a reasonable time limit. Watch for those students who have completed only a little when the faster ones have finished.

RECOMMENDATIONS

For skimming:

A. Hold a class discussion on how skimming can be beneficial. Ask students to tell when it might be appropriate to skim. Their list might be similar to the following:

1. Wanting an idea of what an article or book is about
2. Previewing a chapter in a textbook prior to studying it more carefully
3. Looking quickly at a controversial article or editorial to get an idea of the author's opinion
4. Looking quickly through material to see if it contains the information you are looking for, e.g., skimming an article about a medical condition to see if it applies to you

B. Demonstrate to students how to skim by preparing overhead transparencies of selections that are triple-spaced. Use your finger or a pointer to indicate the speed at which your eyes move over the material. Stop to explain to students what you are reading or glancing at and what thinking is going on in your mind as you are skimming. Take time to thoroughly discuss this and to answer students' questions. Do not be concerned about telling students the *best* way to skim reading materials. What is important is that you model a process of skimming. Once students see that their teacher does this, they will begin to do the same thing when instructed to do so.

C. Give students copies of newspapers, magazine articles, or other short reading selections and ask them to skim the material, without additional directions, to get a general overall impression of the contents. Use a timer and stop the students after the prescribed amount of time has elapsed. Then have the students discuss or summarize in writing what they think the material is about.

D. Using a textbook, have students skim the title, headings, introduction, the first sentence of each paragraph, and the summary to get a general overall impression of the contents. Use a timer and stop the students after the prescribed amount of time has elapsed. Then have the students discuss or summarize in writing what they think the material is about.

E. List three or four broad questions or issues on the chalkboard. Using a textbook or other reading selection, have the students skim to find out if these questions will be answered or if the issues will be discussed in this reading selection.

For scanning:

F. Hold a class discussion on how scanning can be beneficial. Ask students to tell when it might be appropriate to scan. Their list might be similar to the following:

1. Looking for a name in a telephone book
2. Looking for a date in a history book

3. Looking for a certain number of factors to solve a problem
4. Reading the newspaper and searching for a certain article
5. Looking for a word in a dictionary

G. Demonstrate to students how to scan using the same procedure described in item B.

H. Show the students how to move their hands down a page in a telephone directory to find a certain name. After they have practiced and have become proficient with their hands, they can usually do as well without using their hands.

I. Give the students copies of newspapers and have them scan them to find things such as the article about the president, or about a certain baseball pitcher. Another good exercise with a newspaper is to have the students find a phrase on a certain page that describes something or tells a certain fact. After the students have found the phrase, ask them to paraphrase the author's meaning.

J. Give study questions on a reading assignment that can be answered by scanning the material. Keep in mind that this is not always the type of reading one wants to encourage.

K. Have the students scan to find a certain word in the dictionary.

L. Have the students scan to find a certain word (name of a city, etc.) or date in a history book.

M. Tell what a certain paragraph is about and then have the students scan to find the topic sentence of that paragraph. (Make sure there is one!)

N. Show the students that it is possible to get the meaning of some material when many words are missing. Make paragraphs in which some words unnecessary for comprehension are missing. Make sure they understand that they are not to try to supply the missing words. Another variation of this exercise is to give the students paragraphs and have them underline only the words that are really necessary for comprehension. See the example.

The superintendent of schools in Huntsville spoke to a large audience. She discussed reasons for the new building program. To some extent, she covered methods by which new revenue might be made available. Everyone thought her speech was excellent.

GAMES AND EXERCISES

Skim and Sort

Purpose: To provide practice in skimming

Materials: Old textbooks with stories in them that are somewhat varied
Envelope

Procedure:

Cut three stories from a book and then cut each story into either paragraphs or fairly short passages. Make sure each paragraph or passage contains some subject matter that gives a clue to which story it came from. Mix all of the paragraphs or passages together and place them in an envelope. Write the names of the three stories on the outside of the envelope. Give the student this envelope and have him sort through them rapidly, putting each paragraph or passage in one of three piles to match the story title. Number each paragraph or passage. When a student has finished sorting these, give him the number key to check his work. (For example, numbers 1, 3, 5, 7, 9, 13, 15, and 16 may belong in the first story; numbers 2, 6, 8, 14, 17, and 18 may belong in the second story; and numbers 4, 10, 11, 12, 19, and 20 may belong in the third story.)

Finish It

Purpose: To provide practice in scanning

Materials: A book of which all students in the game have a copy

Procedure:

Give students the number of a page from which you are going to read. You then begin reading somewhere on that page. After reading a few words you stop, and those who have found the place continue to read to the end of the sentence.

Scanning Race

Purpose: To provide practice in scanning

Materials: Any book that is available to every student in the game

Procedure:

Divide the students into two groups. Either you or alternating captains ask a question and tell the students in both groups the page where the answer can be found. The first student to find the answer stands by his seat. The first person standing is called on to read the answer. A correct answer scores one point for that side. The object is to see who can get the most points in a specified amount of time or in a specified number of questions. If a student stands and then gives a wrong answer, take away one point from his side.

Rapid Search

Purpose: To provide students with practice in both skimming and scanning

Materials: Several copies of the same articles in magazines, basal readers, or newspapers

Procedure:

One student finds a part of the story that represents some action. He then pantomimes this action, and the rest of the students skim rapidly to try to find the appropriate part of the story, then scan to find the sentence in the story that describes the actions of the student doing the pantomiming.

26

Inability to Locate Information

RECOGNIZED BY

The student is unable to locate information in encyclopedias, the *Reader's Guide to Periodical Literature,* the card catalog or computer files of the library, the *World Almanac,* and other sources.

The student is unable to use cross-references and parts of books such as the table of contents, index, and appendix.

DISCUSSION

It is almost a necessity for students in the intermediate grades and up to be able to use some of the sources of information listed. However, students often lack the skills needed to locate information. Even at the high-school level many students are unfamiliar with the use of the index and table of contents in their own textbooks.

Teachers can locate the types of difficulties students are encountering by giving an informal test similar to the following:

1. Name the part of your textbook that tells the beginning page number of the chapter on atoms.
2. Where would you look in your textbook to locate the meaning of the word *negotiate?*
3. Where in your textbook would you find some reference to the subject of atomic reactors?
4. Find the name of the magazine that published the following article: " _____ ."
5. Explain how you would locate the following book in the library: _____ .
6. How would you locate something on the subject of whales in the following set of encyclopedias: _____ .
7. What city in the United States has the largest population?
8. What is the purpose of the appendix of a book?

RECOMMENDATIONS

A. Discuss with the students the types of information found in encyclopedias. Also give exercises in which the students are required to locate certain volumes and then certain pieces of information using the letter and/or word guides provided.

B. Teach the use of cross-references. Ask the students to find information on certain subjects that are covered under several headings.

C. Explain the use of the library card catalog. (See Appendix P.)

D. Teach the students how to locate information in the *Reader's Guide to Periodical Literature*. Assign reports that require its use for finding a number of references on a certain subject.

E. Explain the use of the *World Almanac*. Give exercises in its use. For example, ask specific questions such as What city has the largest population in the world? and What city covers the most square miles? To increase students' interest in this type of activity, use the *Guinness Book of World Records* in addition to the *World Almanac*.

F. Explain the use of the table of contents, index, and appendix. Do not take it for granted that older students know how to use these. Ask specific questions about their use. For example, What chapter explains the use of maps? What page contains an explanation of photosynthesis? or Where would you find tables showing the relationships between weights and measures in the English and metric systems?

GAMES AND EXERCISES

Reference Hunt

Purpose: To provide practice in using various reference materials

Materials: Encyclopedias
             Dictionaries
             Thesauruses
             World Almanac
             Card catalog
             Other reference materials
             One prepared set of 10 questions for the first reference hunt

Procedure:

The reference hunt should be conducted after you have taught your students how to use the various reference materials. Group your students into 10 teams of 3 to 4 students each. Identify each team by a different number from 1 to 10. Give each team a copy of the prepared set of 10 questions for the first reference hunt. The questions require the students to answer each question and state the source and page number from which the answer came. (See example.) The first group to answer all 10 questions correctly, with the proper page indicated from an acceptable source, is the winner. (The answers to some questions may be found in more than one source.) Reward the students in the winning group by providing them with special class time so that they may prepare the next reference hunt. When the next reference hunt takes place these students can serve as judges. (Caution: Look over the reference hunt questions to be sure that the students' questions are not too difficult for their classmates.)

REFERENCE HUNT

1. How did John Wilkes Booth earn a living? _____
Source _____ Page _____
2. What is the meaning of the word "vitiate"? _____
Source _____ Page _____
3. What is the world's record for the mile run? _____
Source _____ Page _____
4. What is the first sentence of Lincoln's Emancipation Proclamation? _____ Source _____
Page _____
5. Which country leads the world in the production of cotton?
_____ Source _____
Page _____
6. What is the average summer temperature of Juneau, Alaska?
_____ Source _____
Page _____
7. What are two words that are synonyms for the word "lumber" (when used as a verb)? _____ _____
8. For how many years are United States senators elected?
_____ Source _____
Page _____
9. What is the Dewey Decimal Classification of the book *Blue Barns?* _____ Source _____
Page _____
10. What is another name for the gum tree? _____
Source _____ Page _____

Student Travel Bureau

Purpose: To provide practice in research and map study skills

Materials: Globes
Road maps
Travel folders and brochures
Various encyclopedias

Procedure:

When the students are studying a unit on map study, or at any other time you desire, arrange the room as a travel bureau. Advertise the class's service much the same as a travel bureau would. If students bring in information about future trips their family will be taking, student travel agents can

1. Present the traveler with a well-marked road map after studying maps from several companies and after corresponding with state highway departments.
2. List places they may wish to visit along the way.
3. Provide a history of landmarks along the way.
4. Provide other specific information as called for.

Thesaurus Puzzles

Purpose: To help students increase their vocabularies through the use of synonyms and antonyms and to use a thesaurus

Materials: Pocket chart
Word cards
Envelopes

Procedure:

Divide the pocket chart into two columns. In the left-hand column, place a list of words that have synonyms or antonyms. Each student is given an envelope of word cards containing synonyms and antonyms of the word list. Each student then selects a word, which is either the synonym or antonym of one of the given words from her envelope, and places her word card on the right-hand side of the chart. A more advanced arrangement of this game can be made by using a thesaurus. Given a word in column one, the students can use the thesaurus to make their own word cards for column two.

play
white
eager
rare
easy
pleasant
healthy
cleanse
guess
clear
dwarf

List Completion
(For upper grades or junior high school only)

Purpose: To provide practice in the use of the thesaurus

Materials: A thesaurus
    The materials shown

Procedure:

Provide lists of words for the student to complete. Directions: Complete the lists with words that mean almost the same thing.

1. decide	1. erratic	1. charge
2.	2.	2.
3.	3.	3.
1. deck	1. cage	1. charm
2.	2.	2.
3.	3.	3.

Detective

Purpose: To provide practice in locating information and skimming

Materials: Copies of paragraphs from the basal reader, social studies book, or science book the students are using. (From one copy you can make multiple copies of a certain paragraph if you desire.)

Procedure:

Copy a certain paragraph from a book that the student has in her desk. Make sure the paragraph gives enough information to let the reader know from what kind of book it is taken, e.g., a paragraph about clouds would be from a science book. Use paragraphs that give a clue that can be found in the table of contents or in the index of the book. Tables and graphs are appropriate if the book has a list of them. Put one of each of these paragraphs, graphs, or tables in an envelope along with a blank sheet of paper. Each student is given an envelope and the assignment to find where the paragraph came from by using the table of contents, index, list of tables and graphs, or appendix. When the student finds the answer (the same paragraph in her textbook), she writes the information on the blank piece of paper and hands it back to you. Number the envelopes and have the student keep records of which envelopes she has completed.

VI

OTHER ABILITIES

27

Undeveloped Dictionary Skills

RECOGNIZED BY

The student is unable to locate words in a dictionary, to use diacritical markings in determining the correct punctuation of words, or to find the proper meaning for a word as used in a particular context.

DISCUSSION

In addition to the most common errors listed in the "Recognized By" section, there are a number of other dictionary skills with which the student needs to become proficient in order to make the dictionary a useful tool. The following is a list of other skills the students should learn.

1. The use of guide words
2. The use of accent
3. The use of syllabication
4. Interpreting phonetic respellings
5. Using cross-references
6. Determining plural
7. Determining parts of speech
8. Determining verb tense

The dictionary can be a useful tool for independent word analysis. Some students become quite adept at using a dictionary in the second grade; however, most students learn in the third grade, and the skill must be learned no later than the fourth grade.

RECOMMENDATIONS

A. Follow the steps listed for teaching students to locate a word in the dictionary according to alphabetical order. Make sure the students are adept at each skill before beginning the next one.

1. Make sure the student knows the sequence of the letters in the alphabet.
2. Give several letters to be arranged alphabetically: *a, g, d, b, h,* and *m.*
3. Give several words that have different first letters to be arranged alphabetically: *bat, game, calf, dog,* and *man.*
4. Give several words that have the same beginning letters but different second letters to be arranged alphabetically: *pie, pliers, poker,* and *pack.*
5. Give several words that have the same beginning and second letters but different third letters: *pig, pie, pile,* and *picnic.*

B. Explain the purpose of the guide words at the top of the pages in a dictionary. Have the students write the beginning and ending guide words on pages that contain the words they are looking for.

C. Give students two guide words printed at the top of a piece of paper. Then list a number of words and give students a short amount of time to tell whether the words listed would be found on the same page as the two guide words (five to seven seconds). Time them and have them place a plus (+) after each word that would come on the same page as *key* and *kick* and a minus (−) after each word that would not come on the same page. This assignment will enable students to learn to use guide words rapidly.

key	*kick*
keyway	+
kill	−
khan	+
kibe	+
kidney	−

D. Teach the use of diacritical markings. Almost all dictionaries contain a pronunciation key at the bottom of each page that serves as a guide for teaching this skill.

E. Give students lists of words that they are not likely to be able to pronounce. Have them look up their phonetic respellings and write them beside each word. Have students then take turns reading the pronunciation of each word and let other students agree or disagree with each pronunciation.

F. Give students lists of words that have their accent in two places depending upon the part of speech in which they are used (such as *research*). Let students look the words up in their dictionaries and inductively decide where like words are usually accented as nouns and where they are usually accented as verbs. Other examples are *combat* and *contract.*

G. Have the students use the dictionary to find the proper meanings for the way in which certain words are used in sentences. Use words that are clearly defined by the context of the sentences. Have them write the definitions and then use the words with the same meanings in other sentences.

GAMES AND EXERCISES

Today's Words

Purpose: To provide practice in the use of the dictionary and to increase vocabulary

Materials: A dictionary for each student

Procedure:

Each morning place three or four new words on the chalkboard. Use words that the students have not previously studied. Later in the day ask the students questions using the new words. For example, "Miguel, does *pollution* affect our city?"

Synonym Race

Purpose: To provide practice in using the dictionary to find synonyms. This assignment will increase the student's vocabulary and improve his comprehension in silent reading.

Materials: A basal reader
A dictionary for each student

Procedure:

You select sentences from the current reading lesson that include words you wish the students to study. Write these sentences on the board, underlining the words for which the class is to look up synonyms. The students race to see who can supply the most synonyms from their dictionaries.

The starfish does not *please* him.

1. satisfy   3. attract
2. amuse   4. gratify

Water ran in a puddle all over his *clean* house.

1. pure   3. unsoiled
2. spotless   4. immaculate

Written Directions

Purpose: To provide practice in following directions and in the use of the dictionary

Materials: A dictionary for each student in the game
              A set of cards or pieces of paper with directions written on them

Procedure:

Give each student a piece of paper on which there is a set of directions. Be sure that the directions are simple, but also include at least one new word that the student will need to find in the dictionary before he can follow the directions. As the students find the meanings of words they have looked up in the dictionary, they then can take turns pantomiming the action described by the directions. The other students try to guess what they are doing and try to guess the word or a synonym for it. If they guess a synonym for a new word, then both the word and the synonym may be written by each student. This practice will help the whole class to remember the meanings of new words. Some examples of directions for the game are:

1. Pretend you are a vagabond.
2. Pretend you are wicked.
3. Pretend you have a halo.

Categories

Purpose: To provide practice on word meaning

Materials: Envelopes
             Cards with words on them that the students do not know well
             8 ½" × 11" paper or tagboard

Procedure:

At the top of a number of sheets of tagboard write three categories in which words may fall (see the following examples). Place each sheet of tagboard in a manila envelope along with approximately 30 words that will fit one of the categories listed. Pass the envelopes out to the students and have them use their dictionaries to group the words on the small word cards under the proper categories. Number the envelopes and have the students keep a list of the envelopes that they have completed.

What animals do	Things that grow	Things that are not alive
fight	trees	rocks
run	cats	books
play	people	paper
jump	weeds	chalk
eat	frogs	chairs
sleep	elephants	pencils
walk	flowers	magnets

Matching Word Meanings

Purpose: To increase vocabulary through the use of the dictionary or the-saurus

Materials: A word sheet similar to the example given
A dictionary or thesaurus for each student

goodness	stoop	helpfulness	waning	amiability
kind	philanthropy	senile	cambered	knobby
bias	hooked	charitable	inelegant	arch
vulgar	elder	unsmooth	look	rough
aged	rippling	bowlike	chunky	curved
elderly	choppy	geriatrics	turn	

BENT	COARSE	BENEVOLENCE	OLD

Procedure:

Have the students place words from the word list under the capitalized word that would be the best category for them.

28

Written Recall Limited by Spelling Ability

RECOGNIZED BY

The student is unable to spell enough words correctly when engaging in purposeful writing.

DISCUSSION

It is important to distinguish spelling from reading. Reading ability is far more important and may be enhanced through the teaching of generalizations that are not necessarily helpful in spelling. Reading proceeds from symbols to sound (the student sees the symbols and must translate them into meaningful sound), while spelling proceeds from sound to symbols (the student knows the sound of the word she wants to spell and must think of and produce the appropriate symbols that represent that word in writing). Unfortunately, many spelling series confuse these language processes and ask students to apply phonics generalizations to spelling. Such generalizations are not always helpful. The English words most frequently misspelled by nearly all students are those words that are exceptions to the rules of phonics. Therefore, it is usually most helpful to teach students to spell correctly those words that appear most frequently in writing. Although the English language consists of several hundred thousand different words, the following eight words represent 18% of all the words used in writing: *the, of, and, a, to, in, is,* and *you.* The 100 highest frequency words account for 60%, and 1000 words make up nearly 90% of the words used in daily writing. Yet spelling programs may present students with more than 10,000 words.[*]

Discovering that a student makes a great number of mistakes in spelling is not difficult for the teacher. There is a reasonably high correlation between reading and spelling ability. Most good readers are good spellers and most poor readers are poor spellers. However, it is estimated that about 2% of the pop-

---

[*]Sitton, R. (1990). A turning point: Three critical connections in the spelling curriculum for the nineties. *California Reader, 23,* 11–14.

ulation are good readers but poor spellers. It appears that students who are good spellers but poor readers are rare.

A student who is not able to spell correctly as many words as would be normal for her age/grade level should be taught a mastery list of the most commonly used words. If the student must cut down on the total number of words learned, then the words sacrificed should be those of less utility. Be sure that in all subject matter you emphasize spelling. This strategy will help in motivating the students to improve their spelling and will give them the feeling that it is important to spell correctly all the time and not just during the spelling period. Indeed, spelling should not be viewed as a subject, but rather as skill that will enable students to be more effective writers.

Research on the effectiveness of various techniques for teaching spelling suggests that

1. It is not helpful to group and teach words based on phonic generalizations or structural analysis.
2. It is not helpful to teach students to spell words that are introduced as new vocabulary words in reading or content area subjects.
3. It is not helpful to teach too many spelling rules.
4. It is not helpful to color-code parts of words.
5. It is not helpful for students to spell words through an oral presentation, such as a spelling bee.
6. It is helpful if the words taught are words that the students already know the meaning of and that appear on high-frequency lists.
7. It is better to have the student focus on learning the whole word rather than learning to spell the word by focusing on syllables or other parts.
8. It is helpful when students write the word frequently in the context of sentences or stories, rather than writing the word over and over in isolation.
9. It is best to teach only those spelling rules that apply to a great number of words and have few exceptions. It is usually most helpful to teach these rules inductively.
10. It is best to have students use many modalities (such as auditory, visual, and kinesthetic) when learning to spell words.

RECOMMENDATIONS

A. Use the following procedure to teach spelling words:

1. Be sure the student is looking at you.
2. Pronounce the word clearly, then have the student pronounce it.

3. Use the word in a sentence and have the student use it in a different sentence.
4. Write the word on the chalkboard (in manuscript or printing, not cursive); or when working with a single student, write it on a piece of paper. Have the student write the word on a card.
5. Have the student spell the word on her card by pointing to each letter with her pencil, marker, or finger while she says it.
6. The student can use the card for further study. These cards should be kept in a file such as in an old shoe box.

B. Keep increasing the spelling vocabulary by adding previously missed words to new lists as well as some words with which students are more familiar. Most students can learn more words than those normally assigned to them in a spelling book.

C. Teaching the following spelling rules will be helpful; however, keep in mind there will be numerous exceptions to rules in the English language. Whenever possible, teach spelling rules inductively. An example of teaching rules inductively would be to list a number of words that exemplify a particular generalization and then let students develop the rule for themselves. This will take time, but students are more likely to remember the rules. Also, it is better to show students certain exceptions to a rule when they learn it than to let them discover exceptions for themselves. At least make clear that there will be exceptions to nearly all of the rules:

1. Write *ie* when the sound is /ee/, except after *c*, or when sounded as /a/ as in *neighbor* and *weigh*.
2. When the prefixes *il, im, in, un, dis, mis*, and *over* are added to a word, the spelling of the original word remains the same.
3. When the suffixes *ness* and *ly* are added to a word, the spelling of the word remains the same. Examples: *mean + ness = meanness; final + ly = finally.*
4. When a word ends in a consonant + *y*, change the *y* to *i* before adding all suffixes except those beginning with *i*. Do not change the *y* to *i* in suffixes beginning with *i* or those that begin with a vowel + *y*.
5. Drop the final *e* before a suffix beginning with a vowel. Examples: *care + ing = caring, write + ing = writing.* (Exceptions: *noticeable, courageous, dyeing. Dyeing* is spelled as it is to prevent confusion with *dying.*)
6. Keep the final *e* in a suffix beginning with a consonant. Examples: *care + ful = careful, care + less = careless.* (An exception is *argue + ment = argument.*)
7. In one-syllable words that are accented on the last syllable and that end in a single consonant + a single vowel, the final conso-

nant should be doubled when adding a suffix beginning with a vowel. Examples: *beginning, fanning.*

Note: Keep in mind that not all students learn effectively by the use of rules.

D. Make lists of common prefixes and suffixes, as well as families of sounds. (See Appendix 0.)

E. Teach students how to use the dictionary to locate unfamiliar words. Practice this usage on difficult words that can be found by the sounds of the first few letters. Discuss possible spellings for certain words and sounds. Also teach the use of the diacritical markings in the dictionary.

F. Let the students exchange papers and proofread each others' written work. The habit of proofreading will carry over into their own writing.

G. Let the students correct their own papers after taking a spelling test. Use steps 1 through 4 under Recommendation A when students correct their spelling tests. Some students are much more adept at correcting their own work than other students are. You will need to make periodic checks to determine if the students are having difficulty finding and correcting their own errors.

29

Useful Teaching Methods for Students with Reading Difficulties

In this chapter you will find information on some important principles of effective instruction for students who have reading difficulties. Consider these principles when you are organizing your instruction and selecting the techniques to use from various chapters in this book. Next, you will find information on the use of several techniques or approaches that are especially helpful with students with reading difficulties. The first of these approaches is the language-experience approach. Although this approach is used by most primary-grade teachers in a regular developmental reading classroom, certain procedures emphasized here are particularly appropriate for disabled readers of any age. Several highly effective oral reading techniques are then described, including the neurological-impress method, echo reading, repeated readings, and precision reading.

PRINCIPLES OF EFFECTIVE INSTRUCTION

Students often fail to learn to read because large class sizes and multiple demands on the time of classroom teachers make it difficult or impossible for teachers to give students the concentrated instruction they need. Our reading of the considerable literature in the field of reading instruction and our experience in the roles of classroom teacher, reading specialist, school administrator, college teacher, and director of university reading clinics has persuaded us that, with reasonable conditions and appropriate instruction over time, nearly every disabled reader can make significant progress.

The teaching of reading is not a mystical process. Although much remains to be learned about how we can best help those who are failing, we do know which practices succeed most often. The recommendations provided in this book will be most effective if you are mindful of the following principles:

1. Most students require a certain amount of systematic, sequential skill instruction to learn how to decode or pronounce unknown words fluently. The amount of this type of instruction required varies considerably from student to student.

2. Most students require direct instruction, in which the teacher presents information to the students and monitors the pace of their learning of new material.

3. All students should be taught, and should practice, reading at an appropriate level of difficulty so that they can experience frequent success.

4. All students need a substantial amount of practice in the act of reading to ensure that important skills are learned and utilized and to promote an appreciation for the value and joy of reading.

You will notice that some of the recommendations in this book require the teacher to interact with the student, to guide the student in developing strategies to improve reading abilities. These techniques may require the teacher to describe or model a strategy, then assist the student in using it, then provide the student with opportunities to use the strategy on his own. These recommendations are usually the most important and most effective. Other recommendations, while valuable, are less critical. For example, in most chapters you will find suggestions for worksheets, games, or other activities that will give students independent practice on certain skills. These activities may be motivating and may give students beneficial practice when they are working alone or in small groups without the teacher present. But they cannot replace the direct instruction provided initially by the teacher.

For students to benefit most from their reading instruction and practice, activities must be presented at the appropriate level of difficulty. When reading independently students should be able to decode at least 98% of the words on their own. (A procedure for helping students determine if reading material is too difficult is presented in Chapter 21, "Procedures for Improving Overall Comprehension," item B, on p. 132.) If the level of instruction is too high or the material is too difficult, the student will become frustrated. If such frustration occurs frequently, then the "assistance" provided to the student may actually do more harm than good. When in doubt, have the student read easier material. Even if it is too easy, the student will benefit from the practice in reading it.

For new learnings to transfer and become permanent reading abilities, it is essential that students have abundant opportunities for practice in the act of reading. Such practice must consist of the reading of whole, contextual material, not merely flash cards, word lists, or items on a worksheet. This practice should occur both in and out of school and may include both oral and silent reading of magazines, stories, books (both fiction and nonfiction), poems, instructions, recipes, newspapers, child-authored books, manuals, etc. As a teacher of reading you should make every effort to motivate students to read for information and pleasure. While engaged in the act of reading, students put the pieces of reading instruction together and gradually develop the fluency that makes reading an automatic process. Such fluency is also required for adequate reading comprehension.

A number of unusually effective techniques or approaches are presented in the following sections of this chapter. Each of these techniques or approaches embodies the principles described above.

THE LANGUAGE-EXPERIENCE APPROACH

The language-experience approach combines all of the language arts—listening, speaking, reading, and writing. When using the language-experience approach, one need not be concerned about whether the material being read is in the learner's background and will be too difficult to comprehend or whether the student will be interested in the subject. One also need not be concerned about whether the reading material will appear too "babyish" for the student. This is, of course, because in the language-experience approach, the reading material is generated by the student.

The language-experience approach can be used with a single student or with a group of students. Much has been written on the use of the language-experience approach, and varying procedures for its use have been suggested. The material presented here indicates how it might be used with an individual and with a group. Certain procedures are also stressed that may seem, at first, unimportant. However, certain aspects of the language-experience approach are extremely important for its success, and we recommend little variation from these specific procedures. The material that follows is divided into four sections: (1) The theory behind the success of the language-experience approach; (2) Using the language-experience approach with individual students; (3) Using the language-experience approach with small groups of students; and (4) Important procedures and information about the use of the language-experience approach.

The Theory behind the Success of the Language-Experience Approach

The language-experience approach uses the language of the students as the basis for writing materials that will later be read by those same students. When a student dictates something to the teacher or writes something himself, it will naturally be something in which the student is interested and will also be something that the student will understand with no difficulty. Furthermore, it will be written at a reading level appropriate for the student, and its content will not insult the student regardless of age.

Using the Language-Experience Approach with Individual Students

In using the language-experience approach with individual students, the teacher should follow this general procedure:

1. Tell the student that you would like to have him dictate a story to you, so he will have something to read immediately. Spend some time discussing topics that interest him about which he would like to talk or write.

2. When a subject is found, ask the student what he would like to use as a title for the story. You may wish to make suggestions; however, it is *much better* to get the student to use his own language. The student may wish to write about some experience that he has had lately, or he may wish to write about a favorite pet or a brother or sister. There are often hands-on experiences that have taken place in the classroom setting about which the student may wish to write, for example, a science experiment or something the student is making as an art project or social studies assignment.

3. When an appropriate title has been decided, begin to write. Use either manuscript or cursive writing, depending on the age/grade level of the student and what he has previously been taught. If the student has done very little writing of any kind, then you should use manuscript writing. As you write each word, make sure the student is watching. Say each word as you write it. As soon as you have finished writing the title or any sentence, stop and bring your finger down on each word and read it back to the student. It is important to bring your finger down on each word for two reasons. First, it will help the student understand that each set of letters stands for a particular word; second, it will set a pattern for the student to follow when he begins to read. It is also important that you read the material first, so that the words will again be emphasized. This will give the student a second chance to learn each written word.

4. Ask the student to read the title to you. Make sure that the student brings his finger down on each word as he reads it. This will ensure that the student again notes each word carefully and sees each word as a part of the overall title or sentence. A student will, in most cases, be able to read the title or a sentence back to you without carefully looking at what has been written. Having the student bring his finger down on each word will also ensure that he is actually looking at the word being pronounced and not saying one word while looking at another. If the student is allowed to slide his finger under the words as he reads, there is a tendency to read ahead of or behind where his finger is pointing. Students are hesitant to do this at times; they may have had a teacher who told them not to point to words as they were reading. A student may also resist raising his finger up and bringing it down on each word. Insist that it be done this way and you will, in most cases, find that any initial resistance is quickly overcome.

5. Continue to do the rest of the story as you did the title. Stop after each sentence is written and point to each word as you reread the sentence. Bring your finger down on the word and say it at exactly the same time your finger comes down on the word. After reading the sentence, have the student do it in the same manner. Then add a sentence at a time until you have finished the story.

6. After finishing the story, point to each word and read the entire story. Then have the student do the same. If a student miscalls a word, quickly correct him and continue. Depending on the student and his ability to remember, it may be advisable to read the story several times.

7. The length of each story will depend on the characteristics of the student who is dictating it. However, in the beginning stages, be careful not to make the stories too long. The student will lose accuracy in rereading a particularly lengthy story, thus defeating the purpose of having him create his own material. As students continue to improve their reading, you are likely to find that they begin to dictate longer stories.

8. At this point you may let the student illustrate the story or apply stickers or appropriate pictures from other sources.

9. Next, type or print the story using a word processor. If you use a typewriter, use primary or pica type, whichever is appropriate to the age-grade level of the student. If you use a word processor, you may be able to select from a number of fonts and sizes. The student should have the ability to transfer knowledge of words from manuscript or cursive writing to printed type.

10. After a period of time, such as would elapse after doing another activity, have the student reread the original story and then the typewritten or printed copy. You may wish to have the student take the original story, which was illustrated, home and practice reading it to someone in his family. Some students may lose their stories, and having a typed or printed copy will ensure that all stories remain intact.

11. When next meeting with the student, ask him to again read the story written in the previous session. If he reads it without errors, write another story and use the same procedure. Continue this sequence, i.e., rereading all previous stories and writing another one each time you meet.

12. After the student has written a number of stories, you may bind them into a booklet and let the student illustrate the cover.

13. After the student has built up a considerable sight vocabulary and has developed some beginning word-attack skills, you may have him gradually begin to read basal readers or general books.

Using the Language-Experience Approach with Small Groups of Students

In using the language-experience approach with small groups of students, you may wish to follow a sequence such as the following:

1. Find some event or subject of interest to the group, and tell the students that you would like to help them write a story about the event or subject.

2. Ask students to decide on a title for the story. When they have agreed on a title, write it using the exact words given by the students. As you write it, say each word. After finishing the title, instruct the students to watch carefully as you read it. Point to each word as you read it. Be careful to bring your finger down on each word and read it only as your finger touches the word. Then ask the students to read the title as you point to each word. You may have several students read it individually.

3. When writing the story, use these general guidelines:

   ☐ Use the type of writing to which the students are accustomed; i.e., either manuscript or cursive.

   ☐ Use the language that the students suggest and make very few, if any, changes.

   ☐ Write on something that can be saved for future use. Use 24″ × 36″ lined chart paper if it is available.

   ☐ Use a felt-tip pen or marker that will make broad, readable lines.

   ☐ In the beginning stages, use one-line sentences and gradually increase the length of the line as students' reading improves.

   ☐ Emphasize a left-to-right movement.

   ☐ Make sure students see all words as they are written.

4. After the story has been finished, read it to the class, being careful to point to each word as you read it. Be sure to read the story with enthusiasm.

5. Have the students read the story as a choral exercise as you point to each word.

6. Have individual students come to the chart and read the story. The chosen student should point to each word as he reads it, exactly as you have been doing. While this student points and reads, the rest of the students should read the story quietly as a choral exercise. (Although this may seem like a lot of reading of the same story, you will find that it is excellent practice and the students will enjoy participating.)

7. Use a typewriter or word processor to prepare a printed copy of the story after it is finished. Also have the students copy the chart in its exact form.

8. If possible, duplicate the story and give each student a copy to take home to practice reading to someone in his family.

9. After a period of time, ask students to reread the story. You may have students take turns reading a sentence at a time.

10. After the students have practiced reading the story a number of times, you may also duplicate the story on a large piece of tagboard. The tagboard may then be cut into strips with one sentence on each strip. Either you or the students may then place the strips in a pocket chart to re-create the original story. At this time make sure each student can read each sentence in isolation. After you have done this, you may cut the strips of sentences into words and re-create the original story by placing each word in the pocket chart.

11. Each time you meet with the group, read the previously written story and then write another one. Continue this process until stories have been read many times and students know all, or nearly all, of the words as sight words.

12. As students grow in their ability to read, let them begin to write and illustrate their own stories. Then bind these into booklets and let the students illustrate the covers. Let students exchange booklets and read each others' stories.

13. Let students begin to read commercially written materials as their sight vocabulary and word-attack skills permit.

Important Procedures and Information about the Use of the Language-Experience Approach

A. Teachers should remember these important procedures about the language experience approach:

1. When students dictate stories, attempt to use the exact language of the students. However, if you are concerned about students' incorrect usage or inappropriate language, you may modify the transcription of the dictation slightly and tell the students, "That's a good thought; another way we might say this is . . . . " (See item D following.)

2. Make sure that both you and the students point to each word as it is being read. Doing this in the beginning stages of using the language-experience approach ensures that each word is memorized as a separate entity as well as a part of an entire story.

3. Keep words clearly spaced, so students will recognize the difference between *words* and *letters*.

4. In the beginning stages, be sure to use only one-line sentences. Then gradually expand the length of the sentences as the students become more adept at reading.

5. Emphasize a series of events, if possible, so students will see the development of the story.

6. If possible, use 24″ × 36″ chart paper, so capital letters are 2″ high and lowercase letters are 1″ high.

7. Make sure students see the words as they are being written.

8. Duplicate the chart so students can take the materials home to be practiced with another member of the family.

9. Emphasize left-to-right direction and the return sweep in writing and reading the stories.

B. Keep in mind that there are certain limitations to the language-experience approach. For example, a teacher using this approach almost exclusively is not likely to follow a sequential program in teaching word-attack skills. Many studies have shown that structured programs tend to produce better overall achievement from students. For this reason, you would probably want to use the language-experience approach in conjunction with a basal reader program or as a supplemental program for students with reading difficulties.

C. Different types of charts may be written in essentially the same manner as has been described in the preceding material. Some types of charts and their uses are

1. *Summarizing charts.* This chart shows a series of events on a field trip or a step-by-step procedure for doing an experiment in science.

2. *Story charts.* This chart describes an event in the life of a group or an individual.

3. *Planning charts.* This chart lists plans for such things as an anticipated trip or some other event in which the entire class will participate.

4. *Direction charts.* This chart gives specific directions, e.g., for the assembly of a toy or paper folding exercises.

5. *Dictionary charts.* This chart lists new words that have been learned in science, social studies, or other subject areas.

D. There has been considerable controversy over the shaping of the language of students who are using the language-experience approach. For immature speakers and students whose language is somewhat divergent from what might be considered standard English, the question sometimes arises as to whether the teacher should correct certain usage errors made by these students. It is probably true that more fuss is made over this issue than is necessary. If the teacher chooses to modify the students' language slightly, as indicated in the directions above, and if this is done gently, then no damage need occur to either the children's self-esteem or their reading progress.

E. It should be remembered that unless students begin to read trade books and other types of materials as they are developing their sight vocabularies, their reading vocabularies will, of course, be limited to only those words in their speaking vocabularies. Therefore, students using the language experience approach should be encouraged to read other materials along with their language-experience charts and books.

EFFECTIVE ORAL READING TECHNIQUES

A number of oral reading techniques or methods may be used to help students improve their decoding ability and correct various fluency problems, such as reading rate, accuracy, phrasing, or expression. The best known of these techniques are the neurological-impress method, echo reading or imitative reading, repeated readings, and precision reading. We recommend these and similar methods not because oral reading is the goal, but because these techniques often help students to identify and correct specific reading difficulties.

Oral reading is most effective if it is done in a one-to-one fashion or with very small groups, so that students participate as much as possible. Pairing students is a common practice to facilitate oral reading in the classroom. In using these methods, it is important for the teacher to stress to students that oral reading is only one way of reading and that this practice will ultimately lead the student to greater ability in silent reading. Also, oral reading practice is not substituted for silent reading. Rather, it is presented to give students additional experience with the printed word.

The Neurological-Impress Method

The use of the neurological-impress method (NIM) was explained some years ago by H. G. Heckelman.[*] It has been extremely successful with many students with reading difficulties and it is easy to use. NIM is, in fact, *so* easy to use that teachers are often hesitant to use it. A procedure for its use follows.

1. Sit the student slightly in front of you, so you can point to the material the student is reading and read directly into the student's ear.
2. Begin reading material that is at an easy instructional or independent reading level. As you continue to work with the student, you can increase the level of difficulty of the material.
3. Tell the student that you are going to read the material and that he is to read along with you as you point to the words. Then begin to read at a slightly slower than normal rate for you. While reading, be sure to point to each word as it is read. *This part of the procedure is extremely important.* The student may complain, at first, that he is unable to keep up with you. This should not, however, keep you from using the procedure. Explain to the student that he will become a better reader and will probably soon be able to keep up with you.
4. As you work with the student, you are likely to notice a sharp improvement in his ability to read. Begin to increase your rate of reading as the student's reading improves.

---

[*]Heckelman, R. G. (1966). Using the neurological-impress remedial reading technique. *Academic Therapy Quarterly, 1,* 235–239.

5. Read for periods of 5 to 15 minutes two to four times per day. Heckelman suggests that it is common to cover from 10 to 20 pages of material in one session.

6. Heckelman suggests that if periods of approximately 15 minutes are used, then the procedure should be continued until the student has read for an accumulated total of 8 to 12 hours. However, if the student fails to make progress after 4 hours, the method should be discontinued.

Heckelman has emphasized that in using this method you will probably see a great increase in the student's ability to read. He cautions that one of the teacher's most frequent mistakes is to spend too much time reading material written at low levels of difficulty because the teacher does not expect the student to learn so rapidly. For example, Heckelman says that if a student is started at the first-grade level, he might be expected to be reading in materials at the third-grade level after an accumulated total of two hours. After an accumulated total of six hours, the student might be reading materials at the fifth- or sixth-grade level of difficulty.

Heckelman suggests that one of the reasons for the remarkable success that students often experience with NIM is that the student is exposed to many words, many times, in a relatively short period of time. For example, a student reading for approximately 15 minutes may be exposed to from 1000 to 2000 words.

When using NIM, specific correction is seldom, if ever, offered, nor is questioning or testing of the content. As the student's ability improves, he may take over the finger movements and more challenging material may be read.

Studies have been conducted in which teachers have tried to duplicate NIM using tape-recorded materials and having students follow along with the tape-recorded reading. However, this has not produced results comparable to those obtained when working with a student in a one-to-one setting. This is probably because when a student is reading in conjunction with a tape recorder, you have no way of ensuring that the student is actually looking at the words being read. If the student is not actually looking at the words being read, then he is not likely to benefit any more than if he were only listening to the passage.

Echo Reading or Imitative Reading

In echo reading the teacher reads first and the student repeats what the instructor read. Material can be read in either phrases or sentences, and finger pointing is used in this method also. A common variation uses recorded texts; students first listen straight through while following the written text and then read along with the recording. An advantage of this method is that a teacher need not be present. On the other hand, this variation lacks the immediacy and psychological force of the teacher's presence. A number of high-interest, low-vocabulary read-along materials are available in varying formats with accompanying records, tapes, or slides. Students seem to enjoy these, and, if used properly, they can be beneficial.

The teacher must be sure that students *can* read the materials and that they stay on task and *do* read when they are supposed to.

Repeated Readings

Repeated readings is a method suggested by S. Jay Samuels.[*] Students are given selections that consist of 50 to 200 words. The student is instructed to practice the selections and then is timed, after which reading rate and number of errors are recorded on a chart. (See Appendix Q for a blank repeated readings chart and an example of a completed chart.)

While the teacher is checking other students, the student rereads the material along with a recording of the text. The rereading may be done over and over. When the student feels ready, another test is given. Comprehension checks may also take place. Graphing the student's results serves as a motivator for continued progress.

We believe that the repeated-readings method is excellent, but we would add one caution. Our experience has led us to conclude that a primary cause of efficiency or fluency difficulties is that disabled readers often try to read too fast. For most students it is helpful first to encourage them to read accurately and later work to improve their speed.

Precision Reading

Precision reading is an oral reading technique that emphasizes accuracy first, then speed. While the student reads, the teacher records the student's accuracy sentence by sentence on the precision reading form. (See Appendix R for a blank precision reading form and instructions for its use.) The form has spaces to indicate the beginning and ending page numbers of the material read, the total number of *sentences* read, the number of sentences read perfectly, and the number of sentences read with one or more errors. At the beginning the student is given relatively easy material and reads a set number of sentences, such as 25. The teacher records the student's accuracy on each sentence, so that on completion a fraction of correct sentences out of the total is derived; for example, 20/25. This indicates that the student read 20 sentences perfectly and made one or more errors on 5 of the sentences. The fraction is then changed to a percentage—in this case, 80% accuracy—and the percentage figure is graphed daily. (Appendix R also includes a sample accuracy graph.) Students enjoy seeing their performance graphed, and this serves as a powerful motivator for continued progress.

The material selected should not cause the student's accuracy rate to drop below 75%. Also, the teacher may select different material for the student to read each day. However, it is helpful if the passage is chosen at least one day in advance

---

[*]Samuels, S. J. (1979). The method of repeated readings. *Reading Teacher, 32,* 403–406.

so that the student can begin practicing the material in advance as part of his homework. As the student improves and begins to read consistently at or near 100-% accuracy, the teacher may provide more difficult material or add the factor of speed. To do the latter, you may have the student read as many sentences as possible within a prescribed time, as long as the accuracy does not drop below, say, 90%. Then the *number* of sentences read perfectly is graphed daily. (An example of this type of graph is also presented in Appendix R.)

Other Oral Reading Techniques

The following oral reading activities are also effective and provide variety for students:

1. The teacher and student take turns reading the material out loud by alternating paragraphs, sentences, or lines.

2. The student prereads silently first, notes difficult vocabulary, and reviews the vocabulary with the teacher; then the student and teacher read together.

3. The teacher provides choral-reading activities for small groups of students.

4. The teacher provides plays for students to read. A number of kits are available with simple two-, three-, or four-person plays; or teachers and students can write their own plays.

5. Many students enjoy relaxed paired reading. A student and a friend select two copies of a good book and then take turns reading it out loud together.

6. Younger students read selections using puppets.

7. Older students enjoy participating in readers' theater activities.

8. The teacher may provide a reinforcer, such as clicking a counter or putting a chip in a bank, each time the student reads a sentence perfectly.

9. The teacher may use favorite games such as tic-tac-toe, hangman, and dots to score reading accuracy. For example, a student reads while the other draws part of the hangman if the student who is reading makes an error. (Numbers 8 and 9 are variations of the precision reading method described above.)

10. The use of controlled readers or reading pacers is *not* recommended unless great care is taken to guard against the frustration likely to occur if the student is unable to keep up with the machine.

11. A number of suggestions for using an audio tape recorder to help students practice oral reading were presented in Chapter 2, under item L, on page 9.

APPENDICES

A

Code for Marking in Oral Diagnosis

Rd inventories

This section, as explained under the section "How to Use This Book," is designed to teach you a shorthand method of marking oral reading errors. You should find it helpful to read the following information, which should then enable you to use this code effectively.

It is recommended that you tape-record the student's oral reading. In most cases students do not mind being recorded while reading orally. If you record the reading, you may replay it a number of times, if necessary. This will ensure that your original coding was correct or will give you a chance to make any needed changes from the original reading. Also, if you save the recording, you can compare it to a student's later reading of the same material. This is often an excellent way to document a student's progress. By listening to both the earlier and later reading of the same passages, the student, the student's parents, and you can hear noticeable growth in the student's reading ability over time.

PREPARATION FOR USING THE CODE
FOR MARKING IN ORAL DIAGNOSIS

Familiarize yourself with the shorthand method of marking students' oral reading errors before attempting to use it. There are 10 items or 10 notations that are to be made to indicate errors or characteristics that readers are likely to make in oral reading. Each of these notations, of course, denotes a particular kind of error or characteristic of the reader. Once they have been coded and studied, you will find that they will become a blueprint for instruction.

Study each of the 10 notations, so you understand what is meant by such things as an omission, a reversal, a pause, and the like. If you were to analyze the coded passage that follows using the Code for Marking in Oral Diagnosis, you would find the following types of errors made by the students who read this demonstration passage.

Tom drove his automobile to the county fair. He saw no place to park. He drove up and down between the rows of cars. Finally he decided to go home.

1. Circle all omissions.
2. Insert with a caret (ᵥ) all insertions.

3. Draw a line through words for which substitutions or mispronunciations were made and write the substitution or mispronunciation over the word. Determine later whether the word missed was a substitution or mispronunciation.

4. If the student reads too fast to write in all mispronunciations, draw a line through the word and write a *P* over the word for partial mispronunciation or a *G* over the word for gross mispronunciation.

5. Use a dotted or wavy line to indicate repetitions.

6. Mark reversals in the same way as substitutions and later determine whether the mistake was an inversion or a substitution.

7. Use an arched line to connect words in which the student disregarded punctuation. (See line connecting *fair* and *he* in the following example.)

8. Use parentheses ( ) to enclose the words for which the pupil needed help.

9. Make a check (√) over the words that were self-corrected.

10. Make two vertical lines (‖) preceding a word where a pause appeared.

new ⁀ *was* ✓ *pack*
Tom drove his ^automobile to the (county) fair. He ~~saw~~ no (place) to park.

among *g* *P*
He ‖ drove up and down ~~between~~ the rows of cars. ~~Finally~~ he ~~decided~~ to

go home.

Line 1:   The student inserted *new* between the words *his* and *automobile*.

Line 1:   The student omitted the word *county* between *the* and *fair*.

Line 1:   The student did not stop or pause for the period at the end of the sentence ending with the word *fair* and the next sentence beginning with the word *He*.

Line 1:   The student called the word *saw* as *was*. This could be called a substitution; however, in this case it would be referred to as a reversal or inversion since *was* is *saw* spelled backwards. In some coding systems, the authors recommend using a system of marking inversions or reversals using a mark such as the following: ╲s ⌒ a ⌒ w╱ . In this case the mark would indicate that the student said *saw* for the word *was*. However, other than the most common reversals or inversions such as *saw* for *was* or *b* for d, it is usually necessary for the person who coded the material to examine the word in some detail to determine whether it was an inversion or reversal or whether it was a mispronunciation or a substitution. Because the coder is often forced to mark a mistake rapidly, a determination of this type cannot be made instantly. For that reason, it is easier to mark this type of error the same as mispronunciations—i.e., marking a line through the word—and then, after the reader has finished, the teacher can determine whether the mistake was an inversion or reversal or whether it was a substitution or a mispronunciation.

Line 1:   The student made no attempt or did not say the word *place* after a period of time (usually five seconds) and was, therefore, told or given aid with the word *place*.

Line 1:   The student read the word *park* as *pack* and then corrected it without help from the teacher.

Line 2:   The student repeated the word *He* at the beginning of the sentence.

Line 2:   The student paused before the word *drove* for a longer period of time than the scorer believed was normal; however, the period of time was less than five seconds, or *drove* would have had parentheses ( ) around it to indicate that the student had been told the word.

Line 2:   The student repeated the phrase *up and down*.

Line 2:   The student substituted the word *among* for the word *between*.

Line 2:   The student grossly mispronounced the word *Finally*. In some cases, the teacher might note the improper pronunciation since this might be helpful in analyzing the student's problem with word-attack skills. However, when the student reads too rapidly to write in the improper pronunciation, the teacher usually writes a *G* over the word, indicating that it was grossly mispronounced. This means that the pronunciation was so far off that it did not even sound like the original word. If you have recorded the reading, you can indicate the improper pronunciation when you listen to the tape later.

Line 2:   The student partially mispronounced the word *decided*. If possible, it is best to write the incorrect mispronunciation of the word over the correct word. This will be helpful in analyzing what the student seems to be doing wrong in attacking new words. However, when the student reads too rapidly for the coder to keep up with the coding, then a *P* over the word means that it was only partially, rather than grossly, mispronounced. In this case, the student might have pronounced the word with a hard *c* or *k* sound. This could also have been quickly indicated by crossing out the *c* and putting a *k* over it.

PRACTICE IN USING THE CODE FOR MARKING IN ORAL DIAGNOSIS

In using the Code for Marking in Oral Diagnosis, you will need to duplicate something that the student will be reading orally, so you have a copy that reads the same as the one read by the student. It will be helpful if the copy on which you will be coding is double- or triple-spaced, so you can more easily write in notations on various oral reading errors made by the student. You should then seat the student so you can easily hear him as the passage is read. Many examiners find that it is best to seat the student kitty-corner to the opposite side of your handedness. In other words, if you are right-handed, you would seat the student diagonally to your left (see following illustration).

It is a good idea to find a student at a lower grade level who is not a rapid reader when you first begin this procedure since it may become very frustrating to attempt to mark the errors of a student who reads rapidly, especially if the student makes a considerable number of errors.

INTERPRETING A CODED PASSAGE

Once the student has read the passage or has read several passages that are near his high instructional or frustration level, you can begin to interpret the meaning of the various types of errors or miscues. Chapters 2 through 10 deal directly with these kinds of errors. By studying the error pattern, you will often be able to note whether the student has difficulties with the kinds of problems listed in Chapters 12 through 19.

Preparation and Use of Materials for Testing Letter Knowledge

PREPARING FOR THE TEST

Before administering the letter recognition inventory, make multiple copies of the answer sheet on p. 213, so you will have one for each student to be tested. Also remove the stimulus sheet from p. 211 and use rubber cement or tape to fasten it to a 5″ × 8″ card. You may then wish to laminate the card, so it will not become soiled from handling.

SPECIFIC DIRECTIONS FOR GIVING THE LETTER RECOGNITION INVENTORY*

Before beginning this test you may first wish to have the student write all of the letters in both uppercase and lowercase. If this is done correctly, then place a plus (+) mark in the blank by TASK 1 on the answer sheet. If they are not all done correctly, you may wish to note exceptions.

A. Give the student the *Letter Stimulus Sheet* and ask her to read each of the letters in row 1, then row 2, row 3, etc. Mark them as plus (+) if they are answered correctly or you may simply wish to place a plus (+) mark in the blank beside TASK 2 on the answer sheet to indicate that they were all given correctly. If they are not answered correctly, then write the answer given by the student in each blank. If the student can do this task, stop the test. If she cannot name all of the letters, continue with the following tasks.

B. Show the student the *Letter Stimulus Sheet* and ask her to point to letters as you name them. Do them in random order from the lowercase letters and then do them in random order from the uppercase letters. Be sure to do all of them or do enough of them so that you are

---

*The letter recognition inventory is from Ekwall, E. E. (1986). *Teacher's handbook on diagnosis and remediation in reading* (2nd ed.). Boston: Allyn and Bacon. Reprinted by permission of the author and Allyn and Bacon.

certain the student can identify all letters when they are named. If the student can do this, then place a plus (+) mark by TASK 3 on the answer sheet and discontinue the testing. If the student cannot do this task, then note that on TASK 3 and continue with the following tasks.

C. Show the student the *Letter Stimulus Sheet* and ask her to match uppercase letters with lowercase letters, e.g., point to the *n* in the lowercase letters and ask the student to point to the *N* from the letters in the uppercase group. You may wish to alternate by first pointing to a letter in the lowercase and having the student match it with the corresponding letter from the uppercase group; then point to the corresponding letter in the lowercase group. Be sure to do all of them or do enough of them so that you are certain the student can match all letters. If the student can do this, then place a plus (+) mark by TASK 4 on the answer sheet and discontinue the testing. If the student cannot do this task, then note that on TASK 4 and continue with the following task.

D. Show the student the *Letter Stimulus Sheet* and point to a letter from row 11 and ask the student to point to another letter that is exactly the same as that letter. Do this with all of the letters, i.e., first *b,* then *m,* etc., until all pairs have been matched. If the student can do this, then place a plus (+) mark by TASK 5. If the student cannot do this task, then note that on TASK 5.

IMPORTANT POINTS TO REMEMBER

When testing for a student's knowledge of the letters, keep in mind that certain tasks concerning letter knowledge are more difficult than others. For example, note that TASK 2 is more difficult than TASK 3; that is, naming letters in random order from a stimulus sheet is more difficult than pointing to the letters as they are named by the teacher. Likewise, pointing to the letters as they are named by the teacher (TASK 3) is more difficult than being asked to identify a lowercase *g* when shown an uppercase *G* (TASK 4). Therefore, in giving this test, begin with TASK 1 (if you wish), asking the student to write the letters of the alphabet in both uppercase and lowercase. Then the student will do TASK 2. If she can do that task, then there would be no need to do TASK 3. If the student cannot do TASK 3, then she should be asked to do TASK 4, etc.

LETTER STIMULUS SHEET

1.	e	n	i	p	c
2.	v	x	a	j	z
3.	b	o	s	u	q
4.	k	y	f	l	d
5.	g	t	m	r	h	w

6.	C	J	P	H	K
7.	O	G	N	Q	D
8.	L	R	B	Z	Y
9.	A	S	F	M	V
10.	I	W	T	X	U	E

---

11. b m g d r p m b g r p d m o

LETTER KNOWLEDGE ANSWER SHEET

STUDENT'S NAME _____   SCHOOL _____

DATE _____

TESTER _____

See directions.

1. e _____ n _____ i _____ p _____ c _____
2. v _____ x _____ a _____ j _____ z _____
3. b _____ o _____ s _____ u _____ q _____
4. k _____ y _____ f _____ l _____ d _____
5. g _____ t _____ m _____ r _____ h _____ w _____
6. C _____ J _____ P _____ H _____ K _____
7. O _____ G _____ N _____ Q _____ D _____
8. L _____ R _____ B _____ Z _____ Y _____
9. A _____ S _____ F _____ M _____ V _____
10. I _____ W _____ T _____ X _____ U _____ E _____

TASK 1: _____ Student can write all lower case letters correctly

_____ Student can write all upper case letters correctly

Exceptions noted: _____

_____

TASK 2: _____ Student can name all lower case letters correctly

_____ Student can name all upper case letters correctly

TASK 3: _____ Student can identify all lower case letters when named

_____ Student can identify all upper case letters when named

_____ Student cannot identify all lower case letters when named

_____ Student cannot identify all upper case letters when named

Exceptions noted: _____

_____

TASK 4: _____ Student can match all upper and lower case letters

_____ Student cannot match all upper and lower case letters

Exceptions noted: _____

_____

TASK 5: _____ Student can match a letter with another one that is exactly the
same

_____ Student cannot match letters that are exactly the same

Exceptions noted: _____

_____

Preparation and Use of Materials for the *Quick Check for Basic Sight Words*

PREPARING FOR THE TEST

Before administering the *Quick Check for Basic Sight Word Knowledge,* make multiple copies of p. 217, which is the answer sheet to be used in quickly assessing students' knowledge of basic sight words. Also remove p. 219. This page can then be placed on a surface such as tagboard and fastened with rubber cement or transparent tape. After it is cemented in place, you may wish to laminate it to keep it from becoming soiled from handling.

SPECIFIC DIRECTIONS FOR TESTING BASIC SIGHT WORDS

Have your answer sheet ready and give the student the stimulus sheet. Ask the student to read the words in the same order as they are numbered. Tell the student to read each word carefully and skip any word that is not known, or instruct the student to say "I don't know" when a strange word is encountered. Mark the answer sheet as suggested in the directions. If the student pauses more than approximately one second before saying a word, count it as wrong.

IMPORTANT POINTS TO REMEMBER

The *Quick Check for Basic Sight Word Knowledge* is a quick way to test students' knowledge of basic sight words. If there is any doubt in your mind as to whether a student should be given an entire basic sight word test, you may give students this list first. If the student does not miss any words on this test, then he may not need to take the entire basic sight word test. However, if a student misses even one word on this list, he should be given the entire basic word test.

The *Quick Check for Basic Sight Word Knowledge* was developed by giving Ekwall's basic sight word list to 500 students in grades two through six, using a tachistoscopic presentation. One hundred students were tested at each of these five grade levels. A computer analysis then listed, in ascending order of difficulty, the words students most often missed. From this list 36 words were chosen. The first few words are the easier ones. However, following the first few easier words are the ones students tended to miss more often. The list also includes words commonly confused by many students. When giving this test, you should make sure that the student is exposed to each word briefly (approximately one second). Given more time, the student may use word-attack skills instead of his knowledge of basic sight words. A student who misses even one word in this test should be given the basic sight word tests that appear in Appendix D.

Quick Check For Basic Sight Word Knowledge

Answer Sheet

Name_____ Date_____

School_____ Tester_____

Directions: As the student reads the words from the stimulus sheet, mark those words read correctly with a plus (+) and those read incorrectly with a minus (−) or write in the word substituted. If the student says he or she does not know an answer, then mark it with a question mark (?). (If a student misses any words on this test, then he or she should be given the full list of basic sight words.)

1.	I _____	19.	thing _____
2.	the _____	20.	run _____
3.	was _____	21.	thank _____
4.	down _____	22.	once _____
5.	these _____	23.	wish _____
6.	saw _____	24.	think _____
7.	than _____	25.	every _____
8.	start _____	26.	ran _____
9.	this _____	27.	another _____
10.	want _____	28.	leave _____
11.	those _____	29.	should _____
12.	went _____	30.	there _____
13.	both _____	31.	sure _____
14.	then _____	32.	always _____
15.	shall _____	33.	carry _____
16.	upon _____	34.	present _____
17.	while _____	35.	such _____
18.	draw _____	36.	hurt _____

Quick Check for Basic Sight Word Knowledge

1. I	13. both	25. every
2. the	14. then	26. ran
3. was	15. shall	27. another
4. down	16. upon	28. leave
5. these	17. while	29. should
6. saw	18. draw	30. there
7. than	19. thing	31. sure
8. start	20. run	32. always
9. this	21. thank	33. carry
10. want	22. once	34. present
11. those	23. wish	35. such
12. went	24. think	36. hurt

D

Preparation and Use of Materials for Testing Basic Sight Words and Phrases

PREPARING FOR THE TEST

Before administering these tests, make multiple copies of pp. 223–227, the answer sheets to be used in assessing students' knowledge of basic sight words and phrases. You will also need an audio tape recorder and tape. You will need to prepare flash cards for each of the 220 basic sight words and 143 basic sight word phrases. Your flash cards should be arranged in the same order as the words on the answer sheets.

To do this you may purchase 3″ × 5″ or 4″ × 6″ index cards (either blank or lined) or, if you wish, purchase heavier stock cards in a similar or slightly smaller size. Most school supply stores sell cards ready-made for this purpose in various colors. Also, they often have rounded corners, which makes them last longer. You will need 363 cards, but you should purchase a few more in case you make mistakes preparing the cards.

Once you have selected your cards, look at the lists of words on the answer sheets. Print one word on each flash card, using neat lowercase manuscript printing. You may wish to write the list number and the word number on the back of each card. For example, on the back of the first card, *the*, write I-1. (This indicates List I, word 1.) The designation IV-16 would be written on the back of *ride* (List IV, word 16). If your cards ever become mixed up, you will find that it is easy to reassemble them in the correct order if you designate each word on the back as described. You also may wish to use different colored cards for each list.

SPECIFIC DIRECTIONS FOR TESTING BASIC SIGHT WORDS AND PHRASES

Seat the student opposite you and place the microphone near the spot on the table where the cards will be placed after the student has responded to the words on the cards as you flash them. (Make sure the tape recorder is turned on!)

Present the cards in the order they appear on the answer sheet. Say to the student: "I am going to show you some words on flash cards and I want you to say them when you see them. I will be flashing the cards quickly, so, if you don't know a word, don't worry about it and go on." Lift off 20–30 cards from the ordered stack. At a steady rate of approximately one to two cards per second, flash the cards to the student. Do *not* separate the cards into "right" and "wrong" piles, since this may distract you, upset the student being tested, and confuse the order of the flash cards. Continue flashing the cards until the student does not respond to four or five consecutive words or otherwise indicates an inability to successfully complete the test. If the student appears to be pronouncing most of the words correctly, continue the procedure until all cards are flashed.

After you have completed flashing the cards, you may play back the tape and mark the answer sheet with (+) for correct and (−) for incorrect responses. In scoring, *only the first response counts.* Having mastered a word, the student recognizes it instantly. If the student hesitates, the flashed word is not known by *sight*.

You may test the student's knowledge of basic sight word *phrases* by using the procedures described above, this time using the list of basic sight word phrases, also presented in this appendix. You may allow up to two seconds per phrase when flashing the cards. Each sight word test takes approximately six minutes to administer and score.

IMPORTANT POINTS TO REMEMBER

By examining the prepared lists, you can determine specifically which basic sight words and phrases the student has not mastered. These can then be taught without having to misuse instructional time teaching words or phrases that are already known.

A reasonable criterion for mastery of the entire lists is 90% or better. Even students who know all the basic sight words quite well will often miscall a few words because of the speed of the test. You may wish to recheck missed words or phrases a second time to determine whether the errors resulted from the speed of the test or from the student's lack of knowledge.

You must use judgment in evaluating a student's performance on the sight word tests. Young children may have greater difficulty with a speed of one word per second, although ultimately it is essential that the words be recognized at this rate. Similarly, students with speech difficulties may need an adjustment in the rate of flashing.

The modified Dolch list that appears in this appendix includes the 220 Dolch basic sight words reordered according to frequency of occurrence as found in a study conducted by William K. Durr.[*] The 220 individual words are divided into 11 sublists of 20 words each for ease of scoring and instruction.

---

[*]Durr, W. K. (1973). Computer study of high frequency words in popular trade juveniles. *Reading Teacher, 27,* 37–42.

Name _____ Date _____ Scores: (Pretest) _____ /220

School _____ Tester _____ (Posttest) _____ /220

Directions: Turn on the tape recorder and place the microphone on the table. Tell the student what you are going to do. Flash the cards to the student at a rate of one-to-two words per second in the order in which they appear on the list. After you have completed the flashing of the cards, play back the tape and mark the answer sheet with a (+) for correct and (−) for incorrect responses.

Individual Diagnosis of Dolch Words (Listed in Descending Order of Frequency)   pre [/220   ]   post [/220   ]

LIST I

	pre	post
1. the		
2. to		
3. and		
4. he		
5. a		
6. I		
7. you		
8. it		
9. of		
10. in		
11. was		
12. said		
13. his		
14. that		
15. she		
16. for		
17. on		
18. they		
19. but		
20. had		
*	/20	/20

LIST II

	pre	post
1. at		
2. him		
3. with		
4. up		
5. all		
6. look		
7. is		
8. her		
9. there		
10. some		
11. out		
12. as		
13. be		
14. have		
15. go		
16. we		
17. am		
18. then		
19. little		
20. down		
*	/20	/20

LIST III

	pre	post
1. do		
2. can		
3. could		
4. when		
5. did		
6. what		
7. so		
8. see		
9. not		
10. were		
11. get		
12. them		
13. like		
14. one		
15. this		
16. my		
17. would		
18. me		
19. will		
20. yes		
*	/20	/20

LIST IV

	pre	post
1. big		
2. went		
3. are		
4. come		
5. if		
6. now		
7. long		
8. no		
9. came		
10. ask		
11. very		
12. an		
13. over		
14. your		
15. its		
16. ride		
17. into		
18. just		
19. blue		
20. red		
*	/20	/20

LIST V

	pre	post
1. from		
2. good		
3. any		
4. about		
5. around		
6. want		
7. don't		
8. how		
9. know		
10. right		
11. put		
12. too		
13. got		
14. take		
15. where		
16. every		
17. pretty		
18. jump		
19. green		
20. four		
*	/20	/20

LIST VI

	pre	post
1. away		
2. old		
3. by		
4. their		
5. here		
6. saw		
7. call		
8. after		
9. well		
10. think		
11. ran		
12. let		
13. help		
14. make		
15. going		
16. sleep		
17. brown		
18. yellow		
19. five		
20. six		
*	/20	/20

* Number of words read correctly

LIST VII

	pre	post
1. walk		
2. two		
3. or		
4. before		
5. eat		
6. again		
7. play		
8. who		
9. been		
10. may		
11. stop		
12. off		
13. never		
14. seven		
15. eight		
16. cold		
17. today		
18. fly		
19. myself		
20. round		
*	/20	/20

LIST VIII

	pre	post
1. tell		
2. much		
3. keep		
4. give		
5. work		
6. first		
7. try		
8. new		
9. must		
10. start		
11. black		
12. white		
13. ten		
14. does		
15. bring		
16. goes		
17. write		
18. always		
19. drink		
20. once		
*	/20	/20

LIST IX

	pre	post
1. soon		
2. made		
3. run		
4. gave		
5. open		
6. has		
7. find		
8. only		
9. us		
10. three		
11. our		
12. better		
13. hold		
14. buy		
15. funny		
16. warm		
17. ate		
18. full		
19. those		
20. done		
*	/20	/20

LIST X

	pre	post
1. use		
2. fast		
3. say		
4. light		
5. pick		
6. hurt		
7. pull		
8. cut		
9. kind		
10. both		
11. sit		
12. which		
13. fall		
14. carry		
15. small		
16. under		
17. read		
18. why		
19. own		
20. found		
*	/20	/20

LIST XI

	pre	post
1. wash		
2. show		
3. hot		
4. because		
5. far		
6. live		
7. draw		
8. clean		
9. grow		
10. best		
11. upon		
12. these		
13. sing		
14. together		
15. please		
16. thank		
17. wish		
18. many		
19. shall		
20. laugh		
*	/20	/20

SCORE

LIST	pre	post
I		
II		
III		
IV		
V		
VI		
VII		
VIII		
IX		
X		
XI		
TOTAL		

* Number of words read correctly

Name ———————————— Date ———————————— Scores: (Pretest) ————— /143

School ——————————— Tester ——————————— (Posttest) ————— /143

Directions: Turn on the tape recorder and place the microphone on the table. Tell the student what you are going to do. Flash the cards to the student at a rate of one-to-two words per second in the order in which they appear on the list. After you have completed the flashing of the cards, play back the tape and mark the answer sheet with a (+) for correct and (−) for incorrect responses.

Individual Diagnosis of Sight Word Phrases pre [/143] post [/143]

LIST I

	pre	post
1. he had to		
2. she said that		
3. to the		
4. you and I		
5. but they said		
6. on a		
7. for his		
8. of that		
9. that was in		
10. it was		
*	/10	/10

LIST II

	pre	post
1. look at him		
2. as little		
3. at all		
4. I have a		
5. have some		
6. there is		
7. down there		
8. then we have		
9. to go		
10. to be there		
11. look up		
12. look at her		
13. we go out		
14. I am		
*	/14	/14

LIST III

	pre	post
1. look at me		
2. can you		
3. a little one		
4. you will see		
5. what is that		
6. my *cat*		
7. I will get		
8. when did he		
9. like this		
10. get them		
11. so you will see		
12. I could		
13. we were		
14. would not		
15. yes, I do		
*	/15	/15

LIST IV

	pre	post
1. a big ride		
2. went into		
3. if I ask		
4. come over with		
5. they went		
6. I am very		
7. there are blue		
8. a long *book*		
9. an *apple*		
10. your red *book*		
11. its *name*		
12. they came		
13. just now		
*	/13	/13

* Number of phrases read correctly

LIST V

	pre	post
1. I take every		
2. the four green		
3. they don't want		
4. right around		
5. a good jump		
6. a pretty *rabbit*		
7. I know how		
8. where can I		
9. the *duck* got		
10. it is about		
11. don't put any		
12. take from		
13. too little		
*	/13	/13

LIST VI

	pre	post
1. ran away		
2. let me help		
3. going to sleep		
4. five yellow *ducks*		
5. the old *turtle*		
6. by their *mother*		
7. call after *six*		
8. the brown *rabbit*		
9. I am well		
10. will think		
11. will make		
12. you saw		
13. here it is		
*	/13	/13

LIST VII

	pre	post
1. we eat		
2. two may walk		
3. on or off		
4. before seven		
5. today is cold		
6. play by myself		
7. don't stop		
8. it is round		
9. who is eight		
10. have never been		
11. can fly again		
*	/11	/11

LIST VIII

	pre	post
1. black and white		
2. start a new		
3. must try once		
4. don't keep much		
5. it does go		
6. always drink *milk*		
7. will bring ten		
8. *Lad* goes		
9. write and tell		
10. work is first		
11. can give it		
*	/11	/11

LIST IX

	pre	post
1. open and find		
2. *Jill* ate the		
3. those are done		
4. is funny		
5. buy us three		
6. this is only		
7. gave a warm		
8. soon we ate		
9. had a full		
10. run and hold		
11. made a big		
12. it is better		
13. our *duck*		
*	/13	/13

LIST X

	pre	post
1. sit with both		
2. you use it		
3. carry a small		
4. the cut hurt		
5. the fast *car*		
6. then the light		
7. which will fall		
8. pull it in		
9. had found		
10. under here		
11. be kind		
12. pick it up		
13. *Bill* can read		
14. my own *bed*		
15. why is it		
16. I can say		
*	/16	/16

* Number of phrases read correctly

LIST XI

	pre	post
1. wash in hot		
2. because it is		
3. grow best		
4. once upon		
5. sing and laugh		
6. please thank		
7. we draw these		
8. shall we show		
9. the wish is		
10. we clean		
11. they live		
12. too far		
13. all together		
14. many *turtles*		
*	/14	/14

SCORE

LIST	pre	post
I		
II		
III		
IV		
V		
VI		
VII		
VIII		
IX		
X		
XI		
TOTAL		

* Number of phrases read correctly

The list is presented based on the assumption that not all students will master all the words. It is therefore reasonable to begin by teaching the words that appear most often.

The phrase list is compiled so that each word from the isolated words list is presented in a phrase. Only 17 new words are added to complete phrases. These are nouns that are all drawn from the preprimer level of a basal series.

A list of basic sight word *sentences* is provided in Appendix N. These sentences are derived from the phrase list presented in this appendix. It is not suggested that you use the sentences for testing; however, they are quite helpful in *teaching* the student to recognize the individual sight words and sight word phrases in context.

Preparation and Use of the
Quick Survey Word List and the
El Paso Phonics Survey

PREPARATION OF THE *QUICK SURVEY WORD LIST*

Remove p. 231 (*Quick Survey Word List*) and rubber-cement or tape it on a 5″ × 8″ card. After placing it on the card, you may wish to laminate it since it will be handled by students and in the process of usage may become soiled.

DIRECTIONS FOR ADMINISTERING THE *QUICK SURVEY WORD LIST*

The *Quick Survey Word List* is designed to enable the tester to determine quickly if a student has the necessary word-attack skills to successfully read material written at an adult level. It may be given to students at approximately the fourth-grade level or above to determine if it is necessary to administer the *El Paso Phonics Survey*. The student is simply given the word list and asked to pronounce each word. The student should be told, however, that the words that he is about to attempt to pronounce are nonsense words or words that are not real words. The student should also be told that the words are very difficult, but that you would like to know if he is able to pronounce them. If the student can pronounce each of the words correctly, it would not be necessary to administer the *El Paso Phonics Survey* since the ultimate purpose of learning sound-symbol correspondence is to enable the student to attack new words. On the other hand, if it becomes apparent after one or two words that the student is not able to pronounce the words on the *Quick Survey Word List,* then it should be discontinued, and the *El Paso Phonics Survey* administered.

The correct pronunciation of the words on the *Quick Survey Word List* is shown on p. 233. This key shows the correct pronunciation as well as the part of each word that should be stressed. It should be remembered, however, that accent rules or generalizations pertaining to the English language are not consistent. Therefore, if the words are pronounced correctly except for the accent or stress shown on certain syllables, they should be considered correct. It is also suggested that the page with the correct pronunciation of the *Quick Survey Word List* be removed, rubber-cemented or taped to a 5″ × 8″ card, and placed in your diagnostic kit.

IMPORTANT POINTS TO REMEMBER ABOUT THE *QUICK SURVEY WORD LIST*

The *Quick Survey Word List* is also designed to test a student's knowledge of such word-attack skills as syllabication, vowel rules, rules for *C, G,* and *Y,* and accent generalizations. It should, however, be stressed that students who do not do well on the list should be stopped after the first two or three words. Remember, only if the student is able to pronounce all of the words correctly (except for accent) would you continue through the entire list. Having a student attempt to pronounce the words when he is not able to do so without difficulty will only discourage him. If the student does not do well on the first one or two words, then you should simply say, "Let's stop. These words are usually meant for adults, and you would not be expected to be able to read them."

PREPARATION OF THE *EL PASO PHONICS SURVEY*

Remove pp. 239–243 (*El Paso Phonics Survey:* General Directions and *El Paso Phonics Survey:* Special Directions) and rubber-cement them or tape them to a 5″ × 8″ card and laminate them, so they will be available for quick and easy reference in administering the *El Paso Phonics Survey* in the future. You should also remove pp. 249–251 (*El Paso Phonics Survey:* Answer Sheet) and make multiple copies of this material to be used with students when administering the *El Paso Phonics Survey.* These pages should also be protected, so they will be available for duplicating in the future. You should also remove pp. 245–247 and laminate them. These pages are the stimulus sheets for the *El Paso Phonics Survey;* they will be handled by students and if not laminated will become soiled.

DIRECTIONS FOR ADMINISTERING THE *EL PASO PHONICS SURVEY*

As you will note, there are two sets of directions for administering the *El Paso Phonics Survey*—the General Directions and the Special Directions. The General Directions give overall instructions for administering the *El Paso Phonics Survey* and should be read thoroughly before attempting to give it for the first time. The Special Directions give information on specific items that should be helpful for teacher's aides and others not trained in phonics. They should, however, be read by anyone who is administering the *El Paso Phonics Survey* for the first time.

IMPORTANT POINTS TO REMEMBER ABOUT THE *EL PASO PHONICS SURVEY*

At the beginning of the next section, on the rationale for using the *El Paso Phonics Survey,* you will find the advantages of using this survey compared to other types of phonics tests. Be sure to become familiar with these other com-

QUICK SURVEY WORD LIST*

wratbeling	twayfrall
dawsnite	spreanplit
pramminciling	goanbate
whetsplitter	streegran
gincule	glammertickly
cringale	grantellean
slatrungle	aipcid

*Reprinted by permission of Allyn and Bacon from *Teacher's handbook on diagnosis and remediation in reading* (2nd ed.). Boston: Allyn and Bacon, 1986.

PRONUNCIATION OF QUICK SURVEY WORDS*

răt′-bĕl-ĭng

däs′-nīt

prăm′-mĭn-cĭl-ĭng

hwĕt′-splĭt-tər

jĭn′-kyool

crĭn′-gāl

slăt′-rŭn-gəl

twā′-fräl

sprēn′-plĭt

gōn′-bāt

strē′-grăn

glăm′-mər-tĭck-ly

grăn′-tĕl-lēn

āp′-sĭd

PRONUNCIATION KEY

l — litt<u>le</u>

ə — <u>a</u>bout

ä — f<u>a</u>ther

ə — tamp<u>er</u>

hw — <u>wh</u>at

kyoo — <u>cu</u>te

*Reprinted by permission of Allyn and Bacon from Ekwall, E. E. (1986). *Teacher's handbook on diagnosis and remediation in reading* (2nd ed.). Boston: Allyn and Bacon, 1986.

monly used methods and the problems that tend to be encountered in using each of them.

On taking the *El Paso Phonics Survey,* the student is shown three easy words: *in, up,* and *am.* The teacher makes sure the student knows each of these words before beginning the test. The student is then shown a stimulus sheet item such as the following:

1. p am pam
2. n up nup

The student is told to say the *name* of the first letter, to pronounce the word in the middle, and finally to say the word formed by adding the initial consonant to the middle word. Although the final word is usually a nonsense word, the teacher is not giving the student a nonsense word in isolation. By saying the name of the letter and the small word in the center, the student finds that the only new task is to blend the letter sound with a word already known. (Remember the *El Paso Phonics Survey* should not be given unless the student knows each of the three stimulus words—*in, up,* and *am*—before beginning the test.) You will also note that vowels, vowel pairs, and special letter combinations are all put together with one of the first eight initial consonants tested on the survey. The students who get all of the first eight consonant sounds right prove their knowledge of them and show the teacher whether or not they know the vowel sounds that follow. The *El Paso Phonics Survey* does not have any of the disadvantages of the other six methods of testing phonics knowledge (discussed in the following section). In taking the *El Paso Phonics Survey,* some students give the nonsense word the wrong ending sound, even though they pronounced the sound correctly earlier. Extensive use of the *El Paso Phonics Survey* shows that this can happen with the student who is not sure of the initial consonant sound and expends so much thought in pronouncing it, that he simply does not attend to the pronunciation of the final sound. When this happens, do not count the initial consonant sound as correct, even if pronounced correctly.

RATIONALE FOR USING THE *EL PASO PHONICS SURVEY*

In the past, six methods have commonly been used to test students' knowledge of phonics. The rationale for using a test such as the *El Paso Phonics Survey* becomes obvious once one understands the shortcomings of these six methods, as discussed in the following sections.

Method One: *Using real words to test phoneme-grapheme relationships*

With this method, the teacher might ask the student to pronounce the words *dog, do,* and *done* to test the students' knowledge of the /d/ sound. The problem here is that the student probably already knows these words as sight words, and whether he knows the /d/ sound is irrelevant. Many disabled readers have a fairly large sight vocabulary but do not know the initial consonant sound of many words. The student may recognize the beginning /d/ sound but be unable to pronounce words such as *dispart* and *displace,* because he may not know the short /i/, the /s/, the /p/, or other sounds and may make no response at all. Thus, the teacher would receive no useful information, finding only that something in the word was unknown.

Method Two: *Using nonsense words to test phoneme-grapheme relationships*

In this case, the teacher might ask the student to pronounce a word such as *dupe* to test for knowledge of the /d/ sound. If the student can pronounce the word, the student probably knows the /d/ sound. However, if the student makes no response, it might mean one of several things:

1. The student does not know the vowel, consonant, final *e* rule (*v c e* as in *cake*).
2. The student may not know the short /u/, /p/, or /d/ sounds.
3. The student may not be able to blend the sounds together even if they are known.

Method Three: *Testing sounds in isolation*

This method lacks inter-scorer reliability and thus cannot be a valid method of testing students' phonics knowledge. To prove this, ask a student to give the sounds represented by the following letters: *f, r, b, w, l, n, m,* and *v,* while you tape-record the responses. Then ask a group of teachers to listen to the tape and mark each response right or wrong. Next, ask each teacher to tell a response for each sound given by the student. In most cases, the considerable disagreement among the teachers indicates that this procedure is unreliable and, thus, not valid.

Method Four: *Having students write the first letter or letters of a word pronounced by the teacher*

In using this method, the teacher usually pronounces a word such as *shoe* and asks the students to write the first letter or letters that they hear at the beginning of the word on a piece of paper with numbered lines. See the following example:

1. _____
2. _____

When the teacher pronounces the stimulus word, as in *shoe,* the students are to write *sh* in the first blank. Although this method may appear to measure ability to use the *sh* sound in reading, it rarely does so in reality. In a study,

Eldon E. Ekwall found that students who hear a certain sound miss different phoneme-grapheme relationships than students who see the same sound in a strange word.[*] Obviously, hearing a word and writing the initial consonant is a different skill than seeing and pronouncing the same word as tested in the *El Paso Phonics Survey,* or as pronounced in isolation. Reading is, of course, a decoding task, and writing a heard initial consonant sound is an encoding task.

Method Five: *Multiple choice*

In using this method, the teacher pronounces a word, and the students underline or circle one of four choices, as in the following example:

1. f g d b
2. r p n k

Actually, this is also an encoding rather than a decoding task; that is, the students make a written response after hearing an oral stimulus, such as they do in spelling. Furthermore, multiple-choice testing usually allows students to get at least one-fourth of the answers right, regardless of their knowledge.

Method Six: *Multiple choice with a stimulus*

This is almost the same as method five, except that the stimulus word is generated by a picture rather than by the teacher. For example, there might be a picture of a fox next to the choices in the first question. The students are told to look at the picture and say the word that stands for the word's initial sound. This is also an encoding rather than a decoding task and is again multiple choice, allowing a student who knows almost nothing about phonics to get at least one-fourth of the answers right.

---

[*]Ekwall, E. E. (1973). *An analysis of children's test scores when tested with individually administered diagnostic tests and when tested with group administered diagnostic tests* (final research report). El Paso, TX: University Research Institute, University of Texas at El Paso.

EL PASO PHONICS SURVEY
General Directions

1. Before beginning the test, make sure the student has instant recognition of the test words that appear in the box at the top of the first page of the survey. These words should be known instantly by the student. If they are not, reschedule the test at a later date, after the words have been taught and the student has learned them.

2. Give the student the El Paso Phonics Survey stimulus sheet, pages 245–247.

3. Point to the letter in the first column and have the student say the name of that letter (not the sound it represents). Then point to the word in the middle column and have the student pronounce it. Then point to the nonsense word in the third column and have the student pronounce it.

4. If the student can give the name of the letter, the word in the middle column, and the nonsense word in the third column, mark the answer sheet with a plus (+).

5. If the student cannot pronounce the nonsense word after giving the name of the letter and the word in the middle column, mark the answer sheet with a minus (−); or you may wish to write the word phonetically as the student pronounced it. If the student can tell you the name of the letter and the small word in the middle column but cannot pronounce the nonsense word, you may wish to have him or her give the letter sound in isolation. If the student can give the sound in isolation, either the student is unable to "blend" or does not know the letter well enough to give its sound and blend it at the same time.

6. Whenever a superscript letter appears on the answer sheet, refer to the Special Directions sheet on p. 243.

7. To the right of each answer blank on the answer sheet is a grade level designation. This number represents the point at which most basal reading series have already taught that sound. At that point, you should expect it to be known. The designation 1.3 means the third month of the first year.

8. When the student comes to two- or three-letter consonant digraphs or blends, as with the *qu* in number 22, she is to say "*q-u*" as with the single letters. *Remember*: the student never gives letter sounds in isolation when engaged in actual reading.

9. When the student comes to the vowels (number 59), she is to say "short *a*," and so forth, and then the nonsense word in column two. If the student does not know the breve (˘) over the vowels means short *a, e,* and so forth, then explain this. Do the same with the long vowels where the macron (¯) appears.

10. All vowels and vowel combinations are put with only one or two of the first eight consonants. If any of the first eight consonants are not known, they should be taught before you attempt to test for vowel knowledge. You are likely to find that a student who does not know the first eight consonant sounds will seldom know the vowel sounds anyhow.

11. You will note that words appear to the right of some of the blanks on the answer sheet. These words illustrate the correct consonant or vowel sound that should be heard when the student responds.

12. Only phonic elements have been included that have a high enough utility to make them worthwhile learning. For example, the vowel pair *ui* appears very seldom, and when it does, it may stand for the short *i* sound in "build" or the long *oo* sound in "fruit." Therefore, there is really no reason to teach it as a sound. However, some letters, such as *oe,* may stand for several sounds, but most often stand for one particular sound. In the case of *oe,* the long *o* sound should be used. In cases such as this, the most common sound is illustrated by a word to the right of the blank on the answer sheet. If the student gives another correct sound for the letter(s), then say, "Yes, that's right, but what is another way that we could say this nonsense word?" The student must then say it as illustrated in the small word to the right of the blank on the answer sheet. Otherwise, count the answer as wrong.

13. Stop the test after five consecutive misses or if the student appears frustrated from missing a number of items even though she has not missed five consecutive items.

El Paso Phonics Survey

Special Directions

[a]3. If the student uses another *s* sound as in "sugar" (*sh*) in saying the nonsense word "sup" ask, "What is another *s* sound?" The student must use the *s* as in "sack."

[b]15. If the student uses the soft *c* sound as in "cigar" in saying the nonsense word "cam," ask, "What is another *c* sound?" The student must use the hard *c* sound as in "coat."

[c]16. If the student uses the soft *g* sound as in "gentle" in saying the nonsense word "gup," ask, "What is another *g* sound?" The student must use the hard *g* sound as in "gate."

[d]17. Ask, "What is the *y* sound when it comes at the beginning of a word?"

[e]23. The student must use the *ks* sound of *x*, and the nonsense word "mox" must rhyme with "box."

[f]35. If the student uses the *th* sound heard in "that," ask, "What is another *th* sound?" The student must use the *th* sound heard in "thing."

[g]44. If the student uses the *hoo* sound of *wh* in saying the nonsense word "whup," ask, "What is another *wh* sound?" The student must use the *wh* sound as in "when."

[h]72. The student may either give the *ea* sound heard in "head" or the *ea* sound heard in "meat." Be sure to note which one is used.

[i]73. If the same *ea* sound is given this time as was given for item 72, say, "Yes, that's right, but what is another way we could pronounce this nonsense word?" Whichever sound was *not* used in item 72 must be used here; otherwise, it is incorrect.

[j]81. The student may give either the *ow* heard in "cow" or the *ow* heard in "crow." Be sure to note which one is used.

[k]82. If the same *ow* sound is given this time as was given for item 81, say, "Yes, that's right, but what is another way we could pronounce this nonsense word?" Whichever sound was *not* used in item 81 must be used here; otherwise, it is incorrect.

[l]88. The student may give either the *oo* sound heard in "book" or the *oo* sound heard in "moon." Be sure to note which one is used.

[m]89. If the same *oo* sound is given this time as was given for item 88, say, "Yes, that's right, but what is another way we could pronounce this nonsense word?" Whichever sound was *not* used in item 88 must be used here; otherwise, it is incorrect.

El Paso Phonics Survey

> **in   up   am**

1.	p	am	pam	25. sl	in	slin
2.	n	up	nup	26. pl	up	plup
3.	s	up	sup	27. fl	in	flin
4.	r	in	rin	28. st	am	stam
5.	t	up	tup	29. fr	in	frin
6.	m	up	mup	30. bl	am	blam
7.	b	up	bup	31. gr	up	grup
8.	d	up	dup	32. br	in	brin
9.	w	am	wam	33. tr	am	tram
10.	h	up	hup	34. sh	up	shup
11.	f	am	fam	35. th	up	thup
12.	j	up	jup	36. ch	am	cham
13.	k	am	kam	37. dr	up	drup
14.	l	in	lin	38. cl	in	clin
15.	c	am	cam	39. gl	am	glam
16.	g	up	gup	40. sk	up	skup
17.	y	in	yin	41. cr	in	crin
18.	v	am	vam	42. sw	up	swup
19.	z	up	zup	43. sm	in	smin
20.	c	in	cin	44. wh	up	whup
21.	g	in	gin	45. sp	up	spup
22.	qu	am	quam	46. sc	up	scup
23.	m	ox	mox	47. str	am	stram
24.	pr	am	pram	48. thr	up	thrup

49.	scr	in	scrin	77. ar	arb
50.	spr	am	spram	78. er	ert
51.	spl	in	splin	79. ir	irt
52.	squ	am	squam	80. oe	poe
53.	sn	up	snup	81. ow	owd
54.	tw	am	twam	82. ow	fow
55.	wr	in	wrin	83. or	orm
56.	shr	up	shrup	84. ur	urd
57.	dw	in	dwin	85. oy	moy
58.	sch	am	scham	86. ew	bew
59.	ă	tam		87. aw	awp
60.	ĭ	rin		88. oo	oot
61.	ĕ	nep		89. oo	oop
62.	ŏ	sot		90. au	dau
63.	ŭ	tum			
64.	ā	sape			
65.	ō	pote			
66.	ī	tipe			
67.	ē	rete			
68.	ū	pune			
69.	ee	eem			
70.	oa	oan			
71.	ai	ait			
72.	ea	eam			
73.	ea	eap			
74.	ay	tay			
75.	oi	doi			
76.	ou	tou			

El Paso Phonics Survey
Answer Sheet*

Name _____ Sex _____ Date _____

School _____ Examiner _____

Mark answers as follows:
Pass +
Fail - (or write word as pronounced)

PEK = Point at which phonic element is expected to be known

Answers PEK

Initial Consonants

1. p	pam	_____	1.3
2. n	nup	_____	1.3
ª3. s	sup	_____	1.3
4. r	rin	_____	1.3
5. t	tup	_____	1.3
6. m	mup	_____	1.3
7. b	bup	_____	1.3
8. d	dup	_____	1.3
9. w	wam	_____	1.3
10. h	hup	_____	1.3
11. f	fam	_____	1.3
12. j	jup	_____	1.3
13. k	kam	_____	1.3
14. l	lin	_____	1.3
ᵇ15. c	cam	_____	1.3
ᶜ16. g	gup	_____	1.3
ᵈ17. y	yin	_____	1.3
18. v	vam	_____	1.3
19. z.	zup	_____	1.3
20. c	cin	_____	1.3
21. g	gin	_____	1.3
22. qu	quam	_____	1.3

Ending Consonant

ᵉ23. m	mox	_____	1.3

Initial Consonant Clusters

24. pr	pram	_____	1.3
25. sl	slin	_____	1.6
26. pl	plup	_____	1.6
27. fl	flin	_____	1.6

Answers PEK

28. st	stam	_____	1.6
29. fr	frin	_____	1.6
30. bl	blam	_____	1.6
31. gr	grup	_____	1.6
32. tr	tram	_____	1.6
33. br	brin	_____	1.9
34. sh	shup	_____	1.9
ᶠ35. th	thup	_____	1.9 (thing)
36. ch	cham	_____	1.9 (church)
37. dr	drup	_____	1.9
38. cl	clin	_____	1.9
39. gl	glam	_____	1.9
40. sk	skup	_____	1.9
41. cr	crin	_____	1.9
42. sw	swup	_____	1.9
43. sm	smin	_____	2.5
ᵍ44. wh	whup	_____	2.5 (when)
45. sp	spup	_____	2.5
46. sc	scup	_____	2.5
47. str	stram	_____	2.5
48. thr	thrup	_____	2.5
49. scr	scrin	_____	2.5
50. spr	spram	_____	2.5
51. spl	splin	_____	2.5
52. squ	squam	_____	2.9
53. sn	snup	_____	2.9
54. tw	twam	_____	2.9
55. wr	wrin	_____	2.9
56. shr	shrup	_____	3.5
57. dw	dwin	_____	3.5
58. sch	scham	_____	3.9

*The El Paso Phonics Survey is from E. E. Ekwall, *Teacher's Handbook on Diagnosis and Remediation in Reading,* 2nd edition (Boston: Allyn and Bacon, 1986). Reprinted by permission.

Vowels, Vowel Teams, and Special Letter Combinations

Answers PEK

59. a	tam	———	1.6
60. i	rin	———	1.6
61. e	nep	———	1.6
62. o	sot	———	1.6
63. u	tum	———	1.6
64. a	sape	———	1.6
65. o	pote	———	1.6
66. i	tipe	———	1.9
67. e	rete	———	1.9
68. u	pune	———	1.9
69. ee	eem	———	1.9 (heed)
70. oa	oan	———	1.9 (soap)
71. ai	ait	———	1.9 (ape)
[h]72. ea	eam	———	1.9 (meat)
[i]73. ea	eap	———	2.5 (head)
74. ay	tay	———	2.5 (hay)
75. oi	doi	———	2.5 (boy)
76. ou	tou	———	2.5 (cow)
77. ar	arb	———	2.5 (harp)
78. er	ert	———	2.5 (her)
79. ir	irt	———	2.5 (hurt)
80. oe	poe	———	2.9 (hoe)
[j]81. ow	owd	———	2.9 (cow or crow)
[k]82. ow	fow	———	2.9 (cow or crow)
83. or	orm	———	2.9 (corn)
84. ur	urd	———	2.9 (hurt)
85. oy	moy	———	2.9 (boy)
86. ew	bew	———	2.9 (few)
87. aw	awp	———	2.9 (paw)
[l]88. oo	oot	———	2.9 (book or moon)
[m]89. oo	oop	———	3.5 (book or moon)
90. au	dau	———	3.5 (paw)

F

Preparation and Use of Materials for Testing Knowledge of Vowel Rules and Syllable Principles

PREPARING FOR THE TEST

The materials on pp. 259–267 are printed on only one side of the page. You will note that there are 18 rectangles, each with something printed on it. These are meant to be cut out and rubber-cemented or taped to 3″ × 5″ cards. They should then be laminated. The cards are numbered from 1 to 15; however, there is a 1-B, a 7-B, and a 14-B. The 1-B should be cemented to the back of number 1, 7-B should be cemented to the back of number 7, and 14-B should be cemented to the back of number 14. In cementing the materials to the backs of these three cards, make sure that the material on both sides of the cards is placed so that you can read the material on the back of the card while someone is reading the material on the front of the card. When you have finished laminating all the cards, place them in order, faceup on the table, so that they are numbered from 1–15. You may wish to use a rubber band to keep them in this order when not being used.

You will also note that on pp. 255 and 257 there is an answer sheet for each of the vowel rules and syllable principles. These should be removed from the text and duplicated so that you will have a copy for each student being tested.

SPECIFIC DIRECTIONS FOR TESTING VOWEL RULES AND SYLLABLE PRINCIPLES

Have your answer sheet in front of you so you can mark it easily as the student responds. Show the student the first card, which says *Syllable Principles* on the front. At this time read the material on the back of this card to the student. After reading the directions on the back of this card, show the student the first card with words on it (number 2). Take the card marked number 1 and put it on the back of the deck and continue in this order. Ask the student to tell you where she would divide into syllables each of the nonsense words on the stimulus cards. The student must get all responses correct to show that she knows the syllable principle. For example, in principle number 1 there are four stimulus words. The student must get all words right to show that the rule is actually known and that she is not guessing. It is not important that the student can recite the rule, only that she knows where to divide the words. If the student responds to all of the words correctly, then mark syllable principle number 1 as correct with a plus (+), or if it is wrong mark it with a minus (−). Continue in this manner until you have tested all of the syllable principles. The testing of the vowel rules is done by the same procedure as the testing of the syllable principles.

IMPORTANT POINTS TO REMEMBER

You should not attempt to test for students' knowledge of vowel rules unless the student is thoroughly familiar with all vowel and consonant sounds. Therefore, if a student has difficulty with phonics and structural analysis, you should first give the *El Paso Phonics Survey*. If the student knows nearly all initial consonants, consonant clusters, and vowels, then you could logically proceed with testing her knowledge of vowel rules. However, if the student does not know all initial consonants, consonant clusters, and vowel sounds, then testing should be delayed until she has learned these.

When testing for knowledge of vowel rules and syllable principles, remember that the ultimate goal is to enable the student to use, not just to recite, the rule or principle that applies to each word.

Phonics research in the past two decades has not always been used to the best advantage; too many outdated rules appear in textbooks and teacher's manuals even today. The material on the following pages is designed to test the student's knowledge of phonics rules in terms of using the rules and principles, rather than reciting them.

Answer Sheet for Vowel Rules and Syllable Principles Test

Name of Student_____

                      (Last)   (First)   (Middle Initial)

Grade in School_____ Sex_____ Date Tested_____

Syllable Principles

Instructions: Make a plus (+) on the line following the number of the syllable principle if the answer is correct. Make a minus (−) on the line following the number of the syllable principle if the answer is incorrect.

1. ____ Divide wherever there are two consonants surrounded by vowels providing there are no consonant clusters between the vowels. al/pil, op/por, bot/nap, and cur/ron

2. ____ When a word ends in consonant-*le,* the consonant preceding the *le* is included in the syllable with *le.* na/ple, fra/ble, da/ple, and sa/ple

3. ____ Divide between compound words and normal places in the words making up the compound words. cow/per/son, dog/leg, and cow/lick

4. ____ Do not divide between consonant digraphs or blends (consonant clusters). In this case treat the cluster as though it were a single consonant and divide the word so that the cluster goes with the second vowel as in #5 below, or as you would in #1 above. ba/chop, ba/shil, and da/phod

5. ____ In vowel-consonant-vowel situations (VCV) first try dividing so that the consonant goes with the second vowel. mo/nan, fa/dop, and da/lop

Vowel Rules

Instructions: Mark vowel rules the same as the syllable principles above using a (+) or a (−).

1. ___ Single syllable words with only one vowel at the end should usually be pronounced so that the vowel stands for its long sound. ra, de, and po

2. ___ A single vowel at the end of a syllable in a multisyllable word should be given the long sound first. molo, gamo, and ralo

3. ___ A single vowel in a closed syllable usually stands for the short sound of the vowel. loc, pid, and dap

4. ___ Whenever *r* follows a vowel, providing it is in the same syllable, it usually changes the sound of the vowel. (They may be grouped as follows: *er, ur, ir* sound as *ur* in *fur*; *ar* sounds like the *ar* in *car*; and *or* sounds like *or* in *corn*.) der, bir, cur, par, and por

5. ___ The letters *w* and *l* influence the vowel sound preceding them making the vowel neither long nor short. This is true more of the time when there is a double *l*. kaw, rall, baw, and kall

6. ___ When a vowel-consonant-final *e* appears at the end of a word, the first vowel will usually stand for its long sound. Although this is not true an extremely large percentage of the time, it is more true than not. nide, lode, and pake

7. ___ A *y* at the end of a single syllable word, preceded by a consonant, usually stands for the long *i* sound. (Note that in this rule the *y* must be preceded by a consonant.) bly and cly

8. ___ A *y* at the end of a multisyllable word preceded by a consonant usually stands for the long *e* sound. (Note in this rule the *y* must be preceded by a consonant and not a vowel.) noply and dalry

9. ___ A *y* at the beginning of a word usually has the *y* consonant sound as in the word *yard*. yamp and yorp

**Syllable
Principles**

1

Syllable Principles

Say, "Here are some nonsense words. In other words they are not real words. Tell me where you would divide them into syllables if they were real words."

**Optional
Why?**

1–B

---

alpil

oppor

botnap

curron

2

---

naple

frable

daple

saple

3

4

cowperson
dogleg
cowlick

5

bachop
bashil
daphod

6

monan
fadop
dalop

7

Vowel
Rules

Vowel Rules

Say, "I'm going to show you some nonsense words again. This time tell me how you would pronounce each word."

Optional

Why?

7–B

---

ra

de

po

8

---

molo

gamo

ralo

9

---

loc

pid

dap

10

der
bir
cur
par
por

11

kaw
rall
baw
kall

12

nide
lode
pake

13

Rules for "Y"

14

Rules for "Y"

Say, "Here are some
more nonsense words.
They will help me
know if you know how
to pronounce the
'Y' sound."

Optional
Why?

14–B

---

bly

cly

noply

dalry

yamp

yorp

15

G

Preparation and Use of Materials for Testing Knowledge of Contractions[*]

PREPARING FOR THE TEST

Before administering the test, remove p. 271 and duplicate it so that you will have multiple copies to use as answer sheets for testing each student. Also remove p. 273 and use rubber cement or tape to fasten it to a 5″ × 8″ card. You can also laminate it to keep it from being soiled from handling.

SPECIFIC DIRECTIONS FOR TESTING FOR KNOWLEDGE OF CONTRACTIONS

Have your answer sheet ready (p. 271) and give the student the stimulus sheet (p. 273). Then read the directions on the answer sheet.

IMPORTANT POINTS TO REMEMBER

A rather high percentage of students have occasional problems with the pronunciation of contractions; however, you are likely to find a greater percentage who do not know what two words each contraction stands for. Keep in mind that pronunciation is important for reading purposes, but students will not use a contraction in their writing until they know the two words for which each contraction stands.

*Reprinted by permission of Allyn and Bacon from Ekwall, E. E. (1986). *Teacher's handbook on diagnosis and remediation in reading* (2nd ed.). Boston: Allyn and Bacon.

Knowledge of Contractions
Answer Sheet

Name _____ Date _____

School _____ Tester _____

Directions: Say, "here is a list of contractions. I want you to begin with number one and say the contraction and then tell what two words it stands for." Following each contraction are two lines. If the student is able to pronounce the contraction correctly, put a plus (+) in the first blank. If he or she can then tell you what two words it stands for, put a plus (+) in the second blank. Mark wrong answers with a minus (−). The grade-level designation following each blank stands for the point at which the contraction should be known.

1. aren't ____ ____ 1.9			25. there's ____ ____ 2.5		
2. can't ____ ____ 1.9			26. we'll ____ ____ 2.5		
3. don't ____ ____ 1.9			27. there'll ____ ____ 2.5		
4. weren't ____ ____ 1.9			28. what's ____ ____ 2.5		
5. couldn't ____ ____ 1.9			29. you'll ____ ____ 2.5		
6. didn't ____ ____ 1.9			30. doesn't ____ ____ 2.9		
7. wasn't ____ ____ 1.9			31. hasn't ____ ____ 2.9		
8. hadn't ____ ____ 1.9			32. you'd ____ ____ 2.9		
9. won't ____ ____ 1.9			33. he'd ____ ____ 2.9		
10. haven't ____ ____ 1.9			34. you're ____ ____ 2.9		
11. isn't ____ ____ 1.9			35. he's ____ ____ 2.9		
12. wouldn't ____ ____ 1.9			36. I'd ____ ____ 2.9		
13. anybody'd ____ ____ 2.5			37. we've ____ ____ 2.9		
14. he'll ____ ____ 2.5			38. I've ____ ____ 2.9		
15. it's ____ ____ 2.5			39. they've ____ ____ 2.9		
16. here's ____ ____ 2.5			40. she'd ____ ____ 2.9		
17. I'll ____ ____ 2.5			41. who'd ____ ____ 2.9		
18. let's ____ ____ 2.5			42. she's ____ ____ 2.9		
19. she'll ____ ____ 2.5			43. they'd ____ ____ 2.9		
20. that's ____ ____ 2.5			44. we'd ____ ____ 2.9		
21. where's ____ ____ 2.5			45. they're ____ ____ 2.9		
22. they'll ____ ____ 2.5			46. we're ____ ____ 2.9		
23. I'm ____ ____ 2.5			47. you've ____ ____ 2.9		
24. who'll ____ ____ 2.5					

Knowledge of Contractions

1. aren't
2. can't
3. don't
4. weren't
5. couldn't
6. didn't
7. wasn't
8. hadn't
9. won't
10. haven't
11. isn't
12. wouldn't
13. anybody'd
14. he'll
15. it's
16. here's
17. I'll
18. let's
19. she'll
20. that's
21. where's
22. they'll
23. I'm
24. who'll
25. there's
26. we'll
27. there'll
28. what's
29. you'll
30. doesn't
31. hasn't
32. you'd
33. he'd
34. you're
35. he's
36. I'd
37. we've
38. I've
39. they've
40. she'd
41. who'd
42. she's
43. they'd
44. we'd
45. they're
46. we're
47. you've

Preparation and Use of Materials for Testing Ability to Use Context Clues

PREPARING FOR THE TEST

Pages 279–289 contain materials that you may use to test students' ability to use context clues. Each page contains materials for testing context clues at a level from grade one to grade six. To prepare the materials for testing, remove these pages from this appendix. Cut each page in half along the dotted lines and use rubber cement or magic tape to fasten each half of the page to separate sides of a 5″ × 8″ card. You may then wish to laminate the card to keep it from becoming soiled with use. In fastening the materials to the 5″ × 8″ card, make sure that the material on one side of the card is in the same position as the material on the other side, so both you and a student can read the materials at the same time. (An alternative is to place each half page on separate cards, one for the student being tested and the other for you. If you do this you may wish to use different colored cards to distinguish the student's cards from the examiner's cards. This method has the advantage of allowing the student to hold her card so that it will be easier for her to read.)

When all cards are completed, you should place them in grade-level order, so the front of the first card contains the material to be read by a student reading at first-grade level, the second card contains the materials to be read by a student reading at second-grade level, and so on. The other side of the cards (to be read by the tester) will then contain the same passages as those to be read by the student, except that the words omitted on the student's passage will be underlined on the side seen by the tester. This side of the card also shows the grade level at which the material is written.

SPECIFIC DIRECTIONS FOR ADMINISTERING THE TEST

Begin the test at a level at which you are sure the student can function at her low instructional or independent reading level. Hold the card so the student can read the material on her side. Read the directions printed at the top of the card and then let the student proceed to read orally the passage printed on the other side. It should not be necessary to record the student's errors; however, as the student reads, if you believe you have chosen too difficult a passage to begin with, or too easy a passage to begin with, then move to the next passage that is either easier or more difficult. If the student uses a word that is a logical substitute for the one that is omitted, then count it as correct. No norms have been developed for how well students should do in using context clues. However, in these passages it is suggested that you use the following criteria in determining student performance:

No error.......................................Excellent
One error......................................Good
Two errors ....Fair
Three or more errors ....Poor

IMPORTANT POINTS TO REMEMBER

It is often taken for granted that students will automatically attempt to use context clues even though they have not been taught how to do so. This is simply not true. Many readers require a considerable amount of instruction and a great deal of practice in using this skill.

The pages that follow contain materials for testing students' ability to use context clues. It should be stressed that most students will be unable to use context clues effectively unless they are reading at a level that is rather easy for them (their independent or easy instructional level). Therefore, in using the materials, be sure to use only passages that the student would be able to read fairly easily if no words were omitted. If you wish to develop materials for testing students' ability to use context clues, other than those presented on the following pages, the section that follows will be helpful.

DEVELOPING YOUR OWN MATERIALS FOR TESTING STUDENTS' KNOWLEDGE OF CONTEXT CLUES

In constructing materials for testing context clues, you should first keep in mind that students must be aware of context in their oral language. Depending upon the age-grade level of the students with whom you are working, the following sequence is suggested:

1. Make a tape recording of a passage in which certain words are omitted. Replace words that are omitted with the sound of a bell or tone of some type. When the bell or tone sounds, ask the student to give orally the word that she feels should have appeared in place of the tone. In making either a tape recording or a written exercise for testing context clues, make sure the words that are omitted are ones that can be gotten from the context of the sentence, as in the following example:

Lori was going to (beep) a party.
It was going to (beep) on Saturday.
She invited some of (beep) friends to come.
She was (beep) happy.

2. Progress to written materials in which the word omitted is replaced with the first letter of the word omitted, and the rest of the letters are replaced with a blank line as follows:

> Lori was going to h _____ a party.
> It was going to b __ on Saturday.
> She invited some of h _____ friends to come.
> She was v _____ happy.

3. Progress to written materials in which the word omitted is replaced with a _____ for each letter omitted as follows:

> Lori was going to __ __ __ __ a party.
> It was going to __ __ on Saturday.
> She invited some of __ __ __ friends to come.
> She was __ __ __ __ happy.

4. Lastly, progress to written materials in which the word omitted is replaced with a line. At this point, be sure to make all lines equal length.

> Lori was going to _____ a party.
> It was going to _____ on Saturday.
> She invited some of _____ friends to come.
> She was _____ happy.

Teacher reads these directions: Here is a story with some words left out. Each time a word is left out, it has been replaced with a line. When you come to a line, try to figure out what word should be in that blank. Ready—begin.

Jan has a cat.

The cat's <u>name</u> is Tab.

Tab does not <u>like</u> dogs.

One day <u>a</u> dog ran after Tab.

<u>Tab</u> ran up a tree.

The dog could not go <u>up</u> the tree.

Then <u>the</u> dog went away.

Grade one reading level

Jan has a cat.

The cat's _____ is Tab.

Tab does not _____ dogs.

One day _____ dog ran after Tab.

_____ ran up a tree.

The dog could not go _____ the tree.

Then _____ dog went away.

Teacher reads these directions: Here is a story with some words left out. Each time a word is left out, it has been replaced with a line. When you come to a line, try to figure out what word should be in that blank. Ready—begin.

One day Sam was going to school.
He was riding with his father in their car.
He looked out of the window and saw an elephant.
He said, "Look, father, there goes an elephant."
Sam's father did not even look because they were
    in a large city.
  That day Sam's father heard that
    an elephant had escaped from a circus.
  That evening Sam's father said, "I'm sorry, Sam,
    you did see an elephant this morning."

Grade two reading level

One day Sam was going to school.
He was riding with _____ father in their car.
He looked out of the window and _____ an elephant.
He said, "Look, father, _____ goes an elephant."
Sam's _____ did not even look because they were
    in a large city.
  That day _____ father heard that
    an elephant had escaped from a circus.
  That evening Sam's father said, "I'm sorry, Sam,
    you did _____ an elephant this morning."

Teacher reads these directions: Here is a story with some words left out. Each time a word is left out, it has been replaced with a line. When you come to a line, try to figure out what word should be in that blank. Ready—begin.

Ann and her brother Mike like to play basketball in a park that is far from their home. When they <u>want</u> to play, they usually take a bus to get <u>to</u> the park. There are other boys and girls <u>that</u> play there, too. Sometimes when they <u>go</u> to the park, their father and mother go with them. Their father and mother like to take some <u>food</u> and <u>have</u> a picnic while they are at the park.

Grade three reading level

Ann and her brother Mike like to play basketball in a park that is far from their home. When they _____ to play, they usually take a bus to get _____ the park. There are other boys and girls _____ play there, too. Sometimes when they _____ to the park, their father and _____ go with them. Their father and mother like to take some food and _____ a picnic while they are at the park.

Teacher reads these directions: Here is a story with some words left out. Each time a word is left out, it has been replaced with a line. When you come to a line, try to figure out what word should be in that blank. Ready—begin.

Most kinds of dogs make excellent pets. They can learn fast, and they also have an excellent memory. An intelligent dog can learn to respond to many commands. Many dogs that have been taught well can learn more than 100 words and phrases.

Grade four reading level

Most kinds of dogs make excellent pets. They _____ learn fast, _____ they also _____ an excellent memory. An intelligent _____ can learn _____ respond to many commands. Many dogs that have been taught well can learn more _____ 100 words and phrases.

Fire is very important to all of us today. Wherever ruins of early man have been found, there has always been evidence of fire in that civilization. It is thought that early man may have first found fire when lightning struck trees and caused them to burn. Some people think that man might have been able to start fires by getting them from active volcanoes.

Grade five reading level

Fire is very important to all of us today. Wherever ruins of early man have _____ found, there has always been evidence _____ fire in that civilization. It is thought _____ early man may _____ first found fire when lightning struck trees and caused _____ to burn. Some people think that man might have been able _____ start fires by getting them from active volcanoes.

Teacher reads these directions: Here is a story with some words left out. Each time a word is left out, it has been replaced with a line. When you come to a line, try to figure out what word should be in that blank. Ready—begin.

One of the most famous eagles in the entire world is not the one we see on stamps or coins. It was an eagle caught by an Indian named Blue Sky who lived in Wisconsin. Blue Sky sold the eagle to a man that sold him to a soldier in the Civil War who named him Old Abe. Before the eagle died, he had been through four years of war and had survived twenty-two battles.

Grade six reading level

One of the most famous eagles in the entire world is not the one we see on stamps or coins. It was _____ eagle caught by an Indian named Blue Sky _____ lived in Wisconsin. Blue Sky sold _____ eagle to a man that sold him to a soldier _____ the Civil War _____ who named him Old Abe. Before the eagle died, _____ had been through four years _____ war and had survived twenty-two battles.

Using the Cloze Procedure*

DEVELOPING, ADMINISTERING, AND SCORING CLOZE PASSAGES

In constructing cloze passages, you could omit every third, fifth, or 10th word. However, most of the research is based on the deletion of every fifth word. Blank lines of equal length replace each of the deleted words. It should also be stressed that the commonly used percentages for determining students' Independent, Instructional, and Frustration levels are based on the deletion of every fifth word. If every eighth or 10th word were deleted, these commonly used percentages would not apply.

Passages may vary in length depending on the grade level of the students; however, for students of ages equivalent to third- or fourth-grade level or above, passages of about 250 words are often used. The entire first and last sentences are usually left intact. If passages of 250 words plus intact first and last sentences are used, and if every fifth word is omitted, there will be 50 blanks, and every blank or answer will be worth two percentage points.

Cloze passages may be administered in a group situation much as with standardized reading tests. However, in administering cloze passages, there are usually no specific time limits for completion of the work.

For passages in which every fifth word has been deleted, the percentages for the various reading levels are as follows:

Independent Level = 57 to 100%
Instructional Level = 44 through 56%
Frustration Level = 43% or below

In scoring the passages, only the exact word omitted is usually counted as correct—that is, correct synonyms are not counted as correct. Research has shown that the overall percentages change very little regardless of whether synonyms are counted as correct or incorrect. Furthermore, if words other than the exact word omitted were counted, scoring would be much more difficult—that is, what one teacher might consider an adequate answer another teacher may not, and we would tend to lose interscorer reliability. In scoring cloze passages, however, students are not usually penalized for incorrect spelling as long as there is little or no doubt about which word they meant to use.

*Reprinted by permission of Allyn & Bacon from Ekwall, E. E. (1986). *Teacher's handbook on diagnosis and remediation in reading* (2nd ed.). Boston: Allyn & Bacon.

A plastic overlay such as an overhead projector transparency can be made of each cloze passage with the correct answers appearing on the plastic overlay. When this is superimposed on the student's copy, you can readily check the number of right and wrong answers. These can, in turn, be converted to percentages. From these percentages you can then determine whether the material is at the student's Independent, Instructional, or Frustration level.

USING THE CLOZE PROCEDURE TO PLACE STUDENTS IN GRADED MATERIALS

1. Select 6–12 passages from a book or material that students will possibly be using. (If the results of the test show that the book is too easy or difficult for the students, another must be selected.) Pick them randomly but equally distributed from the front to the back of the book.

2. Give the tests to 25–30 students in a class in which the text is commonly used.

3. Calculate the mean score on each test and then the mean of the means (see pp. 293–294).

4. Select the test that is closest to the mean of the means and throw the rest of the scores away.

5. When a test has been selected for each of the texts a teacher is likely to use, the tests can be duplicated and compiled into booklets that can be administered as group tests. When a student's score is 57% or higher, the student is reading at his Independent reading level. A score from 44% to 56% is equivalent to the student's Instructional reading level. A score of 43% or less is considered to be at the student's Frustration level. (In a textbook, of course, one is concerned with placing the student in the textbook that is represented by the passage in which the student scored at his Instructional reading level.)

USING THE CLOZE PROCEDURE TO MEET THE NEEDS OF THE STUDENTS

1. Divide the book into sections and select two or more passages from each section. The same length passages as described earlier can be used.

2. Make a random selection of the students for whom the book will be used.

3. If you are using a great number of students, you may wish to put them into a number of groups and then let each group take some of the tests. (Make sure, however, that the selection of the subgroups is done randomly.)

4. If students are able to score at their Instructional level on the passages from the book, then it would be considered suitable for them. On the other hand, if most students scored at their Frustration level on the passages from the book, it would be considered too difficult for them.

THE RELIABILITY OF THE CLOZE PROCEDURE

The reliability of the cloze procedure will essentially depend on the following factors:

1. If longer tests are used, the students' scores will probably be more accurate, but it will take longer to correct them.
2. If a larger number of tests is used when selecting the one to represent the material, the test selected will more accurately represent the difficulty of the material.
3. Some materials are uneven in difficulty. These materials should be avoided if possible.
4. The procedure outlined here must be followed exactly or the results will not be accurate.

PROCEDURE FOR DETERMINING THE MEAN OF THE MEANS

The following example illustrates how to find the mean of the means. In this example there were 10 passages and 5 students. (In determining the mean of the means one would, of course, be likely to have more than five students.) Note that there are 10 means: 52.4, 34.6, etc. These means were added and their total was 480.6. When this figure (480.6) was divided by the number of means (10), the mean of the means was 48.06. This figure was closest to the mean of passage number 8 (47.4). Therefore, that passage was most representative of the difficulty of the material. As a whole, passage number 8 would be kept, and the rest of the passages would be discarded.

Passage number 8 is then given to new students with whom you may wish to use the text from which number 8 was derived. If they can read passage number 8 with an accuracy of between 44 and 56%, this text would be appropriate for them at their Instructional reading level. If they scored at 43% or lower, the text would be at their Frustration reading level. If they scored at 57% or better, the text would be at their Independent reading level.

	1	2	3	4	5	6	7	8	9	10
Mary	56	42	84	12	48	34	51	47	75	49
Sam	42	41	83	10	40	30	49	50	74	42
Sally	32	36	74	18	42	41	55	51	75	45
Joe	76	26	66	26	47	31	60	38	69	39
Fred	56	28	54	41	49	33	59	51	72	54
Totals	262	173	361	107	226	169	274	237	365	229
Means	52.4	34.6	72.2	21.4	45.2	33.8	54.8	47.4	73.0	45.8

Total of the Means = 480.6

Mean of the Means $\dfrac{480.6}{10} = \boxed{48.06}$

Scope and Sequence of Reading Skills

PURPOSE

The purpose of the reading scope and sequence chart is to help developmental, corrective, and remedial reading teachers know the point at which many basal reader programs present certain reading skills. Use this chart with caution. All students do not learn to read by acquiring the same set of reading skills in the same order. Some students learn to read quite well with the mastery of only a few of the various skills listed.

Format

The following chart lists the various reading skills by the grade level at which they are presented by the authors of six popular basal reading series. This information may be helpful for teachers in determining what skills generally should have been mastered by students at each grade level, as well as what skills students should master during any particular year. For each skill, the vertical line on the chart indicates the point at which the skill should have been mastered. The horizontal line on the chart indicates the range of grade levels at which the skill is taught in various basal readers.

DESIGNATION OF LEVELS

Levels are designated in the scope and sequence chart as follows: below 1.3 equals readiness or kindergarten; 1.3 equals preprimer; 1.6 equals primer; 1.9 equals first reader (or end of first grade); 2.5 equals mid-second grade; 2.9 equals end of second grade; 3.5 equals mid-third grade; 3.9 equals end of third grade; 4.9 equals end of fourth grade; 5.9 equals end of fifth grade; and 6.9 equals end of sixth grade. Note that past the third grade, levels are not split, but are listed only as 4.9, 5.9, and 6.9. Most basal reader companies provide only one book per grade level past the third grade.

IMPORTANT NOTATION CONCERNING GRADE LEVELS

Note that the levels following each skill *do not* represent the level at which the skill is, or should be, taught for the first time. Rather, *the notation represents the first level at which most basal readers agree that the skill should have been mastered or was, at least, taught.* For example, if a grade level of 1.3 appears, it would indicate that most of the basal readers examined would have taught that skill sometime during the first six months of school. Since a "below 1.3" notation did not appear, it would also mean that it had been taught, by most of the series examined, after the first three months or during the fourth, fifth, or sixth months.

DEVELOPMENT

The scope and sequence chart was developed by determining the point at which six major publishers of basal readers teach each of the skills listed. The publishers were: Macmillan (1983); Houghton Mifflin (1987); Economy (1986); Ginn (1984); Harcourt Brace Jovanovich (1982); and Scott, Foresman (1981). For each skill a matrix was developed as follows:

SKILL	*Econ.*	*Ginn*	*HBJ*	*HM*	*Mac.*	*SF*	*Consensus*
fl blend	1.3	1.6	1.6	1.3	1.3	1.3	1.6
soft *c*	1.3	1.9	1.3	1.3	1.3	1.3	1.3

Note that four of the six series examined taught the *fl* blend at the preprimer (1.3) level. However, since two did not teach it until the primer (1.6) level, the designation of 1.6 was used. On the other hand, with the soft *c* sound, five of the six series taught it by the end of the preprimer (1.3) level. Since only one company was in disagreement, the 1.3 designation was used.

In developing the scope and sequence chart, the following rules and notations were generally observed:

1. When only one company was in disagreement with the others, the designation of that company was ignored.

2. When two companies taught the skill after the others, the later designation of these two companies appears.

3. The horizontal line for each listing represents the range, e.g., following the *sc* sound is a range of 1.3 to 2.5. This means that one or more series taught the skill as early as preprimer (1.3), while one or more did not teach it until the 2.5 level.

4. Following some ranges the word *varies* appears, such as with the *sn* blend. This means that the series were in considerable disagreement about the level at which the skill was taught.

5. Following other ranges just as great as for the *sn* blend, the word *varies* does not appear. In this case it means that, although the range varied a great deal, most of the series were in general agreement even though the overall range was great. In such cases, it was usually a case of one series varying considerably from the others.

6. A skill was generally not listed if it appeared in only one series

7. If a skill was listed in only two series, then the words *2 only* appear following the horizontal line that represents the range for that skill.

8. Where the range is limited to only one grade level, it means that all six series, or all series in which that skill appeared, were in agreement as to when it was taught.

9. The designations *K* (for kindergarten) and *R* (for readiness) were both treated as prior to 1.3.

10. Some graphemes, such as *oo* stand for two phonemes (e.g., the /oo/ in *book* and the /oo/ in *moon*). Where this was the case, a word representing each phoneme appears beside that grapheme. Note the word *book* beside one *oo* and the word *moon* beside the other.

11. Only a range is given for recognition of suffixes and prefixes. This is because the six series varied so widely that no one meaningful point could be designated.

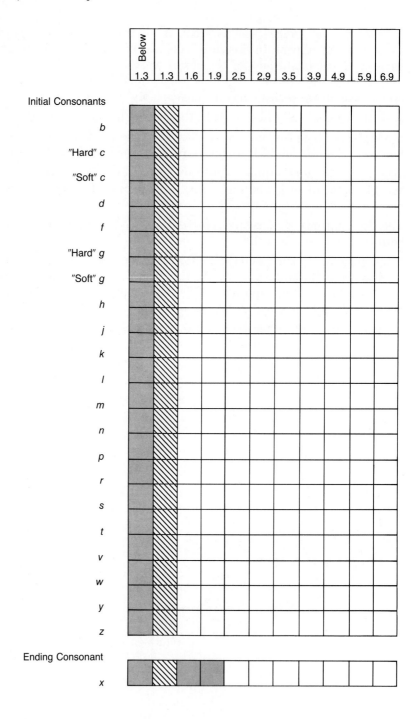

	Below 1.3	1.3	1.6	1.9	2.5	2.9	3.5	3.9	4.9	5.9	6.9

Initial Consonant Clusters

- pr
- qu
- bl
- br
- fl
- fr
- pl
- gr
- sl
- st
- ch
- cl
- cr
- dr
- gl
- sh
- sk
- sw
- th
- tr
- sc
- scr
- sm
- sp

varies

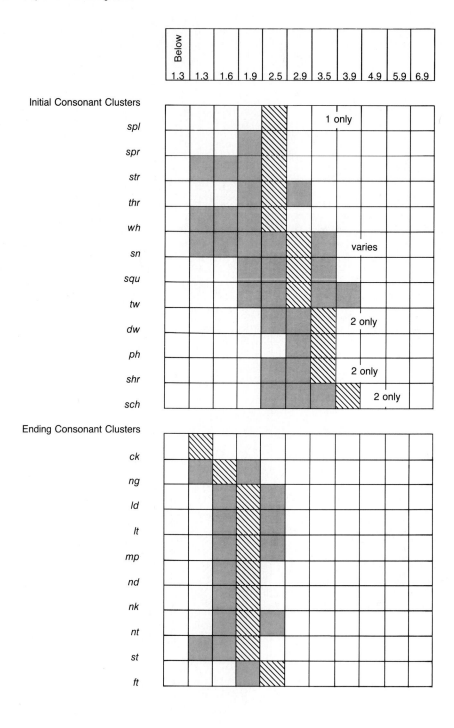

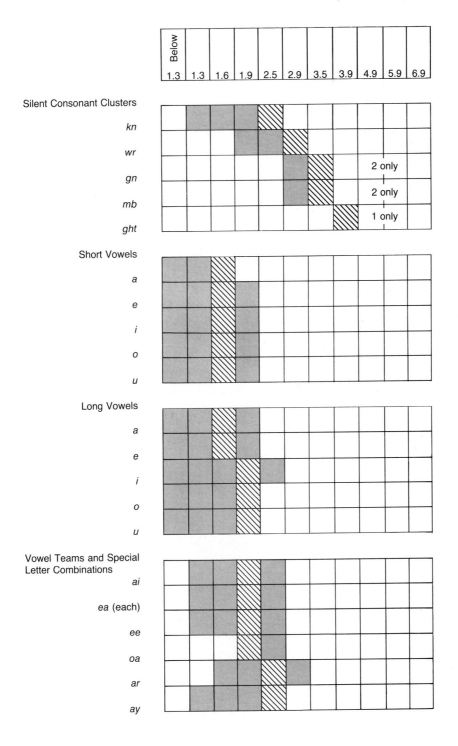

Vowel Teams and Special
Letter Combinations

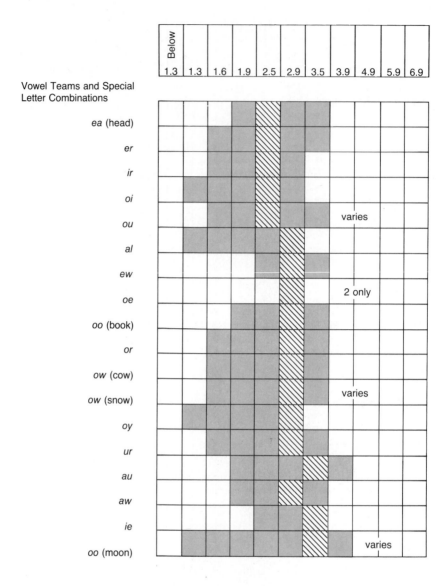

	Below 1.3	1.3	1.6	1.9	2.5	2.9	3.5	3.9	4.9	5.9	6.9
ea (head)											
er											
ir											
oi											
ou								varies			
al											
ew											
oe								2 only			
oo (book)											
or											
ow (cow)											
ow (snow)								varies			
oy											
ur											
au											
aw											
ie											
oo (moon)								varies			

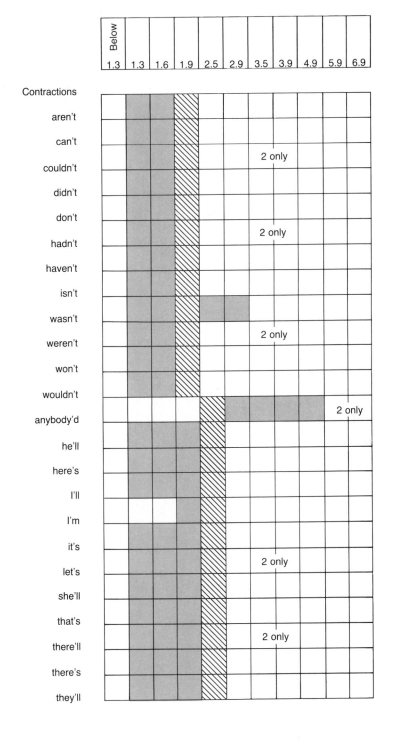

	Below 1.3	1.3	1.6	1.9	2.5	2.9	3.5	3.9	4.9	5.9	6.9
Contractions											
aren't											
can't											
couldn't						2 only					
didn't											
don't											
hadn't						2 only					
haven't											
isn't											
wasn't						2 only					
weren't											
won't											
wouldn't											
anybody'd									2 only		
he'll											
here's											
I'll											
I'm											
it's											
let's						2 only					
she'll											
that's											
there'll						2 only					
there's											
they'll											

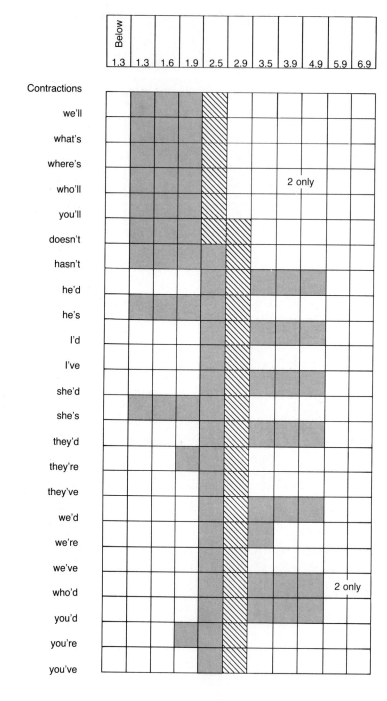

Prefixes (Recognition Only)

	Below 1.3	1.3	1.6	1.9	2.5	2.9	3.5	3.9	4.9	5.9	6.9
a		▓	▓	▓	▓		2 only	2 only			
ad							2 only	2 only		▓	▓
anti							2 only	2 only		▓	▓
be		varies	▓	▓	▓	▓			▓	▓	
com						2 only	2 only		▓	▓	
con						2 only	2 only		▓	▓	
de						2 only	2 only	▓	▓		
dis							▓	▓	▓		
ex					▓	▓		▓	▓		
fore						2 only	2 only	▓	▓	▓	
im							▓	▓	▓	▓	
in							▓	▓	▓		
inter					2 only	2 only			▓		
mid					2 only	2 only	▓	▓	▓		
mis							▓	▓	▓		
non				2 only	2 only			▓	▓		
over				2 only	2 only			▓			
pre							▓	▓	▓	▓	
pro				2 only	2 only		▓	▓	▓		
re					▓	▓					
sub									▓	▓	
trans					2 only	2 only			▓		
un					▓	▓					

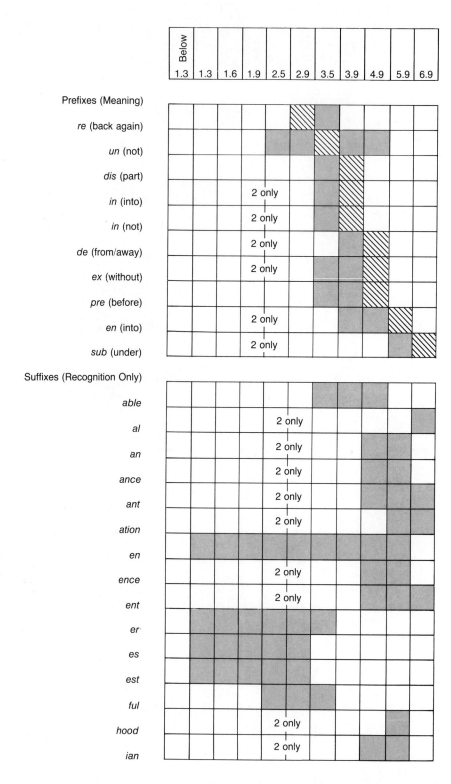

Prefixes (Meaning)
- *re* (back again)
- *un* (not)
- *dis* (part)
- *in* (into)
- *in* (not)
- *de* (from/away)
- *ex* (without)
- *pre* (before)
- *en* (into)
- *sub* (under)

Suffixes (Recognition Only)
- *able*
- *al*
- *an*
- *ance*
- *ant*
- *ation*
- *en*
- *ence*
- *ent*
- *er*
- *es*
- *est*
- *ful*
- *hood*
- *ian*

	Below 1.3	1.3	1.6	1.9	2.5	2.9	3.5	3.9	4.9	5.9	6.9

Suffixes (Recognition Only)

Suffix	Below 1.3	1.3	1.6	1.9	2.5	2.9	3.5	3.9	4.9	5.9	6.9
ible									▓	▓	▓
ic									▓	▓	▓
ion							▓	▓	▓		
ish							▓	▓	▓		
ist							▓	▓			
ity					2 only					▓	
ive										▓	
less				▓	▓						
ly			▓	▓	▓	▓					
ment							▓	▓	▓	▓	
ness						▓	▓	▓	▓		
or						▓	▓	▓	▓		
ous						▓	▓	▓		▓	
ship					2 only						
some					2 only						▓
th					2 only		▓	▓	▓		
tion						▓	▓	▓	▓	▓	
ty			2 only			▓	▓	▓	▓	▓	
ure				2 only						▓	▓
ward				2 only						▓	▓
y						▓	▓				

Below 1.3	1.3	1.6	1.9	2.5	2.9	3.5	3.9	4.9	5.9	6.9

Rules for *y*

1. *y* at the end of a multisyllable word
2. *y* at the end of a single-syllable word

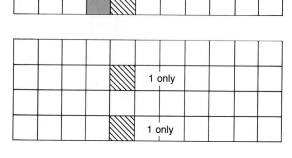

Vowel Rules

1. A single vowel in a closed syllable is usually short.

2. A single vowel at the end of a word is usually long.

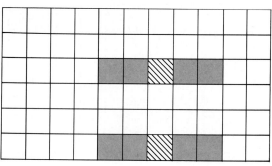

Syllable Principles

1. When two like consonants stand between two vowels, the word is usually divided between the two consonants.

2. When two unlike consonants stand between two vowels, the word is usually divided between the consonants.

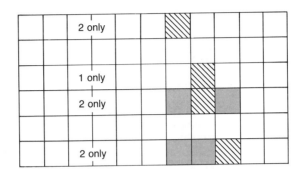

Syllable Principles

3. Prefixes and suffixes are usually separate syllables.

4. When a word ends in a consonant and *le*, the consonant usually begins the last syllable.

5. Divide between compound words.

6. Do not divide between letters in a consonant digraph or consonant blend.

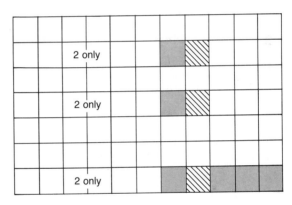

Accent Generalizations

1. In two-syllable words, the first syllable is usually accented.

2. In inflected or derived forms, the primary accent usually falls on the root word.

3. If two vowels are together in the last syllable of a word, it is a clue to an accented final syllable.

Accent Generalizations

4. If there are two unlike
   consonants within a word,
   the syllable before the
   double consonant is
   usually accented.

Dictionary Skills
1. Learning the alphabet
   in order

2. Alphabetizing letters

3. Alphabetizing words
4. Alphabetizing words
   to second letter
5. Selecting word
   meaning from context
6. Alphabetizing words
   to third letter

7. Using guide words

8. Interpreting syllables

9. Estimating location
   of a word in the
   dictionary
10. Interpreting accent
    or stress

Dictionary Skills

11. Interpreting
    pronunciation key
12. Using first and
    second spellings
13. Learning about
    parts of speech
14. Using cross-
    reference
15. Learning about
    word origin

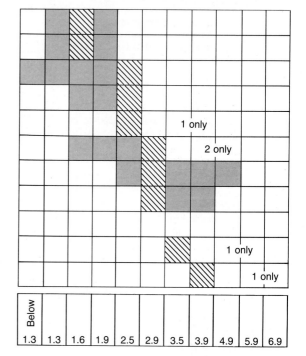

A Phonics Primer

VOWEL SOUNDS

	Short Sounds		Long Sounds
a	bat	a	rake
e	bed	e	jeep
i	pig	i	kite
o	lock	o	rope
u	duck	u	mule

W is sometimes used as a vowel, as in the *ow* and *aw* teams. *W* is usually used as a vowel on word endings and used as a consonant at the beginning of words.

Y is usually a consonant when it appears at the beginning of a word and a vowel in any other position.

Three consonants usually affect or control the sounds of some, or all, of the vowels when they follow these vowels within a syllable. They are *r, w,* and *l.*

r (all vowels)	*w* (*a, e,* and *o*)	*l* (*a*)
car	*law*	*all*
her	*few*	
dirt	*now*	
for		
fur		

CONSONANT SOUNDS

b	bear	*k*	king	*s*	six
c	cat	*l*	lake	*t*	turtle
d	dog	*m*	money	*v*	vase
f	face	*n*	nose	*w*	wagon
g	goat	*p*	pear	*x*	xylophone
h	hen	*q*	queen	*y*	yellow
j	jug	*r*	rat	*z*	zebra

The following consonants have two or more sounds:

c	cat	*g*	goat	*s*	six	*x*	xylophone
c	ice	*g*	germ	*s*	is	*x*	exist
				s	sure	*x*	box

When *g* is followed by *e, i,* or *y,* it often takes the soft sound of *j,* as in *gentle* and *germ.* If it is not followed by these letters, it takes the hard sound illustrated in such words as *got* and *game.*

When *c* is followed by *e, i,* or *y,* it usually takes the soft sound heard in *cent.* If it is not followed by these letters, it usually takes the hard sound heard in *come.*

Qu usually has the sound of *kw;* however, in some words such as *bouquet* it has the sound of *k.*

CONSONANT BLENDS

Beginning

bl	*blue*	*pr*	*pretty*	*tw*	*twelve*
br	*brown*	*sc*	*score*	*wr*	*wrench*
cl	*clown*	*sk*	*skill*	*sch*	*school*
cr	*crown*	*sl*	*slow*	*scr*	*screen*
dr	*dress*	*sm*	*small*	*shr*	*shrink*
dw	*dwell*	*sn*	*snail*	*spl*	*splash*
fl	*flower*	*sp*	*spin*	*spr*	*spring*
fr	*from*	*st*	*story*	*squ*	*squash*
gl	*glue*	*sw*	*swan*	*str*	*string*
gr	*grape*	*tr*	*tree*	*thr*	*throw*
pl	*plate*				

Ending

ld	wi*ld*
mp	la*mp*
nd	wi*nd*
nt	we*nt*
rk	wo*rk*
sk	ri*sk*

CONSONANT AND VOWEL DIAGRAPHS

Consonant

ch	*ch*ute	*sh*	*sh*ip
ch	*ch*oral	*th*	*th*ree
ch	*ch*ur*ch*	*th*	*th*at
gh	cou*gh*	*wh*	*wh*ich
ph	gra*ph*	*wh*	*wh*o

Vowel (Most common phonemes only)

ai	p*ai*n	*ie*	p*ie*ce	(A number of other phonemes are common for *ie*.)
ay	h*ay*			
ea	*ea*ch	*oa*	*oa*ts	
	or	*oo*	b*oo*k	
ea	w*ea*ther	*oo*	m*oo*n	
ei	w*ei*ght	*ou*	t*ou*gh	(*ou* may be either a digraph or diphthong.)
	or			
ei	*ei*ther			
		ow	l*ow*	(*ow* may be either a
			or	digraph or a diphthong.)
		ow	c*ow*	

DIPHTHONGS

au	h*au*l*	*oi*	s*oi*l
au	h*aw*k*	*ou*	tr*ou*t
ew	f*ew*	*ow*	c*ow*
ey	th*ey*	*oy*	b*oy*

---

*Some may hear *au* and *aw* as a digraph.

L

Phonograms and Words for Use in Teaching Phonics

In this appendix you will first find an explanation of how the phonogram list was developed. Following that on pp. 317–320 you will find an explanation of how to use the phonogram list (and word lists on pp. 321–353) to teach phonics. *Be sure to read both of these sections before using the list.*

HOW THE PHONOGRAM LIST WAS DEVELOPED

The phonogram list was developed by taking the phonograms from the words listed in the *Basic Reading Vocabularies.* This is a vocabulary list derived through an analysis of eight sets of basal readers. In the book *Basic Reading Vocabularies,* words are listed alphabetically, by frequency, and by grade level. The phonogram list was developed by using the list by grade level. The list is graded in the following order: Preprimer, primer, first reader, second reader, etc.

The phonogram lists are cumulative, that is to say, in the primer list all phonograms listed at preprimer are shown plus the additional ones at the primer level. Likewise, at first-reader level, you will find the preprimer, primer, and first-reader lists, etc. In developing the final list, the following rules were used:

1. Each word at preprimer, primer, first-reader level, etc., was examined, and the phonogram(s) in those words were listed. For example, in the list shown in *Basic Reading Vocabularies* the following ten words first appear at the preprimer level: *a, all, am, and, are, at, be, bear, big,* and *blue.* From this list one would then have the following phonograms: *all, am, and, are, at, ear, ig,* and *ue.*

2. Because certain of the phonograms listed above begin with vowel pairs or contain a vowel controlled by the consonant following it, e.g., *ea, ar, al,* that are not introduced at the preprimer level, they are not then listed in the phonogram list until that particular vowel pair or vowel-

controlled sound is introduced in the scope and sequence chart shown in appendix J. For example, the vowel pair *ea*, as in the word *each*, is not taught until the first-reader level; therefore, it does not appear in the phonogram list until first-reader level. Likewise the "1"-controlled *a* is not taught in most basal readers until the 2-2 level; therefore, it would not appear in the phonogram list until second-grade level.

3. In some cases words contain phonograms in which the phonogram is different from the sound it takes in most common words, e.g., *are*. When this was the case, it was not used at all. For example, it would be confusing to a student to first say *are* and then *bare, care,* and *dare,* etc.

4. Where a phonogram such as *is* appeared with only one common word such as *his,* it was not included in the list. The author's logic was that such phonograms would be akin to teaching an obscure rule in phonics that pertained to only a few words. The word and phonogram *is* is also somewhat confusing in that it appears in such words as *this* with a different *s* sound. In this case, of course, the student would also probably know *is* and *his* as sight words.

5. Certain phonograms such as *ull,* were omitted. This was done in some cases because the words in which they appear are of rather low utility, such as *dull, gull,* and *skull.* The *ull* sound heard in *gull* also takes on a slightly different pronunciation in words such as *bull.*

6. Only one-syllable words were used in making words from phonograms.

7. Vowel pairs are introduced in the phonogram list at the level at which they appear in the scope and sequence. For example, *oo* appears with the long /o/ sound as in moon at the third-reader level. The *oo* then appears with the short /o/ sound as in *book* at the second-reader level. Therefore, at the third-reader list of phonograms both appear. However, when both appear they are separated by a line so that students will tend to differentiate between the two different sounds. An example of this is shown below:

ook – book, brook, cook, crook, hook, look, shook, took

oof – goof, hoof, proof, spoof, woof

8. Vowel pairs do not appear by themselves (aa, ee, ii, oo, uu). Only vowels or vowel pairs with consonants appear in the phonogram list.

9. There are only about four vowel pairs that are consistent in following the rule that when two vowels appear the long sound of the first one is heard. Or as you may have been taught, "When two vowels go walking the first one does the talking." These vowels are *ai, ay, oa,* and *ee.* Vowel pairs of low utility or vowel pairs that stand for a number of different sounds have, for the most part, been omitted. However, there are several vowel pairs for which two sounds are rather common. Examples of these

are *ea* (each-head), *ow* (crow-owl), *oo* (moon-book). When these appear they are handled as described in number 7 above.

USING THE PHONOGRAM LIST TO TEACH PHONICS

Research in the field of reading shows that the practice of looking for little words in big or longer words is a poor practice since the shorter word often changes in longer words. For example, in the word *government* we would find the words *go, over,* and *men,* yet of these three words only *men* retains the normal sound of the shorter or smaller word. You may wish to experiment with other words.

There is, however, another similar approach that works well for students who need help with word attack skills. In using this approach one looks for phonograms in words. A phonogram, as defined here, is a common word family beginning with a vowel or vowel pair followed by a consonant or consonants, and sometimes ending in *e*. A high percentage of phonograms retain the same sounds in longer words that they stand for in the simple phonograms themselves (See *How the Phonogram List was Developed*). Helping students learn many phonograms will, in turn, help them immediately identify these same sounds in longer words. In learning phonograms, students also learn many consonant and consonant cluster sounds, as well as the sounds for long and short vowels, vowel pairs, and *r,- l,-* and *w*-controlled vowels.

Many students who have problems in learning to read also seem to have problems learning various rules for vowel and consonant sounds. These same students also have difficulty learning sounds in isolation. In using the phonogram approach the student learns automatically and is not required to learn rules. The author has found that many students can greatly expand their knowledge of phonics in a very short time using the phonogram list. Below is an example that illustrates how you can use the phonogram list to teach students vowel sounds as well as the sounds represented by various consonants and consonant clusters.

Recording and Learning Phonograms by Row

You will note that the phonogram list that follows has each of the rows numbered by grade level. The first three rows of phonograms, at the preprimer level, appear as follows:

1. ake – bake, cake, fake, lake, make, take, rake, wake
2. am – ham, dam, jam, ram, Sam, yam
3. ame – came, dame, game, fame, lame, name, same, tame

Using a tape recorder, record the following script:

"I am going to say a number and then some words. As I say the words you are to point to each word and say it right after you hear it on the tape recorder. Be sure to point to the word as you say it. Number one: *ake, bake, cake, fake, lake, make, take, rake, wake.* Number two: *am, ham, dam, jam, ram, Sam, yam.* Number three: *ame, came, dame, game, fame, lame, name, same, tame.*"

In recording the words, pause slightly after each word so that the student will have time to look at the word and say it before you say the next word on the recording. *However, it is very important to keep a rather brisk pace so the student does not become bored. It is also very important that the student be required to point to each word as she says it. The importance of this cannot be overemphasized.*

When teachers first begin to use this method the question is often asked, "How many rows should I expect the student to learn at one time?" The answer to this is not a simple one, but will depend on how fast the student learns. To make this determination, begin with about ten rows on the first recording. Have the student listen to the tape enough times so that she can do the exercise without listening to the tape recording. That is, have her point to the words and say them just as she did when listening to the tape recorder. If you find the student does not know nearly all of the phonograms already studied, or that it takes an inordinate amount of time for her to learn ten rows, then next time do only five rows. Adjust the number of rows so that the student can learn all the words without a great deal of difficulty. However, this is not to say that the student should not have to listen to the tape and go over the words many times.

Another question that you may have is, "How many times should the student have to listen to the tape recording and say the words before she learns them? Again, the answer to this question is not a simple one. The best approach to this is probably to simply tell the student that you want her to listen to the words enough times to learn all of them on the recording. The student will then probably be the best judge of just how many times she needs to listen to the tape to learn all of the words.

If you find that approximately ten rows is best for the student, then continue to give her about ten rows at a time until all of the phonograms and words up to her grade level are known. When she has mastered this task, she will not only know the phonograms found in most words, but also will have learned nearly all of the initial consonants and consonant clusters. The student will probably also have internalized several of the most common vowel rules.

Using the Phonogram List and Word List to Teach the Most Common Vowel Rules

Following the phonogram list you will find a word list for teaching the most common vowel rules. The two vowel rules that beginning readers should learn are as follows:

1. *When a single vowel appears in a closed syllable, it usually stands for the short sound of the vowel.* (This is often referred to as the CVC rule.)

A closed syllable is one that has a consonant at the end; for example, the words *in, did, on,* and *Fred* are all closed syllables. On the other hand, the words *go, he,* and *me* are open syllables. Remember that a closed syllable is one that has a consonant at the end and an open syllable is one that has a vowel at the end.

2. *When a word has a vowel, consonant, and final* e, *the first vowel will be more likely to be long and the final* e *will be silent.* (This is often referred to as the VCE rule.) More accurately, the student should probably be taught that when she encounters a word with a VCE ending, she should try the long sound first.

In order to use the phonogram and word list to teach the two rules listed above, do exercises as follows:

a. Write the following words and ask the student to say each word (or help her, if necessary):

can   cap   dam   pan

After doing this, explain to the student that the *a* sound heard in these words stands for the short *a* sound. Have the student give you more words in which the short *a* sound is heard.

b. Write the following words and then ask the student to say each word (again help her, if necessary):

cane   cape   dame   pane

Following this, explain to the student that the *a* sound heard in these words stands for the long *a* sound. Have her give you some more words in which the long *a* sound is heard.

Now write the word *cane.* Then cross off the *e* at the end. Ask the student what word you now have. Do the same with the words *cape, dame,* and *pane.* Following this, ask the student what happens to the vowel sounds in the words when you remove the *e* from the end. She should, of course, tell you that removing the *e* changes the vowel sound of the first vowel from long to short.

Following this, do words the other way around. That is, take words such as *gag, rag,* and *stag* and have the student pronounce them. (Help her again, if necessary.) Then put an *e* at the end of each word and ask her to pronounce the words as they now appear. Ask her what happens when you add an *e* to the end of words such as these. The student should, of course, tell you that the first vowel sound changes from short to long when an *e* is added.

In doing this it is not necessary to use real words all of the time; therefore, you may wish to use the phonogram list to supplement the word list. Students enjoy doing the same exercises with nonsense words; for example, changing *slam* to *slame,* or *gam* to *game.*

After teaching the two rules stated above, dictate various words and nonsense words to students and have them write them from your dictation. *This is a very important part of the learning of these rules.*

PREPRIMER

1. ake — bake, cake, fake, lake, make, quake, rake, sake, take, wake
2. am — cam, dam, ham, jam, lam, ram, Sam, tam, yam
3. ame — came, dame, game, fame, lame, name, same, tame
4. an — ban, can, Dan, fan, Jan, man, pan, ran, tan, van
5. and — band, hand, land, sand
6. at — bat, cat, fat, hat, mat, pat, rat, sat, tat, vat
7. ed — bed, fed, Jed, led, Ned, red, Ted, wed, Zed
8. elp — help, kelp, yelp
9. et — bet, get, jet, let, met, net, pet, set, wet, yet
10. id — bid, did, hid, kid, lid, mid, rid
11. ide — bide, hide, pride, ride, side, tide, wide
12. ig — big, dig, fig, gig, jig, pig, prig, rig, wig
13. ike — bike, dike, hike, like, Mike, pike
14. ill — bill, dill, fill, gill, hill, Jill, kill, mill, pill, sill, till, will
15. ime — dime, lime, mime, prime, rime, time
16. in — bin, din, fin, gin, kin, pin, sin, tin, win
17. ing — ding, king, ling, ring, sing, wing, zing
18. ish — dish, fish, wish
19. it — bit, fit, hit, kit, lit, pit, quit, sit, wit
20. og — bog, cog, dog, fog, hog, log, tog
21. old — bold, cold, fold, gold, hold, mold, sold, told
22. op — cop, fop, hop, lop, mop, pop, prop, sop, stop, top
23. ot — cot, dot, got, hot, jot, lot, mot, not, pot, rot, sot, tot
24. ump — bump, dump, hump, jump, lump, pump, rump, sump
25. un — bun, dun, fun, gun, nun, pun, run, sun, tun
26. up — cup, pup, sup
27. ut — but, cut, gut, hut, jut, nut, rut

PRIMER

1. ace   — brace, face, grace, lace, mace, pace, place, race
2. ack   — back, black, hack, jack, lack, pack, quack, rack, sack, slack, stack, tack
3. ad   — bad, brad, cad, dad, fad, gad, had, lad, mad, pad, sad
4. ade   — blade, fade, grade, jade, lade, made, wade
5. ag   — bag, brag, flag, gag, hag, lag, nag, rag, sag, slag, stag, tag, wag, zag
6. ake   — bake, brake, cake, fake, flake, lake, make, quake, rake, sake, slake, stake, take, wake
7. alk   — balk, calk, stalk, talk, walk
8. am   — cam, dam, gram, ham, jam, lam, ram, Sam, slam, tam, yam
9. ame — blame, came, dame, fame, flame, frame, game, lame, name, same, tame
10. an   — ban, bran, can, Dan, fan, Jan, man, pan, plan, ran, tan, van
11. and — band, bland, brand, grand, hand, land, sand, stand
12. ank — bank, blank, dank, flank, frank, Hank, plank, rank, sank, stank, tank, yank
13. ask — bask, cask, flask, mask, task
14. ast — blast, cast, fast, last, mast, past, vast
15. at   — bat, brat, cat, fat, flat, hat, mat, pat, plat, rat, sat, slat, vat
16. ate — bate, date, fate, gate, grate, hate, late, mate, Nate, plate, rate, slate, state
17. aw   — caw, flaw, haw, jaw, law, maw, paw, raw, saw, slaw, taw, yaw
18. each — beach, bleach, breach, leach, peach, preach, reach, teach

19. ed   — bed, bled, bred, fed, fled, Jed, led, Ned, pled, red, sled, Ted, wed, Zed

20. ell   — bell, cell, dell, fell, hell, jell, Nell, quell, sell, tell, well, yell

21. elp   — help, kelp, yelp

22. em   — gem, hem, stem

23. en   — Ben, den, fen, hen, Ken, men, pen, ten, yen, wen, zen

24. end   — bend, blend, fend, lend, mend, rend, send, tend, vend, wend

25. ent   — bent, Brent, cent, dent, lent, pent, rent, sent, tent, vent, went

26. et   — bet, fret, get, jet, let, met, net, pet, set, wet, yet

27. ext   — next, text

28. ick   — brick, Dick, flick, kick, lick, nick, pick, prick, quick, sick, slick, stick, wick

29. id   — bid, did, grid, hid, kid, lid, mid, rid, slid

30. ide   — bide, hide, pride, ride, side, slide, tide, wide

31. ig   — big, brig, dig, fig, gig, jig, pig, prig, rig, wig

32. ike   — bike, dike, hike, like, Mike, pike

33. ill   — bill, dill, fill, gill, grill, hill, Jill, kill, mill, pill, sill, still, till, will

34. im   — brim, dim, grim, him, Jim, Kim, rim, slim, Tim

35. ime   — dime, grime, lime, slime, time

36. in   — bin, chin, din, fin, gin, grin, kin, pin, sin, tin, win

37. ing   — bring, ding, fling, king, ling, ping, ring, sing, sling, sting, wing, zing

38. ish   — dish, fish, wish

39. it   — bit, fit, flit, grit, hit, kit, lit, pit, quit, sit, skit, slit, wit

40. ive   — dive, five, hive, live, rive, wive

41. ix — fix, mix, nix, six
42. ob — blob, bob, cob, fob, gob, job, lob, mob, rob, slob, sob
43. og — bog, cog, dog, fog, flog, frog, grog, jog, hog, log, slog, tog
44. old — bold, cold, fold, gold, hold, mold, sold, told
45. op — cop, flop, fop, hop, lop, mop, pop, plop, sop, slop, stop, top
46. ost — host, most, post
47. ot — blot, cot, dot, got, hot, jot, lot, mot, not, pot, plot, rot, sot, slot, tot
48. ox — box, fox, lox, pox, sox
49. uch — much, such
50. uck — buck, duck, luck, muck, puck, pluck, stuck, suck, tuck
51. ump — jump, bump, dump, frump, grump, hump, lump, pump, plump, rump, sump, slump, stump
52. un — bun, dun, fun, gun, nun, pun, stun, sun, tun
53. up — cup, pup, sup
54. us — bus, flus, nus, plus, pus
55. ust — bust, dust, gust, just, must, rust
56. ut — but, cut, gut, hut, jut, nut, rut

FIRST READER

1. able   – cable, table, stable
2. ace   – brace, face, grace, lace, mace, pace, place, race, trace
3. ack   – back, black, hack, jack, lack, pack, quack, rack, sack, slack, shack, stack, tack, track
4. ad   – bad, cad, dad, brad, fad, gad, had, lad, mad, pad, sad
5. ade   – blade, fade, grade, jade, lade, made, wade
6. ag   – bag, brag, drag, flag, gag, hag, lag, nag, rag, sag, slag, stag, tag, wag, zag
7. aid   – braid, laid, maid, paid, raid
8. ail   – bail, brail, fail, frail, hail, jail, mail, nail, pail, quail, rail, sail, tail, trail, wail
9. ain   – brain, chain, drain, gain, grain, lain, main, pain, plain, rain, slain, stain, vain
10. aint   – faint, paint, quaint, saint, taint
11. air   – chair, fair, flair, hair, lair, pair, stair
12. alk   – balk, calk, chalk, talk, stalk, walk
13. ake   – bake, brake, cake, drake, fake, flake, lake, make, quake, rake, sake, shake, slake, stake, take, wake
14. am   – cam, clam, cram, dam, dram, gram, ham, jam, lam, ram, Sam, sham, slam, swam, tam, tram, yam
15. ame   – blame, came, dame, fame, flame, frame, game, lame, name, same, shame, tame
16. an   – ban, bran, can, clan, Dan, fan, Jan, man, pan, plan, ran, tan, than, van
17. and   – band, bland, brand, gland, grand, hand, land, sand, stand
18. ang   – bang, fang, gang, hang, rang, sang, slang

19. ank – bank, dank, blank, flank, frank, Hank, plank, rank, sank, stank, tank, thank, yank
20. ant – pant, plant, slant
21. ask – bask, cask, flask, mask, task
22. ass – bass, brass, class, glass, grass, lass, mass, pass
23. ast – blast, cast, fast, last, mast, past, vast
24. aste – baste, haste, paste, taste, waste
25. at – bat, brat, cat, chat, fat, flat, hat, mat, pat, plat, rat, sat, slat, that, vat
26. ate – bate, crate, date, fate, gate, grate, hate, late, mate, Nate, plate, rate, skate, slate, state
27. ave – brave, cave, crave, Dave, gave, grave, nave, pave, rave, save, shave, slave, stave, wave
28. aw – caw, claw, draw, flaw, haw, jaw, law, maw, paw, raw, saw, taw, thaw, yaw
29. each – beach, bleach, breach, leach, peach, preach, reach, teach
30. eal – deal, heal, meal, peal, real, seal, steal, teal, veal
31. ean – bean, clean, dean, glean, Jean, lean, mean, skean, wean
32. ear – clear, dear, fear, gear, hear, near, rear, sear, shear
33. ease – please, tease
34. eat – beat, bleat, cheat, cleat, feat, heat, meat, neat, peat, pleat, seat, treat
35. ed – bed, bled, bred, fed, fled, Jed, led, Ned, pled, shed, sled, Ted, red, wed, Zed
36. eed – bleed, breed, creed, deed, feed, freed, greed, heed, need, reed, seed, steed, teed, treed, weed
37. eel – creel, feel, keel, peel, reel, steel
38. een – green, keen, peen, queen, seen, sheen, teen
39. eep – beep, cheep, creep, deep, jeep, keep, peep, sheep, sleep, steep, sweep, weep

40. eet — beet, feet, fleet, greet, meet, sheet, sleet, sweet
41. elf — pelf, self, shelf
42. ell — bell, cell, dell, fell, hell, jell, Nell, quell, sell, shell, swell, tell, well, yell
43. elp — help, yelp, kelp
44. em — gem, hem, stem, them
45. en — Ben, den, fen, Glen, hen, Ken, men, pen, ten, then, wen, yen, zen
46. end — bend, blend, fend, lend, mend, rend, send, tend, trend, vend, wend
47. ent — bent, Brent, fent, dent, lent, rent, pent, sent, tent, vent, went
48. ere — here, mere, sere
49. ess — bless, chess, cress, dress, guess, less, mess, press, tress
50. est — best, blest, chest, crest, jest, lest, nest, quest, pest, rest, test, vest, west, zest
51. et — bet, fret, get, jet, let, met, net, pet, set, wet, yet
52. ext — next, text
53. ice — dice, lice, mice, nice, price, rice, slice, trice, vice
54. ick — brick, chick, click, crick, Dick, flick, kick, lick, nick, Rick, pick, prick, quick, sick, slick, stick, thick, trick, wick
55. id — bid, did, grid, hid, kid, lid, mid, rid, skid, slid
56. ide — bide, chide, glide, hide, pride, ride, side, slide, tide, wide
57. ig — big, brig, dig, fig, gig, jig, pig, prig, rig, swig, trig, twig, whig, wig
58. ike — bike, dike, hike, like, Mike, pike
59. ill — bill, chill, dill, drill, fill, gill, grill, hill, Jill, kill, mill, pill, sill, skill, still, thrill, till, will

60. im — brim, dim, grim, him, Jim, Kim, prim, rim, shim, skim, slim, swim, Tim, trim
61. ime — chime, clime, crime, dime, grime, lime, mime, prime, rime, slime, time
62. in — bin, chin, din, fin, gin, grin, kin, pin, shin, sin, skin, tin, thin, win
63. ine — brine, dine, fine, line, mine, nine, pine, shine, swine, tine, thine, wine
64. ing — bring, cling, ding, fling, king, ling, ping, ring, sing, sting, string, swing, thing, wing, zing
65. ink — blink, brink, chink, drink, fink, kink, link, mink, pink, rink, shrink, sink, slink, stink, think, wink
66. int — flint, glint, hint, lint, mint, print, quint, stint, tint
67. ip — blip, chip, clip, dip, drip, flip, grip, hip, jip, kip, lip, nip, pip, quip, rip, ship, sip, skip, slip, tip, trip, zip
68. irl — girl, swirl
69. ish — dish, fish, swish, wish
70. iss — bliss, kiss, hiss, miss, Swiss
71. it — bit, fit, grit, hit, kit, lit, pit, quit, sit, skit, slit, wit
72. ive — chive, dive, drive, five, hive, live, rive, wive
73. ix — fix, mix, nix, six
74. oad — goad, load, road, toad
75. oat — boat, bloat, coat, float, gloat, groat, moat, shoat, stoat, throat
76. ob — bob, blob, cob, fob, glob, gob, job, lob, mob, rob, slob, sob
77. og — bog, clog, cog, dog, fog, flog, frog, grog, jog, hog, log, slog, tog
78. ole — bole, dole, hole, mole, role, pole, sole, stole, tole
79. ood — brood, food, mood, rood
80. oom — bloom, broom, boom, doom, gloom, groom, loom, room, zoom

81. ong   – gong, long, prong, song, thong, tong
82. oon   – boon, coon, croon, loon, moon, noon, soon, swoon
83. op   – cop, chop, crop, drop, fop, flop, glop, hop, lop, mop, pop, plop, sop, shop, slop, stop, top
84. ope   – cope, dope, grope, hope, lope, mope, pope, rope, slope, trope
85. ose   – chose, close, hose, nose, pose, rose, those
86. ost   – host, most, post
87. ot   – blot, clot, cot, dot, got, hot, jot, lot, mot, not, pot, plot, rot, shot, slot, sot, tot, trot
88. ote   – cote, dote, mote, note, quote, rote, tote, vote
89. ove   – clove, cove, drove, grove, stove
90. ox   – box, fox, lox, pox, sox
91. uch   – much, such
92. uck   – buck, chuck, cluck, duck, luck, muck, puck, pluck, shuck, stuck, suck, truck, tuck
93. ump   – bump, chump, clump, dump, frump, grump, hump, jump, lump, plump, pump, rump, slump, stump, sump, thump, trump
94. un   – bun, dun, fun, gun, nun, pun, stun, sun, tun
95. unch   – brunch, bunch, crunch, hunch, lunch, munch, punch
96. ung   – bung, clung, dung, flung, hung, lung, rung, slung, stung, sung, swung
97. up   – cup, pup, sup
98. us   – bus, flus, nus, plus, pus, thus
99. ust   – bust, crust, dust, gust, just, must, rust, trust
100. ut   – but, cut, glut, gut, hut, jut, nut, rut, shut

SECOND READER

1. ab — blab, cab, crab, dab, drab, flab, grab, jab, nab, scab, slab, stab, tab

2. ace — brace, face, grace, lace, mace, pace, place, race, space, trace

3. ack — back, black, clack, crack, hack, jack, lack, pack, quack, rack, sack, shack, slack, smack, snack, stack, tack, track, wack

4. ad — bad, brad, cad, clad, dad, fad, gad, glad, had, lad, mad, pad, sad, shad

5. ade — blade, fade, grade, jade, lade, made, shade, spade, trade, wade

6. afe — chafe, safe, strafe

7. ag — bag, brag, crag, drag, flag, gag, hag, lag, nag, rag, sag, shag, slag, snag, stag, swag, tag, wag, zag

8. age — cage, gage, page, rage, sage, stage, wage

9. aid — braid, laid, maid, paid, raid

10. ail — bail, fail, flail, frail, hail, jail, mail, nail, pail, quail, rail, sail, snail, tail, trail, wail

11. ain — brain, chain, drain, gain, grain, lain, main, pain, plain, rain, slain, Spain, sprain, stain, strain, swain, train, twain, vain

12. aint — faint, paint, plaint, quaint, saint, taint

13. air — chair, fair, flair, hair, lair, pair, stair

14. ake — bake, brake, cake, drake, fake, flake, lake, make, quake, rake, sake, shake, slake, snake, stake, take, wake

15. ale — bale, Dale, gale, hale, Kale, male, pale, sale, scale, shale, stale, tale, wale, whale

16. alk — balk, calk, chalk, stalk, talk, walk

17. all   – ball, call, fall, gall, hall, mall, pall, small, squall, stall, tall, wall
18. am   – cam, clam, cram, dam, dram, gram, ham, jam, lam, ram, Sam, scam, scram, sham, slam, swam, tam, tram, yam
19. amb   – jamb, lamb
20. ame   – blame, came, dame, fame, flame, frame, game, lame, name, same, shame, tame
21. amp   – camp, champ, clamp, cramp, damp, lamp, ramp, scamp, stamp, tamp, tramp, vamp
22. an   – ban, bran, Dan, can, clan, fan, Jan, man, pan, plan, ran, scan, span, tan, than, van
23. and   – band, bland, brand, grand, hand, land, sand, stand, strand
24. ane   – bane, cane, crane, Dane, lane, mane, pane, plane, sane, Shane, vane, wane
25. ang   – bang, clang, fang, gang, hang, pang, rang, sang, slang, sprang, twang
26. ange   – change, grange, mange, range, strange
27. ank   – bank, blank, clank, crank, dank, drank, flank, frank, Hank, lank, plank, prank, rank, sank, shank, spank, stank, swank, tank, thank, yank
28. ant   – pant, plant, slant
29. ap   – cap, chap clap, crap, flap, gap, hap, lap, map, nap, pap, rap, sap, scrap, slap, snap, strap, tap, trap, wrap, yap, zap
30. ape   – cape, drape, grape, nape, scrape, shape, tape
31. ar   – bar, car, char, far, gar, jar, mar, par, scar, spar, star, tar
32. arch   – larch, march, parch, starch
33. ard   – bard, card, guard, hard, lard, sward, yard
34. arge   – barge, charge, large

35. ark — bark, Clark, dark, hark, lark, mark, quark, park, shark, spark, stark
36. arm — charm, farm, harm
37. arn — barn, darn, tarn, yarn
38. arp — carp, harp, sharp
39. art — cart, chart, dart, hart, mart, part, smart, start, tart
40. ase — base, case, chase, vase
41. ash — bash, brash, cash, clash, crash, dash, flash, gash, gnash, hash, lash, mash, rash, sash, slash, smash, stash, splash, thrash, trash
42. ask — bask, cask, flask, mask, task
43. ass — bass, brass, class, crass, glass, grass, lass, mass, pass
44. ast — blast, cast, fast, last, mast, past, vast
45. aste — baste, haste, paste, taste, waste
46. at   — bat, brat, cat, chat, fat, flat, knat, hat, mat, pat, plat, rat, sat, scat, slat, spat, sprat, that, vat
47. ate — bate, crate, date, fate, gate, grate, hate, late, mate, Nate, pate, plate, rate, sate, skate, slate, spate, state
48. ath — bath, lath, math, path
49. ause — cause, clause, pause
50. ave — brave, cave, crave, Dave, gave, grave, lave, nave, pave, rave, save, shave, slave, stave, wave
51. aw   — caw, claw, draw, flaw, gnaw, haw, jaw, law, maw, paw, raw, saw, slaw, squaw, straw, taw, thaw, yaw
52. awl — bawl, brawl, crawl, drawl, pawl, shawl, scrawl, sprawl, trawl, yawl
53. awn — brawn, dawn, drawn, fawn, lawn, pawn, prawn, spawn, yawn

54. ay — bay, bray, cray, day, Fay, flay, fray, gay, gray, hay, jay, lay, may, nay, pay, play, pray, quay, ray, say, slay, spay, splay, spray, stay, stray, sway, tray, way

55. ayed — bayed, brayed, flayed, frayed, grayed, payed, played, prayed, rayed, spayed, sprayed, stayed, swayed

---

56. ead — bread, dead, dread, head, lead, read, spread, thread, tread

---

57. each — beach, bleach, breach, leach, peach, preach, reach, teach

58. ead — bead, lead, plead, read, stead

59. eal — deal, heal, meal, peal, real, seal, squeal, steal, teal, veal

60. eam — beam, cream, dream, gleam, ream, scream, seam, steam, stream, team

61. ean — bean, clean, dean, glean, Jean, lean, mean, skean, wean

62. eap — cheap, heap, leap, reap

63. ease — please, tease

64. east — beast, feast, least, yeast

65. eat — beat, bleat, cheat, cleat, feat, heat, meat, neat, peat, pleat, seat, teat, treat, wheat

66. ear — clear, dear, fear, hear, near, rear, smear, shear, spear, rear, sear

67. earn — learn, yearn

68. eck — check, deck, neck, peck, speck, wreck

69. ed — bed, bled, bred, fed, fled, Jed, led, pled, Ned, shed, sled, sped, red, wed, Zed

70. edge — hedge, ledge, sedge, wedge

71. eed — bleed, breed, creed, deed, feed, freed, greed, heed, need, reed, seed, speed, steed, teed, treed, tweed, weed

72. eek — cheek, creek, Greek, leek, meek, reek, peek, seek, sleek, week

73. eel — creel, feel, heel, keel, kneel, peel, reel, steel, wheel

74. eem — deem, seem, teem

75. een — green, keen, peen, preen, queen, screen, seen, sheen, spleen, teen

76. eep — beep, cheep, creep, deep, jeep, keep, peep, seep, sheep, sleep, steep, sweep, veep, weep

77. eer — beer, cheer, deer, freer, jeer, leer, peer, queer, seer, sheer, sneer, steer, veer

78. eet — beet, feet, fleet, greet, meet, sheet, skeet, sleet, street, sweet, tweet

79. eeze — breeze, freeze, sneeze, squeeze, tweeze, wheeze

80. eft — cleft, deft, left, theft, weft

81. eg — beg, dreg, Greg, keg, leg, peg

82. eld — held, geld, meld, weld

83. elf — pelf, self, shelf

84. ell — bell, cell, dell, fell, hell, jell, Nell, quell, sell, shell, smell, spell, swell, tell, well, yell

85. elp — help, kelp, whelp, yelp

86. elt — belt, felt, melt, pelt, smelt, welt

87. em — gem, hem, stem, them

88. en — Ben, den, fen, hen, Glen, Ken, men, pen, ten, then, when, wen, wren, yen, zen

89. ence — fence, hence, pence, thence, whence

90. ench — bench, blench, clench, drench, French, quench, stench, trench, wrench

91. end — bend, blend, fend, lend, mend, rend, send, spend, tend, trend, vend, wend

92. ent   — bent, Brent, cent, dent, lent, pent, rent, scent,
            sent, spent, tent, vent, went
93. ept   — crept, kept, slept, swept, wept
94. er   — her, per
95. esh   — flesh, fresh, mesh, thresh
96. ess   — bless, chess, cress, dress, guess, less, mess, press,
            stress, tress
97. est   — best, blest, chest, crest, guest, jest, nest, pest,
            quest, rest, test, vest, west, zest
98. et   — bet, fret, get, jet, let, met, net, pet, set, wet, whet,
            yet
99. ew   — blew, brew, chew, clew, crew, dew, drew, few, flew,
            grew, hew, Jew, knew, mew, new, pew, screw, skew,
            slew, spew, stew, strew, threw, yew
100. ext   — next, text
101. ice   — dice, lice, mice, nice, price, rice, slice, spice, splice,
            thrice, trice, twice, vice
102. ick   — brick, chick, click, crick, Dick, flick, kick, lick,
            nick, pick, prick, quick, sick, slick, stick, thick,
            tick, trick, wick
103. id   — bid, did, grid, hid, kid, lid, mid, rid, skid, slid,
            squid
104. ide   — bide, bride, chide, glide, hide, pride, ride, side,
            slide, snide, stride, tide, wide
105. idge   — bridge, midge, ridge
106. ife   — fife, knife, life, rife, strife, wife
107. ift   — drift, gift, lift, rift, sift, shift, swift, thrift
108. ig   — big, brig, dig, fig, gig, jig, pig, prig, rig, sprig, swig,
            trig, twig, whig, wig
109. ike   — bike, dike, hike, like, Mike, pike, spike, strike

110. ile   – bile, file, mile, Nile, pile, rile, smile, stile, tile, vile, while, wile
111. ilk   – bilk, milk, silk
112. ill   – bill, chill, dill, drill, fill, gill, grill, hill, Jill, kill, mill, pill, sill, skill, spill, still, thrill, till, will
113. im   – brim, dim, grim, Jim, Kim, him, prim, rim, shim, skim, slim, swim, Tim, trim, whim, vim
114. ime   – chime, clime, crime, dime, grime, lime, mime, prime, rime, slime, time
115. in   – bin, chin, din, fin, gin, grin, kin, pin, sin, shin, skin, spin, thin, tin, twin, win
116. ince   – mince, prince, quince, since, wince
117. ine   – brine, dine, fine, line, mine, nine, pine, sine, shine, spine, spline, swine, tine, thine, twine, vine, whine, wine
118. ing   – bring, cling, ding, fling, king, ling, ping, ring, sing, sling, spring, sting, string, swing, thing, wing, wring, zing
119. ink   – blink, brink, chink, clink, drink, fink, kink, link, mink, pink, rink, sink, stink, think, wink
120. int   – dint, flint, glint, hint, lint, mint, print, quint, splint, sprint, squint, stint, tint
121. ip   – blip, chip, clip, dip, drip, flip, grip, hip, Kip, lip, nip, pip, quip, rip, scrip, ship, sip, skip, slip, snip, strip, tip, trip, whip, zip
122. ipe   – gripe, pipe, ripe, snipe, stripe, swipe, tripe, wipe
123. ird   – bird, gird, third
124. ire   – dire, fire, hire, lire, mire, quire, shire, spire, squire, sire, tire, wire
125. irl   – girl, twirl, swirl, whirl
126. irt   – dirt, flirt, girt, shirt, skirt, squirt
127. ish   – dish, fish, swish, wish

128. iss — bliss, kiss, hiss, miss, Swiss
129. ist — fist, jist, grist, list, mist, twist, wist, wrist
130. it — bit, fit, flit, grit, hit, kit, knit, lit, pit, quit, sit, skit, slit, spit, split, twit, whit, wit, writ
131. ite — bite, cite, kite, mite, rite, quite, site, smite, spite, sprite, trite, white, write
132. ive — chive, dive, drive, five, hive, live, rive, strive, thrive, wive
133. ix — fix, mix, nix, six
134. ize — prize, size
135. oach — broach, coach, poach, roach
136. oad — goad, load, road, toad
137. oak — cloak, croak, soak
138. oal — coal, foal, goal, shoal
139. oar — boar, roar, soar
140. oast — boast, coast, roast, toast
141. oat — bloat, boat, coat, float, gloat, goat, groat, moat, shoat, stoat, throat
142. ob — blob, bob, cob, fob, glob, gob, job, lob, knob, mob, rob, slob, snob, sob, throb
143. ock — block, bock, chock, clock, cock, crock, dock, flock, frock, hock, knock, lock, mock, pock, rock, shock, smock, sock, stock
144. od — clod, cod, hod, God, mod, nod, plod, pod, prod, rod, scrod, shod, sod, trod
145. ode — bode, code, lode, mode, node, rode, strode
146. oft — loft, soft
147. og — bog, clog, cog, dog, flog, fog, frog, grog, hog, jog, log, slog, smog, tog
148. oice — choice, voice
149. oil — boil, broil, coil, foil, moil, roil, soil, spoil, toil

150. oin   – coin, groin, join, loin, quoin
151. oke   – broke, choke, coke, joke, poke, smoke, spoke, stoke, stroke, woke, yoke
152. old   – bold, cold, fold, gold, hold, mold, scold, sold, told
153. ole   – bole, dole, hole, mole, pole, role, sole, stole, tole, whole
154. ond   – blond, bond, fond, frond, pond
155. ong   – gong, long, prong, song, strong, thong, throng, tong

156. ood   – good, hood, stood, wood

157. ood   – brood, food, mood, rood

158. ook   – book, brook, cook, crook, hook, look, nook, rook, shook, took

159. oof   – goof, poof, proof, spoof
160. ool   – cool, drool, fool, pool, spool, stool, tool
161. oom   – bloom, boom, broom, doom, gloom, groom, loom, room, zoom
162. oon   – boon, coon, croon, moon, noon, soon, spoon, swoon
163. oot   – boot, coot, hoot, loot, moot, root, scoot, shoot, toot
164. op   – cop, chop, crop, drop, fop, flop, glop, hop, lop, mop, plop, pop, prop, sop, shop, slop, stop, top, whop
165. ope   – cope, dope, grope, hope, lope, mope, pope, rope, scope, slope, trope
166. ore   – bore, chore, core, fore, gore, lore, more, pore, score, shore, snore, sore, spore, store, swore, tore, wore, yore
167. ork   – cork, fork, pork, stork, York
168. orn   – born, corn, horn, morn, scorn, shorn, sworn, thorn, torn, worn
169. ort   – fort, port, short, snort, sort, sport, tort, wort

170. ose   — chose, close, hose, nose, pose, prose, rose, those
171. oss   — boss, cross, floss, gloss, loss, moss, toss
172. ost   — host, most, post
173. ot   — blot, clot, cot, dot, got, hot, jot, knot, lot, mot, not, pot, plot, rot, Scot, shot, slot, spot, sot, tot, trot
174. ote   — cote, dote, mote, note, quote, rote, smote, tote, vote, wrote
175. oud   — cloud, loud, proud
176. ought — bought, brought, fought, sought, thought, wrought
177. ould   — could, should, would
178. ound   — bound, found, ground, hound, mound, pound, round, sound, wound
179. ount   — count, fount, mount
180. our   — dour, flour, hour, scour, sour
181. ouse   — blouse, douse, grouse, house, louse, mouse, souse, spouse
182. out   — bout, clout, flout, gout, grout, lout, pout, rout, scout, shout, snout, spout, stout, trout
183. ow   — brow, chow, cow, how, now, plow, pow, prow, scow, vow, wow

184. ow   — blow, crow, flow, glow, grow, low, mow, row, show, slow, snow, throw, tow
185. ox   — box, fox, lox, pox, sox
186. oy   — boy, cloy, coy, joy, ploy, Roy, soy, toy, troy
187. ube   — cube, rube, tube
188. uch   — much, such
189. uck   — buck, chuck, cluck, duck, luck, muck, pluck, puck, shuck, snuck, struck, stuck, suck, truck, tuck
190. udge   — budge, drudge, fudge, grudge, judge, nudge, sludge, smudge, trudge
191. uff   — bluff, cuff, fluff, huff, gruff, muff, puff, ruff, scuff, scruff, sluff, snuff, stuff

192. ug — bug, chug, drug, dug, hug, jug, lug, mug, plug, pug, rug, slug, smug, snug, thug, tug
193. um — bum, chum, drum, glum, gum, hum, plum, rum, scum, slum, strum, sum, swum, thrum
194. umb — crumb, dumb, numb, plumb, thumb
195. ump — bump, chump, clump, dump, frump, grump, hump, jump, lump, plump, pump, rump, slump, stump, sump, thump, trump
196. un — bun, dun, fun, gun, nun, pun, spun, stun, sun, tun
197. unch — brunch, bunch, crunch, hunch, lunch, munch, punch, scrunch
198. une — dune, June, prune, rune, tune
199. ung — bung, clung, dung, flung, hung, lung, rung, slung, sprung, strung, stung, sung, swung
200. up — cup, pup, sup
201. ur — blur, bur, cur, slur, spur, fur
202. ure — cure, lure, pure, sure
203. urn — burn, churn, spurn, turn
204. urse — curse, nurse, purse
205. us — bus, flus, nus, plus, pus, thus
206. usk — dusk, husk, musk, rusk, tusk
207. uss — buss, cuss, fuss, muss, truss
208. ust — bust, crust, dust, gust, just, must, rust, thrust, trust
209. ut — but, cut, glut, gut, hut, jut, nut, rut, shut, smut
210. uzz — buzz, fuzz

THIRD READER

1. ab — blab, cab, crab, dab, drab, flab, grab, jab, nab, scab, slab, stab, tab
2. ace — brace, face, grace, lace, mace, pace, place, race, space, trace
3. ack — back, black, clack, crack, hack, jack, lack, pack, quack, rack, sack, shack, slack, smack, snack, stack, tack, track, wack
4. ad — bad, brad, cad, clad, dad, fad, gad, glad, had, lad, mad, pad, sad, shad
5. ade — blade, fade, grade, jade, lade, made, shade, spade, trade, wade
6. afe — chafe, safe, strafe
7. ag — bag, brag, crag, drag, flag, gag, hag, lag, nag, rag, sag, shag, slag, snag, stag, swag, tag, wag, zag
8. age — cage, gage, page, rage, sage, stage, wage
9. aid — braid, laid, maid, paid, raid
10. ail — bail, fail, flail, frail, hail, jail, mail, nail, pail, quail, rail, sail, snail, tail, trail, wail
11. ain — brain, chain, drain, gain, grain, lain, main, pain, plain, rain, slain, Spain, sprain, stain, strain, swain, train, twain, vain
12. aint — faint, paint, plaint, quaint, saint, taint
13. air — chair, fair, flair, hair, lair, pair, stair
14. ake — bake, brake, cake, drake, fake, flake, lake, make, quake, rake, sake, shake, slake, snake, stake, take, wake
15. ale — bale, Dale, gale, hale, Kale, male, pale, sale, scale, shale, stale, tale, wale, whale
16. alk — balk, calk, chalk, stalk, talk, walk

17. all   – ball, call, fall, gall, hall, mall, pall, small, squall, stall, tall, wall
18. am   – cam, clam, cram, dam, dram, gram, ham, jam, lam, ram, Sam, scam, scram, sham, slam, swam, tam, tram, yam
19. amb   – jamb, lamb
20. ame   – blame, came, dame, fame, flame, frame, game, lame, name, same, shame, tame
21. amp   – camp, champ, clamp, cramp, damp, lamp, ramp, scamp, stamp, tamp, tramp, vamp
22. an   – ban, bran, Dan, can, clan, fan, Jan, man, pan, plan, ran, scan, span, tan, than, van
23. and   – band, bland, brand, grand, hand, land, sand, stand, strand
24. ane   – bane, cane, crane, Dane, lane, mane, pane, plane, sane, Shane, vane, wane
25. ang   – bang, clang, fang, gang, hang, pang, rang, sang, slang, sprang, twang
26. ange – change, grange, mange, range, strange
27. ank   – bank, blank, clank, crank, dank, drank, flank, frank, Hank, lank, plank, prank, rank, sank, shank, shrank, spank, stank, swank, tank, thank, yank
28. ant   – pant, plant, slant
29. ap   – cap, chap, clap, crap, flap, gap, hap, lap, map, nap, pap, rap, sap, scrap, slap, snap, strap, tap, trap, wrap, yap, zap
30. ape   – cape, drape, grape, nape, scrape, shape, tape
31. ar   – bar, car, char, far, gar, jar, mar, par, scar, spar, star, tar
32. arch – larch, march, parch, starch
33. ard   – bard, card, guard, hard, lard, sward, yard

34. arge — barge, charge, large
35. ark — bark, Clark, dark, hark, lark, mark, quark, park, shark, spark, stark
36. arm — charm, farm, harm
37. arn — barn, darn, tarn, yarn
38. arp — carp, harp, sharp
39. art — cart, chart, dart, hart, mart, part, smart, start, tart
40. ase — base, case, chase, vase
41. ash — bash, brash, cash, clash, crash, dash, flash, gash, gnash, hash, lash, mash, rash, sash, slash, smash, stash, splash, thrash, trash
42. ask — bask, cask, flask, mask, task
43. ass — bass, brass, class, crass, glass, grass, lass, mass, pass
44. ast — blast, cast, fast, last, mast, past, vast
45. aste — baste, haste, paste, taste, waste
46. at — bat, brat, cat, chat, fat, flat, gnat, hat, mat, pat, plat, rat, sat, scat, slat, spat, sprat, that, vat
47. ate — bate, crate, date, fate, gate, grate, hate, late, mate, Nate, pate, plate, rate, sate, skate, slate, spate, state
48. ath — bath, lath, math, path
49. ause — cause, clause, pause
50. ave — brave, cave, crave, Dave, gave, grave, lave, nave, pave, rave, save, shave, slave, stave, wave
51. aw — caw, claw, draw, flaw, gnaw, haw, jaw, law, maw, paw, raw, saw, slaw, squaw, straw, taw, thaw, yaw
52. awk — hawk, squawk
53. awl — bawl, brawl, crawl, drawl, pawl, shawl, scrawl, sprawl, trawl, yawl

54. awn   – brawn, dawn, drawn, fawn, lawn, pawn, prawn, swawn, spawn, yawn
55. ay   – bay, bray, cray, day, Fay, flay, fray, gay, gray, hay, jay, lay, may, nay, pay, play, pray, quay, ray, say, slay, spay, splay, spray, stay, stray, sway, tray, way
56. ayed   – bayed, brayed, flayed, frayed, grayed, payed, played, prayed, rayed, spayed, sprayed, stayed, swayed

---

57. ead   – bread, dead, dread, head, lead, read, spread, thread, tread

---

58. each   – beach, bleach, breach, leach, peach, preach, reach, teach
59. ead   – bead, lead, plead, read, stead
60. eal   – deal, heal, meal, peal, real, seal, squeal, steal, teal, veal
61. eam   – beam, cream, dream, gleam, ream, scream, seam, steam, stream, team
62. ean   – bean, clean, dean, glean, Jean, lean, mean, skean, wean
63. eap   – cheap, heap, leap, reap
64. ease   – please, tease
65. east   – beast, feast, least, yeast
66. eat   – beat, bleat, cheat, cleat, feat, heat, meat, neat, peat, pleat, seat, teat, treat, wheat
67. ear   – clear, dear, fear, hear, near, rear, smear, shear, spear, rear, sear
68. earn   – learn, yearn
69. eck   – check, deck, neck, peck, speck, wreck
70. ed   – bed, bled, bred, fed, fled, Jed, led, pled, Ned, shed, sled, sped, red, shred, wed, Zed
71. edge   – hedge, ledge, sedge, wedge

72. eed — bleed, breed, creed, deed, feed, freed, greed, heed, need, reed, seed, speed, steed, teed, treed, tweed, weed

73. eek — cheek, creek, Greek, leek, meek, reek, peek, seek, sleek, week

74. eel — creel, feel, heel, keel, kneel, peel, reel, steel, wheel

75. eem — deem, seem, teem

76. een — green, keen, peen, preen, queen, screen, seen, sheen, spleen, teen

77. eep — beep, cheep, creep, deep, jeep, keep, peep, seep, sheep, sleep, steep, sweep, veep, weep

78. eer — beer, cheer, deer, freer, jeer, leer, peer, queer, seer, sheer, sneer, steer, veer

79. eet — beet, feet, fleet, greet, meet, sheet, skeet, sleet, street, sweet, tweet

80. eeze — breeze, freeze, sneeze, squeeze, tweeze, wheeze

81. eft — cleft, deft, left, theft, weft

82. eg — beg, dreg, Greg, keg, leg, peg

83. eld — held, geld, meld, weld

84. elf — pelf, self, shelf

85. ell — bell, cell, dell, dwell, fell, hell, jell, Nell, quell, sell, shell, smell, spell, swell, tell, well, yell

86. elp — help, kelp, whelp, yelp

87. elt — belt, dwelt, felt, melt, pelt, smelt, welt

88. em — gem, hem, stem, them

89. en — Ben, den, fen, hen, Glen, Ken, men, pen, ten, then, when, wen, wren, yen, zen

90. ence — fence, hence, pence, thence, whence

91. ench — bench, blench, clench, drench, French, quench, stench, trench, wrench

92. end — bend, blend, fend, lend, mend, rend, send, spend, tend, trend, vend, wend

93. ent — bent, Brent, cent, dent, lent, pent, rent, scent, sent, spent, tent, vent, went

94. ept — crept, kept, slept, swept, wept

95. er — her, per

96. ere — here, mere, sere

97. esh — flesh, fresh, mesh, thresh

98. ess — bless, chess, cress, dress, guess, less, mess, press, stress, tress

99. est — best, blest, chest, crest, guest, jest, nest, pest, quest, rest, test, vest, west, zest

100. et — bet, fret, get, jet, let, met, net, pet, set, wet, whet, yet

101. ew — blew, brew, chew, clew, crew, dew, drew, few, flew, grew, hew, Jew, knew, mew, new, pew, shrew, screw, skew, slew, spew, stew, strew, threw, yew

102. ext — next, text

103. ice — dice, lice, mice, nice, price, rice, slice, spice, splice, thrice, trice, twice, vice

104. ick — brick, chick, click, crick, Dick, flick, kick, lick, nick, pick, prick, quick, sick, slick, stick, thick, tick, trick, wick

105. id — bid, did, grid, hid, kid, lid, mid, rid, skid, slid, squid

106. ide — bide, bride, chide, glide, hide, pride, ride, side, slide, snide, stride, tide, wide

107. idge — bridge, midge, ridge

108. ife — fife, knife, life, rife, strife, wife

109. ift — drift, gift, lift, rift, sift, shift, swift, thrift

110. ig — big, brig, dig, fig, gig, jig, pig, prig, rig, sprig, swig trig, twig, whig, wig

111. ike — bike, dike, hike, like, Mike, pike, spike, strike

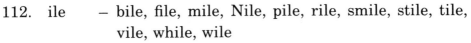

112. ile   — bile, file, mile, Nile, pile, rile, smile, stile, tile, vile, while, wile
113. ilk   — bilk, milk, silk
114. ill   — bill, chill, dill, drill, fill, gill, grill, hill, Jill, kill, mill, pill, sill, shrill, skill, spill, still, thrill, till, will
115. im   — brim, dim, grim, Jim, Kim, him, prim, rim, shim, skim, slim, swim, Tim, trim, whim, vim
116. ime   — chime, clime, crime, dime, grime, lime, mime, prime, rime, slime, time
117. in   — bin, chin, din, fin, gin, grin, kin, pin, sin, shin, skin, spin, thin, tin, twin, win
118. ince   — mince, prince, quince, since, wince
119. inch   — cinch, clinch, finch, flinch, pinch, winch
120. ine   — brine, dine, fine, line, mine, nine, pine, sine, shine, shrine, spine, spline, swine, tine, thine, twine, vine, whine, wine
121. ing   — bring, cling, ding, fling, king, ling, ping, ring, sing, sling, spring, sting, string, swing, thing, wing, wring, zing
122. ink   — blink, brink, chink, clink, drink, fink, kink, link, mink, pink, rink, shrink, slink, sink, stink, think, wink
123. int   — dint, flint, glint, hint, lint, mint, print, quint, splint, sprint, squint, stint, tint
124. ip   — blip, chip, clip, dip, drip, flip, grip, hip, Kip, lip, nip, pip, quip, rip, scrip, ship, sip, skip, slip, snip, strip, tip, trip, whip, zip
125. ipe   — gripe, pipe, ripe, snipe, stripe, swipe, tripe, wipe
126. ird   — bird, gird, third
127. ire   — dire, fire, hire, lire, mire, quire, shire, spire, squire, sire, tire, wire

128.	irl	– girl, twirl, swirl, whirl
129.	irt	– dirt, flirt, girt, shirt, skirt, squirt
130.	ish	– dish, fish, swish, wish
131.	iss	– bliss, kiss, hiss, miss, Swiss
132.	ist	– fist, jist, grist, list, mist, twist, wist, wrist
133.	it	– bit, fit, flit, grit, hit, kit, knit, lit, pit, quit, sit, skit, slit, spit, split, twit, whit, wit, writ
134.	ite	– bite, cite, kite, mite, rite, quite, site, smite, spite, sprite, trite, white, write
135.	ive	– chive, dive, drive, five, hive, live, rive, shrive, strive, thrive, wive
136.	ix	– fix, mix, nix, six
137.	ize	– prize, size
138.	oach	– broach, coach, poach, roach
139.	oad	– goad, load, road, toad
140.	oak	– cloak, croak, soak
141.	oal	– coal, foal, goal, shoal
142.	oar	– boar, roar, soar
143.	oast	– boast, coast, roast, toast
144.	oat	– bloat, boat, coat, float, gloat, goat, groat, moat, shoat, stoat, throat
145.	ob	– blob, bob, cob, fob, glob, gob, job, lob, knob, mob, rob, slob, snob, sob, throb
146.	ock	– block, bock, chock, clock, cock, crock, dock, flock, frock, hock, knock, lock, mock, pock, rock, shock, smock, sock, stock
147.	od	– clod, cod, hod, God, mod, nod, plod, pod, prod, rod, scrod, shod, sod, trod
148.	ode	– bode, code, lode, mode, node, rode, strode
149.	oft	– loft, soft
150.	og	– bog, clog, cog, dog, flog, fog, frog, grog, hog, jog, log, slog, smog, tog

151. oice — choice, voice
152. oil — boil, broil, coil, foil, moil, roil, soil, spoil, toil
153. oin — coin, groin, join, loin, quoin
154. oke — broke, choke, coke, joke, poke, smoke, spoke, stoke, stroke, woke, yoke
155. old — bold, cold, fold, gold, hold, mold, scold, sold, told
156. ole — bole, dole, hole, mole, pole, role, sole, stole, tole, whole
157. olt — bolt, colt, dolt, jolt, molt, volt
158. ond — blond, bond, fond, frond, pond
159. ong — gong, long, prong, song, strong, thong, throng, tong

160. ood — good, hood, stood, wood

161. ood — brood, food, mood, rood

162. ook — book, brook, cook, crook, hook, look, nook, rook, shook, took

163. oof — goof, poof, proof, spoof
164. ool — cool, drool, fool, pool, school, spool, stool, tool
165. oom — bloom, boom, broom, doom, gloom, groom, loom, room, zoom
166. oon — boon, coon, croon, moon, noon, soon, spoon, swoon
167. oop — coop, droop, goop, hoop, loop, scoop, sloop, snoop, stoop, swoop, troop, whoop
168. oose — goose, moose, loose, noose
169. oot — boot, coot, hoot, loot, moot, root, scoot, shoot, toot
170. op — cop, chop, crop, drop, fop, flop, glop, hop, lop, mop, plop, pop, prop, sop, shop, slop, stop, top, whop
171. ope — cope, dope, grope, hope, lope, mope, pope, rope, scope, slope, trope

172. ore   — bore, chore, core, fore, gore, lore, more, pore, score, shore, snore, sore, spore, store, swore, tore, wore, yore

173. ork   — cork, fork, pork, stork, York

174. orn   — born, corn, horn, morn, scorn, shorn, sworn, thorn, torn, worn

175. ort   — fort, port, short, snort, sort, sport, tort, wort

176. ose   — chose, close, hose, nose, pose, prose, rose, those

177. oss   — boss, cross, floss, gloss, loss, moss, toss

178. ost   — host, most, post

179. ot   — blot, clot, cot, dot, got, hot, jot, knot, lot, mot, not, pot, plot, rot, Scot, shot, slot, spot, sot, tot, trot

180. ote   — cote, dote, mote, note, quote, rote, smote, tote, vote, wrote

181. oud   — cloud, loud, proud, shroud

182. ought — bought, brought, fought, sought, thought, wrought

183. ould   — could, should, would

184. ound   — bound, found, ground, hound, mound, pound, round, sound, wound

185. ount   — count, fount, mount

186. our   — dour, flour, hour, scour, sour

187. ouse   — blouse, douse, grouse, house, louse, mouse, souse, spouse

188. out   — bout, clout, flout, gout, grout, lout, pout, rout, scout, shout, snout, spout, stout, trout

189. ove   — clove, cove, drove, grove, stove

190. ow   — brow, chow, cow, how, now, plow, pow, prow, scow, sow, vow, wow

191. ow   — blow, crow, flow, glow, grow, low, mow, row, show, slow, snow, sow, throw, tow

192. ox   — box, fox, lox, pox, sox
193. oy   — boy, cloy, coy, joy, ploy, Roy, soy, toy, troy
194. ube   — cube, rube, tube
195. uch   — much, such
196. uck   — buck, chuck, cluck, duck, luck, muck, pluck, puck, shuck, snuck, struck, stuck, suck, truck, tuck
197. udge   — budge, drudge, fudge, grudge, judge, nudge, sludge, smudge, trudge
198. uff   — bluff, cuff, fluff, huff, gruff, muff, puff, ruff, scuff, scruff, sluff, snuff, stuff
199. ug   — bug, chug, drug, dug, hug, jug, lug, mug, plug, pug, rug, shrug, slug, smug, snug, thug, tug
200. um   — bum, chum, drum, glum, gum, hum, plum, rum, scum, slum, strum, sum, swum, thrum
201. umb   — crumb, dumb, numb, plumb, thumb
202. ump   — bump, chump, clump, dump, frump, grump, hump, jump, lump, plump, pump, rump, slump, stump, sump, thump, trump
203. un   — bun, dun, fun, gun, nun, pun, spun, stun, sun, tun
204. unch   — brunch, bunch, crunch, hunch, lunch, munch, punch, scrunch
205. une   — dune, June, prune, rune, tune
206. ung   — bung, clung, dung, flung, hung, lung, rung, slung, sprung, strung, stung, sung, swung
207. up   — cup, pup, sup
208. ur   — blur, bur, cur, slur, spur, fur
209. ure   — cure, lure, pure, sure
210. urn   — burn, churn, spurn, turn
211. urse   — curse, nurse, purse
212. us   — bus, flus, nus, plus, pus, thus
213. usk   — dusk, husk, musk, rusk, tusk

214. uss — buss, cuss, fuss, muss, truss
215. ust — bust, crust, dust, gust, just, must, rust, thrust, trust
216. ut — but, cut, glut, gut, hut, jut, nut, rut, shut, smut
217. uzz — buzz, fuzz

WORDS FOR TEACHING THE
CVC & CVCE RULE

A Vowels

can	cane
cap	cape
dam	dame
fad	fade
fat	fate
gap	gape
hat	hate
mad	made
mat	mate
nap	nape
pal	pale
pan	pane
Sam	same
tam	tame
tap	tape
plan	plane
scrap	scrape
shad	shade
sham	shame

E Vowels

bed	bede
pet	Pete
met	mete

I Vowels

bid	bide
bit	bite
dim	dime
din	dine
fin	fine
hid	hide
kit	kite
mil	mile
mit	mite
pin	pine
rid	ride
rip	ripe
Sid	side
sit	site
Tim	time

I Vowels (continued)

tin	tine
quit	quite
grim	grime
grip	gripe
prim	prime
shin	shine
slid	slide
slim	slime
snip	snipe
spin	spine
spit	spite
strip	stripe
trip	tripe
twin	twine

O Vowels

rob	robe
cod	code
dot	dote
hop	hope
lop	lope
mop	mope
not	note
pop	pope
rod	rode
rot	rote
ton	tone
tot	tote
glob	globe
slop	slope

U Vowels

Long *u* sound:

cub	cube
cut	cute

Long *oo* sound:

dun	dune
jut	jute
tub	tube
crud	crude
plum	plume

Prepositional Phrases

Appendix M is a list of prepositional phrases that may be used in teaching some of the most common words in the English language as well as the most common prepositions and noun words. Some teachers object, perhaps rightly so, to the teaching of basic sight words or any high-utility word in isolation. For students who are having difficulty with any of the most commonly used prepositions, you may wish to use these phrases as you would the sight word phrases in Appendix D. You may also make an audio tape of the phrases to be sent home with students who are having difficulties with these words. The tape may be made as follows:

1. Copy the first page, so that you will have it for further reference.

2. Number the first 10–15 phrases of the copy you have made. Once you have worked with a student for a short while, you will know how many he is capable of learning. If you find that you send 15 phrases on an audio tape home and the student has easily mastered all of them, send home 20 more the next week. Increase these to the maximum that the student can successfully master in the time between meetings. Place a 1 by the first phrase, a 2 by the second phrase, etc. Then make an audio tape with a script much the same as the one that follows:
"You will hear some phrases on this tape recording. First you will hear a number and then you will hear the phrase. Look at each word as it is pronounced on this tape recording. There will then be a short pause for you to say the phrase. Be sure to point to each of the words as you say them. Number one, *about his dog* (pause); be sure to point to each word as you say it. Number two *about my cat,* (pause); Number three *about dinner, ...*"

It is important that the student point to each word as it is pronounced. This way the student makes the connection between the spoken word and the written word. This seems to be the key to the success of the neurological-impress method and the language-experience approach with students who are lacking in their sight vocabularies. The following are commonly used phrases. Most of the words are also in the Fry list of the 600 most frequently used words in reading and writing the English language.*

*Fry, E. (1972). Reading instruction for classroom and clinic. New York: McGraw-Hill (pp. 55–63).

about
about his dog
about my cat
about dinner
about my sister
about the room

along
along the ground
along the water
along the wall
along the road
along the way

as
as a house
as a girl
as a boy
as a man
as a woman

before
before winter
before bed
before the fire
before eight
before we go

by
by the hair
by the horse
by the week
by the government
by her eyes

after
after we've gone
after three years
after work
after his mother
after the bell

around
around the garden
around the school
around here
around eight o'clock
around the trees

at
at the house
at the door
at the party
at the water
at the half

but
but the outside
but the poor
but the yard
but his head
but her eyes

down
down the hill
down the side
down the front
down the street
down the stairs

for
for the law
for the doctor
for the money
for a guess
for tomorrow

in
in the hour
in the music
in the spring
in the picture
in his voice

like
like the wind
like snow
like you
like her hat
like a bird

next
next turn
next president
next to me
next to him
next in line

off
off the wall
off the water
off the horse
off the table
off of it

out
out of paper
out to study
out of school
out of line
out in public

over
over his clothes
over the ice
over the city
over the thing
over his name

from
from the cows
from her need
from my cousin
from the cold
from the story

into
into the box
into the floor
into the train
into the bank
into the office

near
near the fish
near the war
near the bridge
near the farm
near the airplane

of
of the sun
of my life
of the farm
of the paper
of the church

on
on one afternoon
on Friday morning
on her smile
on the house
on her face

outside
outside the country
outside the woods
outside the town
outside the third grade
outside the grocery store

to
to the summer
to the fair
to the state
to the world
to the house

through
through them
through his heart
through twenty
through the day
through the water

until
until the night
until they come
until tomorrow
until this minute
until he knew

up
up the window
up the river
up the table
up in the air
up to speak

with
with his suit
with my uncle
with her aunt
with a present
with the baby

Basic Sight Word Sentences

Appendix N is a list of basic sight word sentences that may be used to provide students with practice in learning the basic sight words in context. Each of the basic sight word phrases listed in Appendix D were used to create these sentences.

Students may practice these sentences alone, with other students, or with parents at home. You may also make an audio tape of the sentences as described in Appendix M. Since it is important for students to *master* basic sight words, it is appropriate for students to practice these sentences over and over. They may also create their own sentences using the sight word phrases or incorporate them in language-experience activities. The underlined words that appear on the list are nouns drawn from the preprimer level of a basal series.

A common approach that teachers use in teaching the basic sight words, phrases, and sentences follows these steps:

1. First, the student learns the basic sight words from one sublist at a time. (Each sublist contains 20 words.)

2. Then, the student learns the basic sight word phrases from the same sublist.

3. Then, the student learns the basic sight word sentences from the same sublist.

4. Reinforce the learnings in each previous step by having the student read as much as possible from low-level texts that incorporate many basic sight words and by having the student participate in language-experience activities.

5. After the basic sight words from one sublist are mastered, go on to the next sublist and repeat steps 1 through 4.

BASIC SIGHT WORD SENTENCES

List I

1. She said that it was you.
2. He and I had the <u>duck.</u>
3. They said he had to.
4. But she said it was his.
5. It was on that turtle.
6. He said that it was in it.
7. A <u>duck</u> was for you.
8. They had that for you.
9. She said that of you.
10. They said it was for you.

List II

1. Look at him out there.
2. There is some for her.
3. We have to go out there.
4. Then look up at him.
5. I have to go with her.
6. They had as little as he had.
7. All of it is there.
8. Go down there and look.
9. I am little.
10. Be there with him.

List III

1. I will get them a cat.
2. See what you can do.
3. I like this one a little.
4. Would you look at it for me.
5. My turtle is not little.
6. Could you get some for her.
7. When will you see him?
8. Yes, they were there.
9. He did it for them.
10. Get it so I can see it.

List IV

1. Get the big blue book.
2. When it's over, come to see me.
3. Its ride is very long.
4. No one came to ask her.
5. I would like an apple that is red.
6. He came in just now.
7. If you ask, they will come.
8. They went into see him.
9. They are your books.
10. He will ride out.

List V

1. I can take it from there.
2. They don't want to do it now.
3. How did you know it was right?
4. She got her four pretty little rabbits.
5. Don't jump around there?
6. Where did he put the good one?
7. It was too little for me.
8. I take every red and green one.
9. It is about this long.
10. Don't put any around there.

List VI

1. They ran away from here.
2. Call after six, then come over.
3. He ran and got his yellow duck.
4. I think I saw the brown turtle.
5. He can help to make her well.
6. I like going to sleep here.
7. Five old turtles are there.
8. Let me ask her to come.
9. He will come by after five.
10. Their cat ran around here.

List VII

1. We can help you eat.
2. The two ducks may walk over there.
3. He will take off the round can.
4. Help him to come before seven.
5. It is very cold today.
6. I do not like to play by myself.
7. I don't know where to stop.
8. When can it fly again?
9. They have never been there.
10. Who had eight yellow ducks?

List VIII

1. Their cat was black and white.
2. May we start to play?
3. You must try once, then try again.
4. Always write your name before you start.
5. Tell her to give it to him.
6. You must drink all of it.
7. Do the work first, then play.
8. You may keep the ten new turtles.
9. How much does he bring?
10. He goes to him for help.

List IX

1. Soon they will find only three of us there.
2. He ate it before it got warm.
3. Our work gave them much help.
4. Will you buy those funny yellow ducks?
5. Hold it open for her.
6. He has made a cold drink.
7. Better start to work right now.
8. It is all done for you.
9. It is cold, so run and jump around.
10. He said he can make it fall.

List X

1. Use the right light when you read.
2. Both of you will sit here.
3. Run too fast and you may fall.
4. They found it under here.
5. Can you pick it up?
6. The cut hurt very much.
7. Say which one you want.
8. I will carry the small one myself.
9. Why pull it up there?
10. My own work is kind of good.

List XI

1. Please thank him for the cold drink.
2. I live far from here.
3. It will grow best over here.
4. I like to laugh and sing, don't you?
5. I wish these were together.
6. How many shall come here?
7. Wash, because you must keep clean.
8. Draw it, then show it to him.
9. She gave him a hot drink.
10. She will start to say, "Once upon. . . . "

Prefixes and Suffixes

PREFIXES

Prefix	Meaning	Examples
a	on, in, at	alive asleep abed
a (an)	not, without	anhydrous anhydride anarchy
*ab, abs	*from*	abduct abrogate abstain
*ad (ac, af, ag, al, an, ap, ar, as, at)	*to,* at, toward	adapt accuse aggrade acclaim affirm
ambi (amb)	both	ambicoloration ambivalent ambidextrous
amphi (amph)	both, around	amphibian amphitheatre amphibolite

---

*Prefixes that appeared most frequently and accounted for 82 percent of the 61 different basic forms of prefixes studied by Stauffer. The italicized word represents the meaning of the prefix in the study referred to here. From Stauffer, R. G. (1969). *Teaching reading as a thinking process.* New York: Harper & Row (p. 348).

Prefix	Meaning	Examples
ana	back, again, up, similar to	analysis analogy anabaptist
ante	before, earlier date	antechamber antedate antetype
anti (ant, anth)	against, counteracts, prevents	antilabor antiaircraft antitoxin
apo (ap)	off, away from, used before	apology aphelion apocrine
archi (arch)	chief, extreme	architect archenemy archfiend
auto	self-propelling, self	automobile autotruck autobiography
*be	to make, about, *by*	belittle beguile befriend
bene	well	benefit benefactor benevolent
bi	having two, double	bicycle bilingual biweekly
by	near, extra	bystander by-pass by-product
cata (cat, cath)	down, against	catastrophic catacomb catheter
centi	one hundred	centigrade centimeter centipede

Prefix	Meaning	Examples
circum	around, about	circumnavigate circumpolar circumspect
*com (co, col, con, cor)	*with,* together, intensification	combine copilot collect confided corrupt
contra	against	contradict contraband contrarious
counter	opposite, in retaliation, opposed to but like	counterclockwise counterattack counterpart
*de	*from,* away	deport detract devitalize
deca (dec, deka, dek)	ten	decimal decade decagon
di (dis)	twice, double	dissect dichroism dichloride
dia	through, across	diagonal diagram diagnose
*dis	opposite, refuse to, *apart*	disagree disintegrate disable disengage
ec (ex)	out of, from	eccentric exodus exaggerate
*en	*in,* into make	encircle enact encourage

Prefix	Meaning	Examples
enter	to go into, among	enterprise entered entertain
epi (ep)	upon, after, over	epitaph epilogue epicene
equi	equal	equilibrium equilateral equiangular
*ex	*out*	exile exhale exhaust
eu	well	euphony euphonism eugenic
extra	beyond	extraordinary extrajudicial extracurricular
for	very, neglect, away	forlorn forbid forget
fore	before, in front	forepaws forehand foreleg
geo	earth, ground, soil	geography geographic geology
hemi	half	hemisphere hemicycle hemistich
hexa (hex)	six	hexagon hexapod hexachord
hyper	over, above	hypersensitive hyperactive hyperacid

Prefix	Meaning	Examples
hypo	under, beneath	hypocrite hypocycloid hypodermic
*in (il, im, ir)	in, within, *into*	inbreed instigate infect
*in (il, im, ir)	no, *not,* without	illiterate immaterial insignificant irresponsible
inter	between, with	interurban interlock interact
intra	within, inside of	intrastate intravenous intramural
intro	into, within	introvert introspective introduce
kilo	one thousand	kilowatt kilogram kilocycle
mal (male)	bad, wrong, ill	maladjust malediction maladroit
meta (met)	after, change in place or form	metacarpal metabolism metaprotein
milli	one thousand	milligram millimeter milliard
mis (miso)	wrong	misplace misadventure misanthrope
mono (mon)	one	monosyllable monologue monolayer

Prefix	Meaning	Examples
multi	many	multitude multiply multiphase
non	not	nonunion nondemocratic nonzero
ob (oc, of, op)	to, upon, totally	object occur offer oppose
oct (octa, octo)	eight	octopus octagon octopod
off	from	offspring offset offstage
out	beyond, excels	outtalk outweigh outmaneuver
over	too much	overactive overheated overage
par (para)	by, past, accessory	parallel paragraph parasympathetic
penta (pent)	five	pentagon Pentateuch pentane
per	through, completely	perceive persuade perchloride
peri	around, about	perimeter periphery periscope
phono (phon, phone)	voice, sound	phonograph phonate phoneme

Prefix	**Meaning**	**Examples**
poly	many	polygon polygamy polysulfide
post	later, behind	postgraduate postaxial postlude
*pre	*before,* in front (of), superior	prewar preaxial pre-eminent
*pro	moving forward, acting for, defending, favoring, *in* *front of*	progress pronoun prosecutor prolabor prologue
quadr	four	quadrant quadrangle quadrennial
quint	five	quintuplets quintet quintillion
*re (red)	*back,* again	review regain recall
retro	backwards	retroactive retrospect retroflex
semi	half, partly, twice in (period)	semicircle semicivilized semiannually
sex (sexi)	six	sextant sexpartite sexivalent
*sub (suc, suf, sug, sup, sur, sus)	*under*	submarine succeed suffix
super	above, exceeding	superior superstructure superscribe

Prefix	Meaning	Examples
sur	over, above, beyond	surcoat surface surbase
syn (sym)	with, together	sympathy synthesis symptom
tele (tel)	afar, of, in, or by	television telescope telephoto
trans	across	transcontinental transport transatlantic
tri	three	triangle tricycle triweekly
ultra	beyond, excessively	ultraviolet ultramodern ultramarine
*un	not, opposite	unannounced unburden uncrowned
uni	consisting of only one	unicellular uniform unicorn
under	below	underpaid underworked underpass
vice	in place of	viceroy vice-president vice-consul
with	against, away	withstand withdraw withhold

SUFFIXES

Suffix	Meaning	Examples	Used to Form
able (ible, ble)	able to, worthy of	obtainable divisible breakable	adjectives
ac (ic, al, an)	characteristic of, having to do with, caused by	cardiac alcoholic comical American	adjectives
aceous (acious)	characterized by, like	carbonaceous crustaceous tenacious	adjectives
ade	action, product	blockade limeade lemonade	nouns
age	act of, cost of	tillage passage postage	nouns
al	relating to, of, pertaining to	directional fictional dismissal	adjectives
al	action process	rehearsal arrival acquittal	nouns
an (ian, ean)	pertaining to, of, born in	diocesan Christian European	adjectives
an	one who, belonging to	artisan African American	nouns
ance (ence)	act of, state of being	continuance reference performance	nouns
ancy (ency)	state of being, act	efficiency piquancy emergency	nouns

Suffix	Meaning	Examples	Used to Form
ant (ent)	one who	accountant suppliant superintendent	nouns
ant	performing, promoting	litigant expectorant expectant	adjectives
ar	relating to, like, of the nature of	regular polar singular	adjectives
ard (art)	one who (excessively)	braggart dullard pollard	nouns
arium	place relating to	planetarium sanitarium aquarium	nouns
ary (ar)	relating to	military dictionary scholar	nouns
ate	office, function	directorate vicarate magistrate	nouns
ate	acted on	temperate determinate animate	adjectives
ate	to become, com- bine, arrange for	evaporate chlorinate orchestrate	verbs
ation (ition)	state of	translation realization nutrition	nouns
cle	little, small	article particle corpuscle	nouns
dom	state of being	wisdom martyrdom freedom	nouns

Suffix	Meaning	Examples	Used to Form
ed	tending to, having	cultured versed bigoted	adjectives
en	cause to have, made of	strengthen woolen wooden	nouns
en	to make, made of	deepen strengthen fasten	verbs
ent (ence)	quality, act, degree	solvent emergence despondence	nouns
er (ar ior, yer)	a thing or action, connected with, or associated	batter beggar interior lawyer	nouns
ery (erie)	place to or for collection of	nunnery jewelry tanneries	nouns
esce	to begin	effervesce fluoresce coalesce	verbs
escent	starting to be	obsolescent fluorescent alkalescent	adjectives
esque	like, having quality or style of	picturesque Romanesque statuesque	adjectives
ess	female	patroness giantess princess	nouns
et (ette)	little, female	dinette suffragette pullet	nouns
ful	full of	hopeful playful joyful	adjectives

Suffix	Meaning	Examples	Used to Form
fy	to make, become	liquefy purify glorify	verbs
hood	state of, condition	womanhood childhood priesthood	nouns
eer	one who, calling or profession	auctioneer buccaneer profiteer	nouns
ic (ics)	relating to, affected with	alcoholic allergic volcanic	adjectives
ic (ical)	one that produces	magic cosmetic radical	nouns
ice	condition or quality of	malice justice practice	nouns
ie	small, little	doggie lassie	nouns
ile (il)	appropriate to, suited for, capable of	docile missile civil	adjectives
ing	related to, made of	farthing banking cooking	nouns
ion (sion)	result of act, state	regulation hydration correction	nouns
ise (ize)	to make, treat with	sterilize summarize finalize	verbs
ish	having	boyish purplish fortyish	adjectives

Suffix	Meaning	Examples	Used to Form
ism	act of, state of	baptism invalidism animalism	nouns
ist	practicer or believer in one who, the doer	evangelist pianist violinist	nouns
ive	related to, tending to	creative massive amusive	adjectives
ize	to become, become like	Americanize crystallize socialize	verbs
kin	little	catkin manikin napkin	nouns
le (el)	small, a thing used for for doing	icicle handle mantle	nouns
less	without, lacking	careless hopeless painless	adjectives
ling	young, small	duckling hireling suckling	nouns
ly	in a way, manner	softly quietly hoarsely	adverbs
ment	concrete result, state, process	embankment development amazement	nouns
ness	state of being	happiness cheerfulness hopefulness	nouns
ock	small one	hillock bullock paddock	nouns

Suffix	Meaning	Examples	Used to Form
or	state of, does certain thing	pallor grantor elevator	nouns
orium	place for, giving	sanatorium auditorium haustorium	nouns
ory	tending to, producing	auditory gustatory justificatory	adjectives
ose	full of, containing, like	verbose cymose morose	adjectives
ous	having, full of	religious generous poisonous	adjectives
ship	state of, office, art	friendship clerkship horsemanship	nouns
ster	one that does or is	spinster teamster youngster	nouns
th	act of, state of	growth length spilth	nouns
tude	condition	certitude gratitude finitude	nouns
ty (ity)	state of, degree, quality	masculinity priority timidity	nouns
ulent	tending to, abounds in	fraudulent flocculent opulent	adjectives
ure	act, office	exposure legislature procedure	nouns

Suffix	Meaning	Examples	Used to Form
ward	in specified direction	southward seaward backward	adverbs
wise	manner, way	likewise clockwise lengthwise	adverbs
y	like a, full of	rosy fishy glassy	adjectives
y (acy)	state of, action, condition, position	jealousy inquiry celibacy	nouns

P

Samples of the Author, Title, and Subject Cards

AUTHOR CARD

Call number

Author

Title

Publisher & date
of publication

Total number of
pages in book

Indicates subject
heading in library
card catalog
Indicates there is
a title card in
card catalog

```
395
  G
        Parker, Pamela

        Table Manners around the World.
        Illus. by Lilia Lavender
        Merrill, 1989.


              260p. illus.


           1. Etiquette      I. Title
```

TITLE CARD

Call number

Title

Author

Publisher & date
of publication

Total number of
pages in book

Indicates subject
heading in library
card catalog
Indicates there is
a title card in
card catalog

395 G	
	Table Manners around the World
	Parker, Pamela Table Manners around the World. Illus. by Lilia Lavender Merrill, 1989.
	260p. illus.
	1. Etiquette I. Title

SUBJECT CARD

Call number

Subject

Author
Title

Publisher & date
of publication

Indicates subject
heading in library
card catalog
Indicates there is
a title card in
card catalog

395 G	
	Etiquette
	Parker, Pamela Table Manners around the World. Illus. by Lilia Lavender Merrill, 1989.
	1. Etiquette I. Title 64

Repeated Readings Chart

The method of repeated readings is described in Chapter 29. On page 382 is an example of a repeated readings chart in which the student began reading at 35 words/minute and, after 8 trials, was reading at 120 words/minute. The student also began this passage with 26 errors and, after 8 trials, made no errors. To compute words/minute, count the number of words the student is to read and then determine the time it takes the student to read that passage in seconds.

The words/minute equals the number of words read divided by the number of seconds it took to read the passage, multiplied by 60. A student who reads 220 words in 110 seconds would then be reading at: $220/110 = 2.0 \times 60 = 120$ words/minute. In doing repeated readings, it is recommended that you use 100 words/grade level times .75. Thus a student in the fourth grade should read $400 \times .75$ or 300 words. A student in the fifth grade should read $500 \times .75$ or a 375-word passage, etc.

On page 383 is a blank repeated readings chart that you may wish to detach and duplicate for students' use.

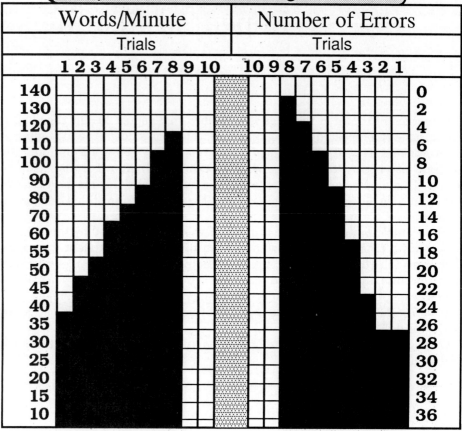

Repeated Readings Chart

Words/Minute		Number of Errors	
Trials		Trials	
1 2 3 4 5 6 7 8 9 10		10 9 8 7 6 5 4 3 2 1	
140			0
130			2
120			4
110			6
100			8
90			10
80			12
70			14
60			16
55			18
50			20
45			22
40			24
35			26
30			28
25			30
20			32
15			34
10			36

Name of Student: _____

Number of Words in Passage: _____

R

Precision Reading Form and Charts

The precision reading technique is described in Chapter 29. On page 387 is a blank form that may be used to record the student's performance during three separate precision reading trials.

At the top of the form are blank spaces to record the following information: student's name, teacher's name, date(s) of trials, the page the passage begins on (if it was taken from a book), and the page the passage ends on.

The form is easy to use. The numbers above the boxes correspond to the *sentences* that the student reads. The teacher merely writes a + (plus) or a 0 (zero) in each box, as the student finishes the sentence, to indicate whether the student read the sentence correctly (+) or with one or more errors (0). At the completion of the reading (up to 50 sentences per trial on this form), the teacher and student count the number of +'s, then tabulate the Efficiency Rate as described below.

The Efficiency Rate is a percentage, obtained by dividing the number of sentences read without error, by the total number of sentences, and multipying this figure by 100.

The Efficiency Rate = the total number of *correct* sentences (+) ÷ the total number of sentences × 100.

Example: 42 correct sentences ÷ 50 total sentences × 100 = Efficiency Rate of 84% (or, if total of 50 sentences is always used, multiply the # of correct sentences by 2)

After the student's reading performance is tabulated, the teacher or student then completes the Graphing Accuracy chart, such as the example on p. 389. If the technique is used daily, the student will see improvement on his reading of the same passage over time by looking at the chart. When the student achieves 100% on two successive readings, a new, more difficult, passage may be selected.

This method is designed to stress *accuracy* over speed. Only after the student is able to read material at grade level with consistent accuracy should the technique be modified to encourage reading speed. To do this, the same recording chart is used; however, the student is asked to read for a specified time (which may be indicated in the *Time* space on the recording form). At the end of the specified time, the teacher or student then graphs the number of correct sentences read correctly on the second chart that appears on p. 389.

Before using this technique, it is suggested that you read the more complete description in Chapter 29.

PRECISION READING FORM
AND CHARTS

Student _____   Teacher _____

Date(s) _____   Begin on _____   End on _____

TRIAL # ____
Scoring by Sentences

1	2	3	4	5	6	7	8	9	10	11	12	13	14	15	16	17
18	19	20	21	22	23	24	25	26	27	28	29	30	31	32	33	34
35	36	37	38	39	40	41	42	43	44	45	46	47	48	49	50	

Tabulating Efficiency   [TIME: _____]

_____ ÷ _____ × 100 = _____

correct sentences   total sentences   efficiency rate

TRIAL # ____
Scoring by Sentences

1	2	3	4	5	6	7	8	9	10	11	12	13	14	15	16	17
18	19	20	21	22	23	24	25	26	27	28	29	30	31	32	33	34
35	36	37	38	39	40	41	42	43	44	45	46	47	48	49	50	

Tabulating Efficiency   [TIME: _____]

_____ ÷ _____ × 100 = _____

correct sentences   total sentences   efficiency rate

Graph Samples

GRAPHING ACCURACY

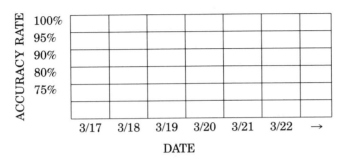

This graph begins at 75% accuracy because the student should not be reading any material at a lower rate.

GRAPHING THE NUMBER OF CORRECT SENTENCES

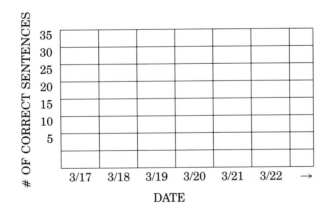

Charts for Graphing Words per Minute and Comprehension

Appendix S is for students to use in graphing their reading rate in words per minute, as well as graphing their percentage of comprehension. As noted in the description of the precision reading technique in Chapter 29 and the previous appendix, emphasis should be placed on *speed* of reading only after the student demonstrates an ability to read materials at grade level with consistent *accuracy*.

A number of available study skills and reading rate books present passages to be read by the student. These are usually followed by comprehension questions, most often 10, for the student to answer. You may wish to use the system of graphing each factor separately that appears on page 394 or the single chart system on the preceding page that takes both percentage of comprehension and reading rate in words per minute into account. It will, of course, do the student little good to improve reading rate if comprehension suffers considerably in the process. In using the combination chart on page 393, multiply the number of words per minute by the percentage of comprehension and then graph the combination of these two factors. On page 392 you will find a sample of Fred's reading scores graphed for six trials. Note that there are blank lines on the left side of the graph to be filled in by the student. The lines have been left blank because every student will tend to read at a different rate. As the student gains in competence, he will probably improve in overall comprehension. Although percentage of comprehension may decrease as the child increases reading speed, it will usually increase after practice. Start the numbers representing the combination of the words per minute and percentage of comprehension on the third line from the bottom (as shown in Fred's example), since it is quite possible that the student may decrease in overall score slightly before beginning to increase that score. The method of computing Fred's scores is shown below the graph of Fred's reading performance. This is the system that you should, of course, use if you wish to graph the students' scores yourself.

On Fred's first trial, he read at 150 words per minute and had a comprehension score of 60%. His score was $150 \times 60 = 9000$. This score was then put as the first trial using the third line from the bottom, in case in any future trials his score might decrease instead of increase.

Name <u>**Fred**</u>

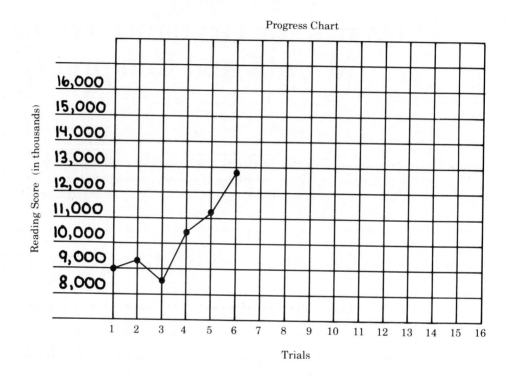

Progress Chart

On the following five trials, Fred's scores are shown below and graphed above.

Trial 2:   155 words per minute with a comprehension score of 60% = 9,300

Trial 3:   170 words per minute with a comprehension score of 50% = 8,500

Trial 4:   175 words per minute with a comprehension score of 60% = 10,500

Trial 5:   185 words per minute with a comprehension score of 60% = 11,100

Trial 6:   185 words per minute with a comprehension score of 70% = 12,950

Name _____

Progress Chart

Reading Score (in thousands)

1 2 3 4 5 6 7 8 9 10 11 12 13 14 15 16

ILLUSTRATING WORDS PER MINUTE AND
PERCENT OF COMPREHENSION

Name _____

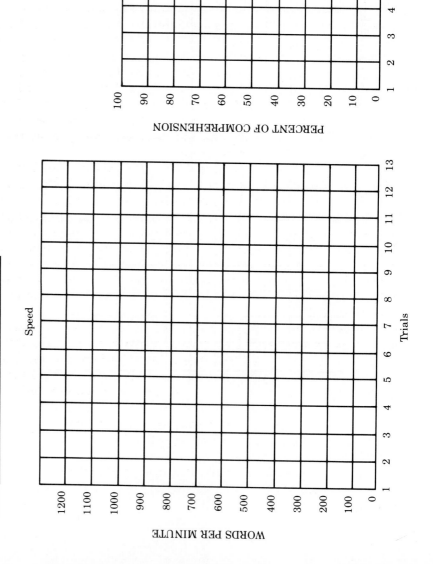

Speed

WORDS PER MINUTE

PERCENT OF COMPREHENSION

Trials

Suggestions for Interviewing Parents of Disabled Readers

Interviewing the parent or parents of a student with reading difficulties is important for several reasons. In the interview you often will be able to discover certain things that parents may hesitate to put in writing. For example, in an interview parents often will give information concerning *their* perception of their child's capabilities. If the parents have other children, they will be able to give important information on their feelings concerning the child's ability to learn compared with their other children. This will provide you with important information, not only about the child but also about the parents' feelings toward the child's capabilities. It is important that parents believe that their child has the ability to learn and that they are willing to do their part in carrying out a program of remediation.

Parents can also provide accurate information on when they first noticed the reading problem. For example, if the child has had problems from the very beginning of school, it would indicate that the reading difficulties may be severe and take longer to remediate. However, if the child suddenly started having reading problems at a later grade level, then it might indicate that the child has developed some emotional problem because of a divorce, a death in the family, or some other traumatic event. The development of a reading problem might also indicate that there was an onset of a physical problem such as a need for eyeglasses, a hearing difficulty, or a side-effect to a prescribed medication.

The initial interview should also reveal, to some extent, if counseling is needed. The parents may need guidance to help them make the child feel confident in her ability to learn. The parents, perhaps unintentionally, may have given their child the impression that she does not have the ability to learn. The parent interview can also provide important information on whether the parents have been consistent in dealing with the child. For example, do the parents tell their child to do something and then not carry through with requiring it to be done, or is the child allowed to find excuses for not performing certain tasks?

In the initial parents' interview, it is also important that you get a verbal commitment from the parents that they are willing to do such things as the following:

1. Be prompt and responsible in providing transportation to tutoring sessions, if required.

2. Follow up in scheduling appointments for physical examinations, including vision and hearing examinations, if necessary.

3. Set aside a specific time each day when the student is required to do homework assignments or recreational reading.

4. Provide a reading environment in which the student sees his parents reading.

5. Provide a quiet place where the student can concentrate on homework or recreational reading without being interrupted by brothers or sisters or without interference from a television.

6. Check to see that homework is done.

7. Take the student to the library and learn techniques for selecting books to be read for pleasure.

Index

ISBN 0-02-332181-4

9 780023 321818